The Politics of Parenthood

MARY FRANCES BERRY

The Politics of Parenthood

Child Care, Women's
Rights, and the Myth of
the Good Mother

V I K I N G

VIKING
Published by the Penguin Group
Penguin Books USA Inc., 375 Hudson Street, New York, New York 10014, U.S.A.
Penguin Books Ltd, 27 Wrights Lane, London W8 5TZ, England
Penguin Books Australia Ltd, Ringwood, Victoria, Australia
Penguin Books Canada Ltd, 10 Alcorn Avenue,
Toronto, Ontario, Canada M4V 3B2
Penguin Books (N.Z.) Ltd, 182–190 Wairau Road,
Auckland 10, New Zealand

Penguin Books Ltd, Registered Offices:
Harmondsworth, Middlesex, England

First published in 1993 by Viking Penguin,
a division of Penguin Books USA Inc.

10 9 8 7 6 5 4 3 2

23°²

LIBRARY OF CONGRESS CATALOGING IN PUBLICATION DATA
Berry, Mary Frances.
The politics of parenthood : child care, women's rights, and the
myth of the good mother / Mary Frances Berry.
p.   cm.
Includes index.
ISBN 0-670-83705-9
1. Child care—Government policy—United States.   2. Child care
services—Government policy—United States.   3. Women—Employment—
United States.   4. Women's rights—United States.   5. Work and
family—United States.   I. Title.
HQ778.7.U6B49   1993
362.7'12'0973—dc20   92-50388

Printed in the United States of America
Set in Bodoni

For Mindy

and

Connie and David

Preface and Acknowledgments

Despair compelled me to write this book. Some of my best friends failed to understand that defining women as primarily responsible for child care prevented women from enjoying the equality of rights and access to power they sought.

The idea grew in my University of Pennsylvania seminar in the History of Law and Social Policy. In discussing the history of day care, I discovered that my students, male and female, felt they had few real options. Mothers were destined to care for children and fathers had always been employed outside the home. They thought that women just had to accept the responsibility for child care along with a job and anything else they needed or wanted to do.

I explain in this book that fathers (and even men and women who are not relatives) have cared for children as successfully as mothers or other relatives. The mother-care tradition persists because we are acculturated to accept it and because it reinforces existing power arrangements. The tradition is, however, neither traditional nor necessary.

I owe an enormous debt to the students in my undergraduate and graduate seminars who have contended over the data and the interpretations in this study for the last five years. I also thank my graduate student researchers James Johnson, Herman Graham, and Anne Bailey.

In Washington, Domenic Ruscio put his unparalleled experience with the congressional legislative process at my disposal. Tom Nardone of the Bureau of Labor Statistics was unfailingly helpful in answering my questions about data on women's employment. Martin O'Connell of the Population Fertility Branch at the Census Bureau responded cheerfully to my data requests and questions concerning child-care responsibilities. Melissa Goodsight of the Administration of Youth, Families and Children and Terry Herron of the Title XX Social Services Block Grant Program at the Department of Health and Human Services helped me to understand the process for implementing the child-care and welfare-reform legislation.

Over the years, the scholars who commented on this topic at conventions and in departmental seminars helped immensely. I want to thank Joan Hoff, Genna Rae McNeil, Eileen Boris, John Blassingame, Linda Kerber, Joan Scott, Michael Blakeley, Ellen Carol DuBois, Jane DeHart, and Evelyn Brooks-Higginbotham for their comments and suggestions. My colleague, Carroll Smith-Rosenberg, warrants special gratitude for reading and rereading the manuscript as it evolved over time. Mindy Chateauvert read and commented unmercifully. She was my best critic.

I also benefited from being able to talk and listen to a number of remarkable women as this project proceeded. They include Blandina Cardenas Ramirez, Judith Lichtman, Marcia Greenberger, Elaine Jones, Melanne Verveer, Barbara Arnwine, Phyllis Schlafly, Clare Coss, Mindy Shapiro, Carol Muehling Frausto, and Elizabeth Abramowitz. Virginia Insley gave me insight into the history of children's programs in the federal government, where she directed the Maternal and Child Health programs for so many years. Three male friends also deserve special notice. Roger Wilkins, DeWayne Wickham, and John White kept reminding me that the remedies suggested here are easier said than done.

Krishna Toolsie enabled me to complete this project. My agent, Charlotte Sheedy, proved to be formidable. Her advice and moral support made it possible to bring this project to completion. My editor, Mindy Werner, made this a better book. The Viking copy editing so carefully done by Lois Adams is greatly appreciated.

Mary Frances Berry
North Truro, Massachusetts, 1992

Contents

The Politics of Parenthood

Introduction: The Problem

Connie Chandler is a lawyer in a major New York–Washington law firm. She and her husband, David, a member of the same firm, have two children, ages three and five. The firm reimburses the couple for day care up to five thousand dollars a year, and grants parental leave when a child is ill. The children are enrolled at an excellent for-profit day-care center located in the same downtown Washington building as the law firm.

Both Connie and David attended Harvard Law School, where they were on the law review. Although Connie is considered one of the brightest lawyers in the firm, David has been promoted to partner, while her career has stalled. She handles a few tax matters but mostly deals with leases and other real estate transactions. He started in mergers and acquisitions and has moved into bankruptcy, one of the hottest departments in the firm.

Connie and David agree that Connie should be employed but not to the detriment of the children's welfare, which they both believe requires more mother care than father care. David sees himself as the principal breadwinner and Connie sees no reason to disagree. She enjoys being a lawyer, although she sometimes feels stressed out and exhausted.

1

Connie and David agree she has principal responsibility for the children. She picks them up after the day-care center closes and arranges for the night-care center or a baby-sitter when she works evenings. David helps when he can, but they understand his first priority is to do an outstanding job for the firm.

Penny Davis is a motor vehicle emissions inspector at a state transportation department. A diligent and conscientious worker, Penny is a divorced mother of two boys, three and seven years old. Since the divorce two years ago, the children's father has taken little interest in them. He even resents the child-support payments deducted from his wages as a hospital lab technician. Penny's youngest son spends his day at the child-care center subsidized by the transportation department. His brother is enrolled there in an after-school program. Penny is lucky because her portion of the day-care cost is only sixty dollars a week.

It appeared that Penny's luck ran out when she had to pass up a promotion because she could not work the longer hours sometimes required. She makes less than eighteen thousand dollars a year after taxes and certainly could have used the higher salary, but Penny decided the promotion was not worth the increased time away from her children. Another female co-worker chose for the same reason not to compete for the promotion.

The department director is now deciding between three other candidates who appear to be equally qualified. One is a single woman. He knows it would be illegal to exclude her from consideration, but he privately worries she might marry, become pregnant, and have child-care problems.

The director thinks the second candidate, Vernon Johnson, is peculiar and should be ruled out because he seems to spend a large amount of time with his family. Vernon recently asked for several hours off to take his son to the dentist. He also talks a great deal about putting his family first and helping his wife, who is a secretary, care for the children. The Johnson children are cared for by a next-door neighbor who has several children in her home during the workday.

Finally, the director decided to promote the third candidate, a single man.

I decided to write this book because of people like Connie, David, Penny, and Vernon. They live in an era when the salad days of the 1960s, when the women's movement demanded that women receive treatment equal to men, seem old-fashioned. The movement's demand for autonomy—the right to define and express one's own sexuality, reproductive choice, economic independence, and a sense of identity independent of others—is seen as selfish and exaggerated in this "post-feminist" era. Those pro-family advocates who believe women should be child-centered see a continued focus on women's rights as undermining woman's most important role.

The achievements of Alice Paul, Susan B. Anthony, Elizabeth Cady Stanton, and their sixties' successors, Betty Friedan and Gloria Steinem, is an old story to some in the nineties—interesting in the telling but irrelevant to our daily lives. The women's rights struggle becomes an important part of history, not a present reality.

Most people assume that the women's movement's demands for equal rights have been realized. Conceptually and practically, however, constraints on women's equality and rights remain. Women have made tremendous gains in education: women make up a majority of undergraduate college students, 42 percent of law and medical students, and one-third of M.B.A. students. Yet, on the average, employed women still take home 71 cents for every dollar a man makes. Moreover, sexual freedom and the future of a woman's right to reproductive choice remain in doubt.

Women who responded to the women's movement's call to autonomy and individual rights by rejecting marriage and childbearing in the 1960s complained by the 1970s and 1980s that work without love and family was unfulfilling.

But women in nuclear families who tried to hold a job and be responsible in the family too often found inadequate resources and child-care help. They discovered what large numbers of women who are poor and/or the heads of households have always experienced. The help was not there. The time, place, and manner in which employers organize work and the attitude of fathers toward child care had changed too little to ease the burden.

Because good child care is scarce and expensive, men and women had to compromise their desires for job success and personal autonomy. These realities led to suggestions that women renounce their individual rights and return to marriage, family, and children as their primary goals. The rejection of the Equal Rights Amendment in 1982, when it failed ratification by a three-state margin, made a fitting endpoint for the struggle to define equality for women by emphasizing their individual goals, aspirations, and freedom.

Betty Friedan and others responded to the new realities by redefining women's equality. Friedan, who was so instrumental in the development of the women's movement in the sixties, heralded the movement's retrenchment in her book, *The Second Stage* (1981). She publicly affirmed the importance of the heterosexual biological family, deemphasized women's rights, and emphasized the importance of women's responsibilities for children and family while holding a job.

Friedan and others wanted to shift some of the responsibility for children to fathers, or to government and employers, to help employed women with their care-giving functions. Congressional women's rights advocates such as Pat Schroeder, Barbara Boxer, and Mary Rose Oakar, as well as groups such as the National Organization for Women, joined child-care activists Elinor Guggenheimer, longtime president of the Child Care Action Media Campaign, and Marian Wright Edelman, president of the Children's Defense Fund, in asking for privately and publicly funded child-care programs.

This approach seemed immensely satisfying for a time. Business and industry slowly began to provide motherhood supports. The federal government debated child-care proposals and in 1990 Congress passed a national child-care policy with bipartisan support. A few states passed leave laws permitting parents to take unpaid leave to care for a sick child or other close relatives.[1]

Meanwhile, a new concept of modern women gradually arrived on the scene. Formulated as a new feminine mystique, the "supermom" is an exemplary woman who successfully combines child care with employment and everything else she desires.

This new feminine mystique at first brought a certain amount of internal satisfaction, but eventually it spawned a growing disquiet among women. Even when women with children have motherhood supports such as leave for child care or subsidies from employers or government, a deep discontent surfaces. They enjoy the sanction the "supermom" image gives to their commitment to caring for their families, but they are also aware that women remain unequal competitors in the world of work and still lack enough autonomy in their lives.

The availability of options is made more complicated by the constraints of race and class. Regardless of sex, race, class, or political persuasion, everyone expresses a desire for children to have quality care. The wealthy, however, can afford high-quality, educationally enriching day care, but the middle class has fewer choices and the poor can only afford the cheapest care, from relatives or unregulated institutions, or, alternatively, leaving the children alone.

Distress over a new feminine mystique flows directly from women's acceptance of being defined as mother, which leads to a devaluing of their individual rights. Redefined women's rights places too little pressure on the need to restructure work, and to rethink what is necessary for child care and for adult self-fulfillment. Women still must try to compete at work while raising children without adequate supports. They experience a double burden, and if they are part of a racial minority, a triple one. This devaluing and redefinition occurred across the country in the 1980s and still lives on in the 1990s.

For Connie, Penny, and Vernon, the new feminine mystique and its accompanying assumptions about male and female roles is even more confining than the old mystique. The old mystique said mothers should stay home with their children, while fathers are the breadwinners. The new mystique says mothers should try to compete at work while raising children.

Advertisers quickly seized upon the idea that these superwomen could be both workers and mothers. "Superwoman," carrying baby, briefcase, purse, and wearing a cape, began appearing on the covers of women's magazines. The comic-book heroine got her own television series starring Lynda Carter, but the televised superwoman was single and without children.

Commentators—husbands, child development experts, and antifeminists led by Phyllis Schlafly—denounced the women's liberation movement for undermining "family values." Schlafly, a Republican conservative, former vice president of the National Federation of Republican Women, founder of the Eagle Forum, and author or coauthor of several books, including *A Choice Not an Echo*, written with Barry Goldwater, successfully led the fight to defeat the ERA. By "family," they meant the nuclear, white, middle-class family, and by "values," they meant a stay-at-home mother with principal responsibility for household and children, under the control of father the breadwinner.

From what *Time* magazine called the "smoldering wreckage" of antiwar protests, civil rights campaigns, and other battles for change in the 1960s, a new conservatism emerged. In the 1970s, Americans seemed selfish, apolitical, a "me" generation fatigued by a lost war, political scandal, and causes only partially won. By the 1980 presidential election, conservatism had taken root.[2]

Increasingly, people doubted the power of government to solve social problems. Rising illegal drug use, crime, and declining educational standards were all blamed to some degree on divorce and the displacement of the old feminine mystique. Schlafly and other antifeminists blamed employed mothers for the tripling of the divorce rate between 1960 and 1980. Barbara Ehrenreich noted, however, in *The Hearts of Men*, that the decision to end a marriage was often made by the husband in search of the pleasures of bachelorhood as depicted in *Playboy* and other men's magazines.[3]

The Moral Majority, founded by the Reverend Jerry Falwell and other Christian evangelicals in 1979, brought the traditional family, anti-abortion, and conservative, fundamentalist religious groups together as an organized force in politics. The New Right distorted the themes of individual rights and personal freedom that were key parts of the women's movement and turned them against feminists. To the New Right, freedom meant the father's authority to preserve Christian values in the family and the privacy of the home unregulated by the state.[4]

Ronald Reagan, a divorced father distanced from his children and grandchildren, whose personal behavior strayed far from their ideal, would not seem to have been the obvious presidential candidate for New Right moralists. But he united the New Right with the old anti-communist and laissez-faire-economics wings of the Republican party.

As the New Right gained strength, interest in civil rights and women's rights declined. Reagan's election in 1980 began the Reagan Revolution of reduced government regulation, cuts in federal social programs, and restoration of "traditional family values." Reagan's leadership gained him overwhelming public support and reelection in 1984. The support for these issues carried over to 1988 and a win for George Bush.

The emergence of new issues like AIDS and increased drug use, especially of crack cocaine, and the explosion in drug-related homicides added firepower to those who crusaded for traditional values. Republicans blamed liberal Democrats for these problems and Democrats were afraid to attack their opponents for fear of conservative public opinion. The Republicans insisted that the country retreat to "old values," including the traditional family, as a restorative.

Caught in the contradictions of the prevailing political atmosphere, many women began to lose their illusions about the new feminine mystique during the Reagan-Bush era. Idealizing motherhood in the traditional family seemed quaint when Wall Street proclaimed that greed is good. Female-headed or two-paycheck families needed more income, and women wanted to compete for high salaries, too. The replacement of selfish, too-thin, fashion-conscious Nancy Reagan by the wholesome, family-oriented Barbara Bush in 1988 only highlighted the differences between the way most working people could afford to live and the political myth of family life.

When Betty Friedan wrote *The Feminine Mystique* in 1963, she addressed white middle-class mothers who did not work outside the home. These young women with young children were popular images in the media, but they represented only a quarter of the married women at the time. In 1960, half of all mothers with young children had part-time jobs. Another 25 percent, mainly African-American, Hispanic, and poor women, worked full-time jobs and took care of young children.[5]

Today, those numbers have drastically changed. In 1992 at least three out of four mothers of young children work, including 52 percent whose children are below the age of two, and more than one-half of these mothers have full-time jobs. Only about 20 percent of women are full-time homemakers. The labor force participation rate of white and black women is practically the same. Hispanic women's participation has risen to about 55 percent but they are still less likely than white or black women to be in the labor force.[6]

The media's glamorous depiction of women at the top of their professions is a reality for only a small, privileged group. For the most part, women are segregated into a narrow band of relatively low-paying service and caring occupations such as sales, teaching, nursing, waitressing, and clerical jobs.[7]

As more and more women share the experience of balancing jobs, children, and the desire for personal autonomy, discontent is becoming contagious. Nearly half of the work force is made up of two-career couples and single parents. Over half of all recent mothers (women with children under one year of age) are either employed or seeking paid work.[8]

In the next ten years, more than half of the work force will be female and most working women will have children. The number of employed women increased to 53,130,000 in November 1991, from 53,049,000, in November 1990. This was the slowest rate of growth in women's employment since 1948. Statisticians attribute the slowdown to the recession, which hit hard the mix of jobs in the service sector in which women were involved. They also note that some mothers in well-off two-earner families decided to leave the work force to concentrate on family and child care.[9]

Because of economic necessity and choice, however, the increases in women's employment are expected to continue. Workplace policies and parental responsibilities are not responding to the reality of employed women fast enough to spread the possibility of real equality of rights beyond an elite. Unless women and men change their attitudes toward children and who cares for them soon, there will be growing discontent in the next decade, and children and their parents will suffer.

For most families, it has become increasingly difficult to find good, affordable child care. Employed parents spent over fourteen billion dollars for child care in 1988, the most recent year for which statistics were available from the Census Bureau. About one-third, or six million, of the nation's working mothers with children under the age of fourteen paid an average of $45 per week, or 6 percent of their monthly family income, for child care. Poor women, whose annual income is less than $13,360 for a family of four, paid a far greater portion for child care. About one-fourth of their earnings, an average of $32 per week, was spent for child care.[10]

Over thirty-two million children, nine million of whom were under age five, had mothers who worked full- or part-time. One-fifth of those children were in day-care centers, another 28 percent were cared for in their own homes. A majority, like Vernon Johnson's children, were cared for by another woman, a relative, a neighbor, or a friend in her home. For children over five, the lion's share of the care between September and June was provided by school. During the summer, however, almost 13.2 percent of school-age children were unwatched, left to fend for themselves.[11]

Many parents rotate day and night jobs with split-shift parenting to solve their child-care problems. While one parent stays at home with the children during the day, the other goes out to work. At night, the roles are reversed. This method is cheaper but very exhausting for the parents and leaves little time for emotional involvement with each other.[12]

Employed parents who hire care-givers to work in their homes today face new legal restrictions. The 1988 welfare-reform legislation makes the child-care tax credit more difficult for some middle-class parents to receive, thus decreasing its value. Parents who claim tax benefits for child care are required to report the Social Security number of their care-giver to the Internal Revenue Service.[13]

Many people have slowly discovered that under-the-table payments to relatives and illegal aliens hired as care-givers can no longer be claimed. Kay Hollestelle of the National Association for Family Day Care, a nonprofit Washington group representing women who care for other people's children in their own homes, called this aspect of the law "a well-kept secret" that catches people by surprise. Sidney Kess, a New York accountant, mused, "whatever the law says, many people hire illegal aliens who may be wonderful at caring for their children, and if you have a wonderful baby-sitter, you'll probably sacrifice the tax credit rather than find a new one." Some better-informed people dropped out of company-sponsored plans for the reasons Kess gave. Their care-giver did not have a Social Security number and did not want to be reported. [14]

Affluent families handle child-care problems by hiring experienced nannies or au pairs. The two terms are used interchangeably, though an au pair is usually a young European woman temporarily in the United States and nannies are American citizens or illegal aliens. Nanny placement services have become a growth industry in the last decade, with more than eight hundred nanny employment agencies operating across the country. [15]

At the end of 1991 some nannies worked sixty-hour weeks for less than $80 a week including room and board, but most made between $100 and $500 a week. These amounts had increased from an average of $94 a week nationwide and $250 a week in Washington and New York in 1988. Two out of three nannies leave their jobs each year, giving this job the highest turnover rate of any predominantly female occupation. [16]

Maureen White, an investment banker, complained about what she called the "tyranny of the nannies" and the importance of keeping the nanny satisfied. "You think, if the nanny is happy, the baby is happy. If the baby's happy, you're happy, your husband's happy," said White. But nannies do not see it that way. Marie Gaston, a nanny in Aspen, Colorado, complained that being a nanny can be a twenty-four-hour job when you travel with your employer. "Sometimes it's two or three weeks before you get time off," said Gaston. "And there's no overtime." [17]

Aliens who work as nannies said that when they seek legal status, employers sometimes take advantage of them. "They seem nice at first and then when they know they're going to sponsor you they start to treat you differently because they know if you don't work with them you're going to have to start over with someone else again. Some of them treat you like a slave." [18]

If care-givers fall ill or become pregnant, new problems arise. Some parents hire only women without children. A few are willing to hire single mothers with children and permit the care-giver's children to become integrated with their own households.[19]

For-profit child-care centers, like the one Connie Chandler uses, are a viable option for parents who can afford it. Such centers have become big business. Kinder Care, organized in 1969, had enrolled more than a million children by 1992 and had twenty thousand employees in forty states and Canada. Sheila Kamerman, a child-care expert at Columbia University's School of Social Work, notes that because of research findings concerning the value of preschool enrichment programs, "more and more middle class parents now want to enroll their children in some kind of organized program when they are two or three years old." Kinder Care and similar facilities offer some educational services along with custodial care. But the expense of sending your child to a for-profit center can be phenomenal. In some cases, it may be more than the tuition for a prestigious private school.[20]

A few employers, such as hospitals, high-growth service industries, and high-technology firms, which have large numbers of female employees and labor shortages, offer parents financial help for day care. Smaller employers are less likely to provide such help, but such firms employ the vast majority of working parents. Part-timers, newly hired, and temporary workers are the least likely to have access to child-care help from employers.[21]

Many large companies offer either day care at the work site or some other kind of child-care benefits. Much of the resources companies invest in child care, however, are spent on referring parents to child-care services or providing information about existing services in the community. This is cheaper than establishing a child-care center. Since the Economic Recovery Act of 1981 made child benefits taxable, many firms have adopted dependent care assistance plans for employees. They are financed by salary reductions that allow employees to pay for child care with pre-tax dollars. Employees' savings equal the amount they would have paid in taxes on child-care expenses, up to $5,000 a year. The employer spends practically nothing and the cost is borne by the federal treasury in taxes not collected. This cost the government $150 million in fiscal 1989.[22]

Employers have found that assisting workers with child care is popular. The Work and Family Information Center of the Conference Board, which is funded by the Fortune 500 companies, reported that in 1991 some 5,500 companies with more than one hundred employees offer child-care benefits ranging from financial assistance, alternative work schedules, and family leave options, to on-site child-care services. This was a major increase over the 3,300 companies that did so just two years before, and a dramatic rise from the 110 that did so in 1978. Yet companies still describe these policies as a way to retain female workers in a period of labor shortages. They do not view child care as a serious problem for male employees. [23]

Company child-care programs please women workers like Renee Mardis of Dayton, Ohio, who works for the Stride Rite Company, a maker of children's shoes. Mardis's young daughter, Ashley, attends the company's day-care center. Mardis was exultant because "now I pay $44.80 per week for Ashley, who goes to work with me and leaves with me." Some companies also have free back-up care centers. For example, Wilmer, Cutler & Pickering, a Washington law firm with over 1,700 lawyers, has made available a small emergency-only care facility for lawyers and support staff since 1980. [24]

Increasingly, employers offer unpaid leave that can be used for child care. The Work and Family Information Center of the Conference Board reported in 1991 that over one-third of the largest manufacturing and service companies provided some kind of unpaid leave for child care. The federal Equal Employment Opportunity Commission issued a guideline in December 1990 that employers offering leave to mothers must offer the same leave to fathers; however, almost all of the leave is taken by women. [25]

International Business Machines (IBM) since October 1988 has implemented a policy that gives employees either up to three years' unpaid leave for "serious reasons," such as child care or the need to care for a sick or elderly relative, or a once-in-a-lifetime educational opportunity. [26]

The leave policies of IBM, like those of many companies, apply to women and men but clearly assume that mothers are primarily responsible for child-rearing. Jesse Henderson, an IBM official, explained that the leave policy was extended to three years so that a mother with a new baby could remain at home until the child was ready for day care. He thought that policies such as flextime, extended leave, and work-at-home programs were important options.[27]

Henderson said that because of "the changing demographics, companies will have to do that to be more competitive. They're going to have to have more flexibility." It has become bad business practice to appear less than willing to address child-care problems. Henderson added, "I would like to think we are in the vanguard."[28]

But unpaid leave for child care is not as flexible a policy as it may appear. The structure of work itself does not change. One woman at IBM, who worked part-time because of child-care responsibilities, complained that her career was in a holding pattern with no promotions in sight. IBM's Henderson conceded that taking these options really was not a good decision for those who wanted to get ahead in their careers. In the long run, "you're really taking yourself out of the running for other things," he said.[29]

Expansion of work-at-home policies like those at IBM might be an attractive option to those who want to make the child care burden easier, but widespread adoption of these policies is a long way off. Link Resources, a Manhattan consulting group, reported that 11.2 million homeworkers were self-employed in 1990. The numbers had increased 11.9 percent since 1989. This was out of a total work force of 122.7 million employees. Link's studies survey 2,500 U.S. households annually. According to earlier government studies, a large number of male homeworkers are farmers, but Link reported that the greatest increases now are in white-collar jobs such as information processing.[30]

Child care has little to do with many men's decisions to work at home. Many of those surveyed were professional men who had the freedom to work either at home or at the office. They expressed more concern about avoiding commuting, with its problems of traffic and pollution.[31]

The majority of homeworkers, however, are women and many are working at home out of necessity. A survey of fourteen thousand women working at home finds that those with low skills do it because they have few options and have to care for small children or elderly relatives.

Working at home can result in a sense of isolation and a loss of upward mobility unless the homeworker owns the business.[32]

Increasingly, public and private employers seek advice on options to meet their workers' child-care needs. In California, the Child Initiative, established by the Bank of America Foundation in 1985, works with federal, state, and local government agencies and twenty-four corporations to train and license family day-care providers. Corporations shoulder two-thirds of the program's $3-million budget. The program claims to have provided about 1,100 new child-care spaces in 231 newly licensed family day-care homes in its first year. In 1988, Minnesota passed a law to award grants of $200 to $30,000 to individuals and companies for child-care start-up costs. These initiatives and others have helped families to find child care.[33]

On-site day care is marketed as the wave of the future. Leonard C. Kuhn, senior vice president for development at Kinder Care, the largest day-care chain, claims such centers will be cheaper and more convenient. This is a growth area that his company is "pursuing aggressively." Some child development scholars predict child-care centers like Kinder Care will become like fast-food chains, "coat-checking the kids." Large department stores and shopping centers have begun to set aside playrooms for children to stay in while their parents shop.[34]

The trend toward including day-care centers in office buildings is growing. Yvonne Ali, vice president of the Learning Center Inc., a Washington, D.C., firm that runs child-care facilities in office buildings, said that at first, "developers were against it." Ali said developers are worried about insurance and security needs required by child-care facilities. But this is changing as parents demand these services. "Now it seems that every office building has to have all the amenities: restaurants, a health club, and child-care center," she said. Ali said that rather than regarding the facility as a place to leave the children, "the parents here are very involved. They drop in for lunch, they help out, they come with us on field trips."[35]

Interestingly, Ali claims, "Fathers are getting more involved and the kids are beginning to understand the other part of their parents' lives." Bill Howard, a director for the Learning Center Inc., sees developmental benefits for the children. They "get a kind of undergraduate experience in socialization" before they reach kindergarten, Howard said. "They already know what a teacher does and what relations with peers are all about."[36]

But the parental involvement cited by the Learning Center was absent at another corporate facility widely cited as an example of good on-site child care. In Camden, New Jersey, the Campbell Soup Company's day-care center operates five days a week from 7 A.M. to 6 P.M. for up to 120 children, with a state-certified full-day kindergarten program for children up to age six. The work site has 1,800 employees. Campbell's pays about half of each child's tuition, no matter how many children a family enrolls. Total tuition ranged from $140 a week for the children younger than one year, to $92 a week for five- and six-year-olds.[37]

Executive secretary Diane Ronketty dropped off six-year-old Lisa at the company center each day. While Ronketty said she thought of Lisa often, she rarely walked the 200 feet to the day-care building until she got off work at 4:30. No more than six parents visited their children during a reporter's two-day visit.[38]

Two of the workers who visited the center were parents of infants. Among the others were the mother and father of a two-year-old girl who was spending her first day at the center and Ronketty, who broke her usual routine to take Lisa to the company's cafeteria for lunch. Apparently engrossed in their routine, the children paid little attention to their own parents who did come by. Ronketty liked "knowing you can get to your child in an emergency within minutes and knowing you can see them if and when you want during the day." She said "[it] relieves a lot of tension and anxiety."[39]

Some companies continue to change in order to meet the demands of work and family. Stride Rite, not content to be a leader in providing day care at the work site, expanded its child-care operations to the opening of an inter-generational care facility. Here employees can bring not only children from the ages of fifteen months on up, but aged relatives as well. The inter-generational care facility at their Cambridge, Massachusetts, headquarters serves fifty-five children and twenty-five adults. Companies developing such programs recognize that women most often perform the care-giving role for the entire family and that many employed women have parents to care for as well as children or grandchildren.[40]

In a promising new departure, the president of the Postal Workers Union persuaded management at the regional postal center in Syracuse, New York, to open a twenty-four-hour child-care facility. The Little Eagles Child Care Center sets a good example. Not only the postal service, but hospitals, supermarkets, service stations, and three-shift factories all need this kind of service for employed parents who lack other options for their children.[41]

Some small companies are exerting themselves to provide child-care services. Many of the owners are parents with small children of their own. They may give flextime, offer financial subsidies, or at the very least referral services.[42]

Some large companies have started opening their on-site centers to the public, setting a new community standard for high-quality care. Others are offering new benefits to child-care workers, recognizing the need to improve their skills and wages, which now average $183 per week. Still others are financing efforts by child-care centers to win accreditation. These corporations believe that information and referral services are cheap and popular but do little good where there are few openings. They also worry that their employees in the branches are not being helped as well as those at headquarters.[43]

In Charlotte, North Carolina, in 1991, IBM, American Express, Allstate, Duke Power, and a research park developer financed a new center, which is open to the public and to employees' children. They are following the example of Stride Rite, whose Roxbury center was started in 1971 as a service to the poor black community near its Cambridge, Massachusetts, headquarters. Only later was it opened to employees. The center in Charlotte has cut the teacher-child ratio to half of what is required by state law.[44]

Dayton-Hudson Corporation decided to address the lack of trained child-care workers by financing training. One of those sponsored was Sacramento, California, home-care provider Rosemarie Peebles. She learned how to take inventory of her toys to determine what new types she needs to foster broad skills in the children in her care. She also learned to keep computer records on naps, activities, and diaper changes, thus improving her communication with parents. IBM and Burroughs Wellcome Company paid for efforts by approximately twenty North Carolina child-care centers to win accreditation from the National Association for the Education of Young Children, the largest professional association of early childhood educators. Given the costs and needs, collaborations "are the only way corporations are going to be able to afford to go," according to Barbara Katersky, director of employee relations for American Express.[45]

Whether provided by parents or by care-givers at home or in day-care centers, child care raises questions of quality and safety as well as availability and cost. Abuse of children by their own parents has been acknowledged as a national problem at least since 1973, when Congress began appropriating funds to the states for child protection services. The services are largely underfunded and short-staffed but their existence acknowledges the problem and provides a recourse to help for some children.[46]

Widely publicized incidents of custodial child abuse create additional worries about the well-being of their children for employed parents. In January 1989, less than two weeks after she was hired by a Washington couple, forty-one-year-old Linda Johnson banged the head of the couple's nine-month-old daughter against a wall. The child died and Johnson was convicted of voluntary manslaughter. She said she was trying to stop the baby from "fussing and crying." In December 1991, Olivia Riner, a twenty-year-old au pair from Switzerland, was charged with second-degree murder and arson in the death of a three-month-old girl in her care. The police said she started fires in three bedrooms of the home of Denise and William Fischer in Thornwood, New York, and probably poured charcoal lighter fluid on the baby, Kristie. Riner pleaded innocent. As one family cautioned, when you hire nannies you "do take your risks" because "there are crazies in this world."[47] Riner, however, was aquitted on July 7, 1992, and returned home to Switzerland.

In early 1992, right after the Riner incident, Walt Disney's film *The Hand That Rocks the Cradle* came to theaters. The film depicts an emotionally disturbed and financially needy woman who gets herself hired as a nanny to an unsuspecting family. A series of macabre events leads up to a deadly confrontation between the two women. *Washington Post* reviewer Rita Kempley thought "this anti-feminist parable is both a labor and a pain." Screenwriter Amanda Silver expressed surprise at criticism that the film, her first, was "sexist" and implies women "should stay home and not hire nannies," which was not her point at all. She has a nanny for her three-month-old son and was only writing about "women's fears," especially the most "trenchant example," which is "bringing someone into your home to care for your children."[48]

The nanny industry in film and in real life is essentially unregulated. Child-care centers are regulated by the states, but abuses occur. An ABC television "Prime Time Live" show on June 20, 1991, used hidden cameras to film three day-care centers in the New Orleans area where middle-class parents sent their children. One center displayed a kind, loving environment; the film of one of the others showed children being slapped, playing on filthy floors, or being left in cribs all day with no adults around. The parents were paying from forty-five to sixty-five dollars a week. One parent, Debra Onnebane, watching her five-month-old son getting slapped, reacted angrily: "It makes me furious."[49]

Experts on the show gave helpful advice to concerned parents of the approximately two million children in sixty thousand child-care centers nationwide. Ellen Galinsky of the Families and Work Institute in New York advised, "If you know your program has someone who takes responsibility for your child, has a caring relationship with him, then don't worry." Barbara Willer of the National Association for the Education of Young Children (NAEYC) suggested, "Drop by unexpectedly to see what is happening."[50]

The standards for day-care centers recommended by NAEYC require that the director have a college degree, preferably a master's in child development, and three years' experience. The staff should have some training and experience. There should be no more than three to four babies or six to seven toddlers for each adult and the ambience should show that they care about children. Slapping a child should be absolutely forbidden. There should be careful attention to health and safety standards, fire drills, well-maintained play equipment, smoke detectors, first-aid supplies, and hazard-free play areas.[51]

California, Iowa, Florida, Minnesota, Texas, and Washington have established a registry of convicted child abusers so that day-care centers can run background checks on job applicants. Oprah Winfrey, who was sexually abused as a child, testified before the Senate Judiciary Committee in support of a National Child Protection Act which would extend the registry nationwide. According to Senator Joseph Biden of Delaware, chairman of the Senate Judiciary Committee, 6,200 convicted criminals have been detected seeking these jobs.[52]

Those who insist on mother care of children are upset by the increasing use of day care, even when that day care is safe and supportive. Not only "celebrity antifeminists" like Phyllis Schlafly but "regular" women raise their voices against the trend. The views of Barbara Shroyer of Fairhope, Alabama, are representative of the complaints. She expresses amazement at her "generation," accusing parents of pursuing "any avenue" to assure a "perfect baby" but being willing to have an institutional care-giver "during its most vulnerable developmental period." She worries about the effects on "day-care children of . . . early pressures to conform."

Shroyer, a former practicing lawyer, at home with her baby, hopes her views on day care are erroneous. If so, "it certainly won't alter the way I feel about the time spent with my daughter, but it will lessen my fears for the future of childhood in the United States." She forgets that many employed mothers cannot choose to stay home with their babies. Ironically, the town of Fairhope where Shroyer lives was founded in 1894 as a utopian community, whose residents supported a kindergarten for local children.[53]

Barbara Bush has added her voice to those who criticize mothers who have jobs. The First Lady thought a woman could not be a bank president and a mother at the same time. "What are you going to do about these children? Why do we have these crises in the schools? The working women opted to have children. You can't be the President of the United States and also be a mother." When it was pointed out to Mrs. Bush that the reality of most mothers' lives included employment and children, she wavered. ". . . But we're talking about the single parent, mother or father."[54]

Meeting the expectations of the new feminine mystique brings approval from family members but exhaustion for mothers. The difficulty of holding a job and caring for children is repeatedly confirmed in surveys and studies. No matter how many hours they work, employed mothers spend as much time at household labor as unpaid housewives did in the 1950s. Employed women continue to spend nearly eleven hours more than men each week on such unpaid chores as cooking and keeping track of money. Regardless of income, hours, or status outside the home, women do more housework than their husbands.[55]

Yet spouses discuss their housework as if they shared it equally despite this disparity. And some wives, like those in immigrant and African-American families who have long persuaded their husbands that they were working just to "help out" when, in fact, their incomes were absolutely necessary, have little inclination to emphasize the unequal burdens and to insist on change.[56]

In every category of income and employment status, mothers spend more time than fathers in activities solely devoted to child care. Men in households in the $35,000-and-over income category spend more time in these activities (four hours per week) than men in lower income categories. Mothers in that same $35,000-and-over income category spend twice as much time (eight hours a week) with their children. Men take children on trips to the zoo or the park. Women feed, bathe, and clothe them, and deal with their emotional problems. As one supportive father put it when his five-year-old had problems at school, "Handle it the best way you can, honey. I'm a hundred percent behind you."[57]

A 1991 poll done by the Roper Organization for *Playboy* magazine reported that men were increasing their parenting and housekeeping duties, but change is slow to come. Martha Farnsworth Riche of the Population Reference Bureau says studies show men do not care as much as women do about whether a house is neat. John Robinson, director of America's Use of Time Project at the University of Maryland, College Park, says wives often redo whatever housework a husband does anyway.[58]

The nation's most stressed-out men are those who have young children and wives who do not have jobs. Their stress arises from financial problems. The most stressed-out women are those who are employed and have young children at home. Three out of four mothers are in this category. Forty percent of employed women suffer frequent job-related tension, perceived pay inequities, and overwork, along with the demands of child care and housework.[59]

This unequal burden of housework, child care, and job stress brings several kinds of response from women. Some women see the need for more day care and other supports for employed mothers. Others say that if women insist that husbands do more, divorce will be the result. In the 1970s, such insistence on husbands sharing household burdens led to discontent and criticism. Now, says syndicated columnist Ellen Goodman, "he is doing more than his father and feeling under-appreciated. She is doing more than her husband and feeling under-valued." But taking a different tack, economist Robert Kuttner calls discussion of the unequal household burden a "standard feminist plaint." He notes that upper-income people generally used their income to hire "small armies of surrogate wives." They became workaholics who "almost totally parceled out the role of mother into purchased services . . ." He worries about children in these economically ad-vantaged families becoming "spoiled rotten."[60]

In newspapers and magazines, today's well-educated professionals discuss how career women balance work, a marriage, and family. Sharing of housework and child care occurs primarily among uniquely advantaged, middle-class professionals. One recent mother insists that housework will only be devalued if parents convey to their children that it is an unimportant activity. Her little girl sees that she and her husband, a physicist, are both professionals, but "both shop and cook and clean and take care of her"; she would understand that "work and housekeeping are integral parts of a well-balanced, healthy life." Though the mother is an economist, she disregards the fact that em-ployment is valued in our society by how much employees are paid, and that household workers are paid less than either physicists or economists.[61]

A male professor notes that in six years of marriage, he has "done the majority of the domestic chores . . ." Ignoring the effect a four-year-old's activities might have on a classroom environment and the many choices available to him in academia, he "frequently" takes his child to his college classes, where the child draws on the blackboard while he lectures or sits with him while he monitors examinations. The professor can also take three months off from his research while his wife attends a seminar far from home. He wants it understood that he is just an average person and not a "new man." However, "No man in his right mind is going to sign up for the role traditionally relegated to women."[62]

Other proof of changing roles was found in a 1989 nationwide survey by Robert Half International, an executive recruitment firm. Eight out of ten employees were willing to sacrifice rapid career advancement to have more time with their families. In a 1990 poll done by Half, over 50 percent of the men surveyed said they would be willing to have their salaries cut 25 percent to have more personal or family time. The *Playboy*-Roper poll of 1991 shows increasing numbers of men in the 18–44 age group who believe leisure time, including time spent with children, is more important than their job. Such attitudes, analysts note, undercut the assumption that only women want a mommy track with flexible hours and time off to care for children and slower advancement in the workplace.[63]

They suggest encouraging a "parent track" for men and women who might accept reduced incomes and less upward mobility to spend time with their families. One man calls this a "sanity track" but recognizes it would interfere with his progress on the job. According to James Levine, director of The Fatherhood Project of the nonprofit Families and Work Institute in New York, flexibility for working fathers will be a significant issue in the 1990s. Companies must "realize it's not just moms, but dads, that want to use the policies," Levine said.[64]

Levine gives seminars on Daddy stress of the kind claimed by Jeffrey Coulter, who complains that Microsoft Corporation's New York office fired him for not spending more time at after-hours training sessions and social events. Coulter, age thirty-six, said he worked fifty-six hours a week but had to be home because his wife often travelled as a flight attendant. Company spokeswoman Pam Edstrom said he was fired for poor performance. Levine noted that "lack of time for families is an underground phenomenon that men aren't talking about. That's because corporate culture tends to be macho culture. You don't talk about your problems. It's a big 'no-no,' an 'invisible dilemma.' "[65]

Attitudes toward gender roles and child care are slowly changing, but in a 1989 nationwide poll only 43 percent of black women felt that men were beginning to think differently about child care and the need for women's equality. More attention is being focused on the issue. *Ebony*, the leading magazine subscribed to by African-Americans, remains ambivalent about the necessity of change. One article, somewhat marred by class bias, praised women who "make it work by balancing the diverse demands of a career or job, and children and family." All but one of the women profiled by *Ebony* were employed as a manager.[66]

In the same issue, Harvard psychiatrist Alvin Poussaint provided a persuasive rationale to men for sharing the burden of housework and child care. He explains that "it's not just a question of equality, but also a question of making a better home life . . . when a man pitches in, it helps build a better relationship with the child and provides a good model for the youngster as well."[67]

Ebony's changing views on the subject are displayed in a 1991 article on "Secrets About Black Men That Every Black Woman Should Know." The magazine advised a black woman who wanted successful relationships to remember that "In American society men are socialized to be the providers and protectors of women." Challenging this view would be counterproductive, according to the magazine.[68]

For many women in the labor force, discussion about changing roles is beside the point. A flight attendant, divorced and in her early thirties, described to me her situation, which is typical for many women, during a weather-induced delay somewhere in upstate New York. She had been in a long joint custody arrangement with her former husband, who was angry because she left him. As so many women do in the heat of a divorce, she had given up the house and barely made enough to support herself and contribute her part of the children's expenses, including child care.

Moreover, she had incurred additional legal expenses when her ex-husband sought revenge by trying to obtain complete child custody. She had met a pilot with whom she had a good relationship and he seemed to want to marry her. "If he does," she said, "we've agreed that I can stop working. I've been working constantly since I was eighteen and I'm tired. I'm glad I had the experience, but I'll be happy to stay home. Up to now I've never had that choice."

When asked about his choices, she answered that he did not have many, but "he's perfectly happy and wants what I want. We don't want to change the world." Perhaps after she stays home awhile she will go back to her job. Maybe he will change his mind, maybe they will divorce, but at least for now she sees a choice.[69]

Instead of getting men to take more responsibility for children, we could try to change the way work is performed, including schedules, travel, meetings, and deadlines. This reform is proving more difficult than providing employer-sponsored child care. In many supervisory, well-paying jobs, a workday is nine to five and beyond, with many meetings and frequent travel a necessity. More companies are showing flexibility, but conference calls, teleconferencing, and other means of minimizing disruption of employees' lives are underutilized.[70]

However, we should not be too surprised by this. On almost every issue, from long hair to button-down shirts, corporate culture has proved decidedly resistant to change. Most corporate leaders do not want to change the culture. They attribute their success to long hours and devotion to their jobs. After years of predicting that corporate life would grow easier, executives report that it has become harder, with longer hours, more weekend work, and more travel.

Corporate culture changes when a sufficient number of workers demand change. But many employees prefer the workplace as it is, and demand motherhood supports so that they or their husbands can take time from work to care for children. In a nationwide poll taken in August 1989, 63 percent of women and 70 percent of men thought women still had to be as tough as men to succeed on the job. Furthermore, only 35 percent of women and 26 percent of men hoped the workplace would become transformed as more women became bosses. If women still have to be as tough as men to succeed, employed mothers must insist on sharing child care with fathers. Otherwise slow change in the structure of work combined with slowness in changing child-care roles make it less likely that women will move up.[71]

The needed change is readily apparent. When they can afford it, more women and men have started part-time or job-sharing arrangements. More and more companies provide child-care services at the work site. [72]

In 1981, in *The Second Stage*, Betty Friedan suggested that changes in the workplace and child care would occur when they were understood to benefit the "well-being of families" and not just women. "The solutions will come about only because more and more men demand them too . . . because of their own new problems and needs and choices, as fathers and for themselves as men. Single-parent households headed by men increased to about 1.4 million in 1990, and more men are expressing a desire to help with the care of their children. But the change is still not occurring fast enough in most sectors of the population to relieve the discontent generated by mothers trying to juggle the dual chores of child care and employment."[73]

If data showing an increase in younger women who plan to have children are correct, these problems are likely to worsen. A woman, as any individual, has rights and responsibilities, but society's assumption that she is automatically responsible for child care means she will remain discontented.

Mothers are not "supposed" to work as long as men do or make as much money or think single-mindedly about something other than children and mate. They are expected to subsume their own personality to family. This means having no other real interests, but only substitute or contingent ones, depending on other family members' desires.

There was a time in our country's history when fathers took responsibility for the care of their offspring. A complete reversal of roles today is neither required nor necessary. If women, however, are to have an equal opportunity for successful careers and families, both fathers and mothers must share child care.

I

Searching for Solutions

Developing strategies to address women's complaints about employment and child care requires an organized challenge to gender relations and patriarchy. This is because the child care–employment problem arises in the context of a traditional family ideal. This ideal legitimates gender relations that continue to restrict women's economic opportunities, reproductive choice, sexual freedom, and sense of independent identity.

This book explains that the idealized traditional family is a modern invention. Mothers have not always had primary responsibility for children. The history of child care indicates that children have been taken care of by fathers, mothers, wet nurses, nannies, boarding schools, kindergartens, and nurseries, sometimes for better and sometimes for worse, depending on the quality of the care.

Our modern idea of a traditional family is that mothers take care of children alone while fathers work. Yet this version, which was reflected in 1950s television shows such as "Father Knows Best," "Leave It to Beaver," and "The Jane Wyman Show" was more fiction than fact. Even in the 1950s, many mothers did not do it alone, especially in the South, where black domestic workers did some, if not all, of the housework in white middle-class homes.[1]

Research and theories about gender roles, child care, and infant development to which we have been exposed encourage us to cling to the mother-care tradition today despite the economic burdens women face. Much of the research on gender roles and infant development reinforces existing roles. The research that does not is usually obscured or rejected because most people seek reinforcement for their behavior rather than impetus to change.

The researchers and theorists diligently propose remedies to relieve the stress women shoulder in their dual roles as mothers and employees. They are looking hard to find ways to ease the discontent of middle-class "Supermoms." They worry about the next generation of women who face a similar fate when they marry and have children and jobs.

The large numbers of researchers issue even larger numbers of studies proposing everything from more child-care centers to the total restructuring of American society. A few reports, including A *Mother's Work* (1985) by Deborah Fallows, a linguist and wife of former White House speech writer and journalist James Fallows, describe economically able mothers who have chosen full-time motherhood over paid work.[2]

Most studies, however, deal with the difficulty of balancing jobs and children. Researchers chiefly propose changes that are already occurring: fathers should help mothers more or government should aid parents with "motherhood supports" such as more and better child-care centers, parental leave, and flextime.[3]

More sweeping solutions include giving tax credits to real estate developers to build affordable housing near the workplaces and shopping centers, with nearby meal preparation facilities. Implementing these suggestions, say researchers, may make it easier for families to enjoy happier marriages and help some women to balance jobs and children.[4]

Virtually all of the studies overlook race and class differences among families, the problems of female-headed households, and families who work on anything other than nine-to-five shifts. One of the most influential experts on infant development, seventy-three-year-old Harvard pediatrician Dr. T. Berry Brazelton, acknowledged in 1991 that neither he nor eighty-two-year-old Benjamin Spock nor any of the other most-cited experts speaks for poor people. "I wish we did," he says. "But the poor in this country don't have enough self-image left to even know what they want to do for their children. It's been taken away from them. There's absolutely no feeling of importance." Many of the findings, therefore, apply largely to white middle-class families.[5]

The child-care and employment researchers also uniformly ignore the possibility that helping Supermom put on her cape is not just a matter of giving her more help with the children and housework or making things easier on the job. When researchers advise helping Supermom with her "responsibilities," they are dismissing her rights as a person. The choices she makes about how to spend her time and what interests to pursue become automatically more constrained than those of fathers. Her opportunity for self-realization goes unnoticed. This is one result of defining a woman's rights mainly as her responsibilities for family and child care.

These researchers are not anonymous government employees but are often well-respected university professors with best-selling books. Pulitzer Prize–winning journalist Susan Faludi discusses some of these works in her 1991 study, *Backlash: The Undeclared War Against American Women*. She examines how the media, politicians, and experts undercut the struggle for women's rights in the 1980s and made employed mothers feel guilty about their achievements, which supposedly neglected children and family.[6]

Feminism was indeed undercut by female experts, who behaved like Phyllis Schlafly, a professional career woman who graduated from law school and ran for Congress, then became a regular on the national lecture circuit leading a movement demanding that women should be only homemakers. These experts authored studies and were "having it all" themselves, but seemed not to understand that they were indirectly urging most women to abandon the strategies that made it possible to compete, that they were essentially urging women not to try. Their views resonated deeply among women who read them seeking comfort for their predicament or affirmation of their acculturated beliefs that the problem was a lack of child-care services or a personal inability to cope, not gender roles and discrimination.

In one of the most influential studies, *A Lesser Life* (1986), Sylvia Hewlett suggests that "motherhood supports" would truly liberate women. Such support systems have been widely adopted in Western Europe; she praises the extensive government-funded child-care system in Sweden as a model for the United States. Hewlett concludes that women should demand a similar system in this country, instead of organizing for laws against sex discrimination on the job. Hewlett's book strengthened the movement for government-funded child care but at the cost of defining women as mothers, not persons. It would have been more helpful to urge women to work against sex discrimination and then to use the same organizing tactics to gain child care. Furthermore, Hewlett did not analyze carefully how these programs affect the lives of West German or French or British women, or how European governments, such as Sweden's, pay for them.[7]

As Eleanor Smeal, president of the Fund for a Feminist Majority, described her conversations with several Swedish women, she was told, "Don't be fooled. We don't have enough child care and when we do, it's women who are the child-care workers." She found that European women complained generally about having access only to traditional female jobs. They also predicted that if the United States government funds expanded child care, those "traditional" jobs would remain poorly paid and female-dominated.[8]

The Women's Research and Education Institute examined European countries' funding of motherhood supports after Hewlett's book was published. They found that no European country funded enough child care for children and that employed women are principally in occupationally segregated, lower-paying jobs.[9]

By the end of the decade, with much less attention and policy persuasion, more insightful books such as Arlie Hochschild's *The Second Shift* (1989) were published. Hochschild's study is based on interviews with fifty mostly middle-class, double-income couples in the San Francisco Bay area and forty-five other people including baby-sitters, day-care workers, and divorcees with children. She described the disadvantages mothers in husband-wife families face on the job and at home. The "second shift" starts when the mother gets home from her job and begins her "mother" work. Hochschild's solution to reducing Supermom's workload is to have fathers share more in housework and parenting.[10]

Books such as Hochschild's raise public awareness about the issues. Most people now agree that more child-care services should be available for mothers who take paid jobs. However, the suggested transformation of women's and men's roles is still happening slowly.

Only in a small but growing number of professional middle- and upper-class families are such role changes considered desirable. The fathers who give primary care to their children are still widely regarded, except among some intellectuals and highly paid professionals, as unduly burdened.

Reflecting the weight of public opinion, when developing child-care and family-leave policies, politicians in Congress and the White House assume that mother care is best for children. They and their New Right supporters of the "traditional family" believe that mothers should not have jobs when their children are young, except if the mother is poor. During a "Modern Maturity" television talk show discussion, Phyllis Schlafly's principal objection to child care was that most women have jobs because they want a more expensive life-style, not because they really need to work.[11]

Child development experts accept the historical evidence that children require care, of course, but they do not agree that care has to come from the family or from their mothers. Dr. Brazelton says he worries more about how taking a child to a day-care center affects the parents than how it affects the children. Some child development experts, such as Dr. Jay Belsky of Pennsylvania State University, feel that maternal bonding is important for the first few months for infants; others, such as psychologist Burton White, director of the Massachusetts-based Center for Parent Education, maintain that parent or grandparent care until age three is absolutely the best for children. His reason is that parents and grandparents are more reliable. University of Virginia psychologist Sandra Scarr insists that either parental or nonparental care will serve. She prefers professional day care because it is likely to be high-quality care where relationships with other children and adults are sometimes better than the care some families give.[12]

All experts agree that the most important ingredient for a child's healthy psychological development is nonabusive and consistent care, whether from a parent, a nanny, or a child-care worker in a center. Most people prefer parental care, nonetheless, for their own psychological comfort and because they believe it is best for children. They are unlikely to satisfy this desire, however, because in one-parent families, that parent must have a job, and in two-parent families both often work.[13]

When a preference is established for parental care, the obvious question is whether there is a reason that it should be mother care. On this issue, child development experts equivocate. Most say it depends on the circumstances and on the interest and abilities of individual parents.

Religious and political proponents, however, feel strongly about the issue. Some argue mother care is best for economic reasons. Brigitte and Peter Berger, in *The War Over the Family*, are convinced that the customary pattern of dividing work into specific tasks for men and women is more efficient and that, besides, women are happier when their families come first. Harvard economist George Gilder takes the argument a step further in *Wealth and Poverty*. He believes the heterosexual nuclear family with the male as breadwinner is essential to national economic productivity and thus is important to everyone. Men in our society, Gilder asserts, are defined by how much they can produce, and need to have traditional families. Bachelors without family responsibilities involve themselves in nonproductive activities because of the absence of responsibility for women and children. Consequently, he argues, the government should not encourage or fund child care, parental leave, or any programs that interfere with the traditional family.[14]

Religious beliefs concerning appropriate roles lead some parents to prefer mother care over father care. In Genesis, they note, God created woman from the rib of Adam, thus subordinating her from the beginning. Further, Eve's tempting of Adam in the Garden of Eden made them sexual creatures. Woman's sexuality therefore must find expression in motherhood. She must submit to her husband and bring forth children in pain and he must work by the sweat of his brow to support the family. As Rev. Jerry Falwell and other fundamentalists argue, religious imperatives mean that gender roles are permanent. The traditional sexual division of labor is consequently natural and ordained by God.[15]

Mother-care proponents consider the strong attachments children form to their mothers sufficient proof that mother care is a biological rule rather than acculturation. A young man who attended one of my lectures insisted that substances binding a mother and child were found in mother's milk and therefore to disturb breast-feeding or any part of the mother-child relationship would jeopardize the child's future. He based his comments on the theories of anthropologists Lionel Tiger and Robin Fox, which posit that studies of the animal kingdom, in general, apply to man because all animal behavior is rooted in biology. Fox and Tiger, however, present no evidence that good care by someone other than mother is harmful to children.[16]

Phyllis Schlafly argues in *The Power of the Positive Woman* (1978), as well as in other writings and personal appearances, that motherhood is woman's calling. A rare woman such as Mother Teresa can find satisfaction outside the home, and some women may successfully pursue a marriage and a career, but this works only if they can do it within their own resources and not let career stand in the way of marriage and family, according to those who believe as Schlafly does. She agrees with Rev. Falwell that the maternal instinct is innate.[17]

Anthropologist Nancy Makepeace Tanner in *On Becoming Human* cites theories of human evolution as evidence of an environmental basis for the existence of mother care. As the theory goes, a major characteristic distinguishing humans from other primates is the physical helplessness of infants. This happened because the birth canal narrowed when humans began to stand upright. Human babies, therefore, are born physically less mature than other primates, with relatively smaller heads in order to ease passage through the birth canal. Unlike apes, human babies are born without a hair covering, and have a greater need for warmth from some other source. They lack the apes' movable toe and cannot grasp another human being for steady support, hence the need for cradling. Under these conditions, theorists conclude, the sheltering of infants and breast-feeding by mothers were instrumental to survival.[18]

Tanner and neurophysiologist Ruth Bleier believe that over the three million years of human evolution, infancy and nursing were prolonged. High infant death rates meant multiple pregnancies were necessary for human survival. The system of dividing work into specific tasks for men and women began very early. Encumbered by children, women were unable to hunt but could pursue agriculture. Women's occupations were functional to the extent that they were compatible with child-rearing and mothering. In some cultures older people worked as child tenders while mothers traveled afar for hunting and gathering. According to Tanner's and Bleier's theories, environmental imperatives help to explain nurturing and the sexual division of labor dating from the earliest period of human existence.[19]

Tanner and Bleier agree that theories based on the early stages of human evolution imply that mother care was a cultural adaptation. No automatic generalizations can be made that such behavior is timeless or that modern conditions require mother care. Most biologists explain that it is always difficult to ascertain cause and effect in human behavior; verifying the influence of biology, rather than culture or learned behavior, on the mother-care tradition is probably impossible. There is no exact answer.[20]

Analyses of human evolution do help us to understand why mother care is easily seen as important. When today's mothers choose to breastfeed babies and spend more time with them than other people do, strong mother-child bonds can be expected to form. Conversely, if fathers feed infants and children and care for them as frequently as mothers do, father-child bonds could be expected. The reality of human adaptability means we can respond to the real conditions of life for fathers, mothers, and children today.

Researchers in other fields of human behavior are also trying to explain why child care became a mother's responsibility. Their ideas are also used to reinforce the widespread reluctance to adapt gender roles to modern conditions. In 1974, sociologist Nancy Chodorow advanced the proposition that basic sex differences exist in personality development. The female personality is defined more in relation and connection with other people than is the masculine personality. This happens, she argues, because of the way in which children are raised.[21]

As infants, boys and girls strongly identify with their mothers. For boys to grow up to become men, they must repress this early identification with their mothers, and in the process they repress their capacity for intimacy. Girls continue to identify with their mothers because they grow up to become women. As a result, throughout their lives females see themselves as connected to others. Care and love remain identified as feminine so long as women are the primary caretakers of infants.[22]

Historian Carroll Smith-Rosenberg affirmed the validity of a distinct women's culture in an enormously influential 1975 *Signs* article, "The Female World of Love and Ritual." Other historians had argued that the nineteenth-century emphasis on domesticity and separate spheres for women and men oppressed women. Smith-Rosenberg turned those beliefs upside down when she praised the importance of women's networks of love and caring. The women she described actually reveled in a separate female culture.[23]

The most visible and influential work on women's separate culture was psychologist Carol Gilligan's 1982 book, *In a Different Voice*. Gilligan applied Chodorow's theories in her study of eleven-year-old male and female children in a sixth-grade class. Gilligan's findings are based on the children's different reactions to acculturation. Gilligan affirmed Chodorow's speculations that women and men develop distinct characteristic behavior. Boys justify moral choices by balancing one option against another in sequence, choosing what they think is best according to an abstract idea of moral justice.[24]

According to established psychological theory, girls often do not consider the concept of justice. Psychologists have long considered this a failure to reach "higher" levels of moral thinking. Instead of using abstract rules to decide whether an action is right or wrong, girls focus on who would suffer by the action. They then decide that the best choice is the one causing the least personal harm. When asked whether a man should steal a drug he cannot afford to buy in order to save his wife's life, a boy weighs the factors, decides property is less valuable than life, that laws are sometimes more honored in the breach than in the observance, and is entirely comfortable in saying the man should steal. The boy assumes his assessment is totally logical and that anyone would reach his conclusion. Asked the same question, an eleven-year-old girl equivocates, unable to decide. She wonders not about property and life and law along a calculus, but what effect the theft could have on the relationship between the man and his wife. Contrary to established interpretations, this pattern of responses, Gilligan insists, does not mean that women's moral reasoning is underdeveloped, just different.[25]

Such affirmations of women's culture—valuing womanly responsibility, connection, altruism, and caring—have supported a negative redefinition of women's rights. Men's rights are defined as reflecting separation, autonomy, and hierarchy while women's rights are seen in the context of care and responsibility for others, including child care. Those who believe in the primacy of mother care can use the "difference theories" of Chodorow, Smith-Rosenberg, Gilligan, and others as proof for their position even though they were not intended for that purpose.[26]

These ideas are also useful in arguing for changing the time, place, and manner of work to accommodate the ethic of care rather than requiring women to adjust to work's current realities. The analysis is embraced by many women because it describes their acculturated responses to the same sort of moral dilemmas. Such thinking, however, extrapolated to policy issues is dangerous, because it rationalizes the continued exploitation of women. Opponents of equal pay insist that many women choose jobs with less pay and responsibility in order to care for their families and that therefore these women are not victims of wage discrimination.

While women express an ethic of care and connection, men continue to exercise power and authority in traditional ways. The woman who comes home from work, cooks, and does housework because she "cares" while her husband watches the evening news is not comforted by the difference theory. She begins to believe it would be better to acculturate both men and women so that both sexes express an ethic of care. Emphasizing the distinctiveness of women only leads to more dishes, diapers, and domesticity.

Difference theory, when pushed very hard, has other pernicious consequences. For example, it adversely affects the pay equity claims of women in traditional female jobs such as nursing. Nurses and school teachers argue that their pay should be evaluated in terms of their effort, skill, and responsibility. They have been traditionally paid less than men in jobs that are objectively no more difficult because of the identification of theirs as women's jobs. The assumption that women work for "extras" while men work to support a family leads to a situation where electricians and tree trimmers are paid more than teachers and nurses. In disputes over these pay equity issues, Gilligan's theories are misused to defeat those who would like to see paycheck sexism abolished.

Difference theory also defeats those who would like to end job segregation. In the *EEOC* v. *Sears, Roebuck* (1986) case, the Equal Employment Opportunity Commission proved women were underrepresented in relatively high-paying commission jobs selling appliances and furniture. Sears defended itself successfully against sex discrimination charges by citing Gilligan and others. In their defense, Sears insisted women preferred the lower-paying jobs because they did not want the hard-sell pressure. Women's primary concern with relationships at home and at work could be presumed to make them sacrifice worldly advancement in favor of less-demanding jobs and limited hours to accommodate their devotion to family.[27]

The *Sears* decision awakened many observers to the dangers of difference theories when used in the real world. Such theories imply that men are appropriately judged by their economic success and cannot be expected to make care in personal relationships a priority. Difference theory also perpetuates "glass ceilings" and "mommy tracks," limiting women's career possibilities. Those who use difference theory to oppose women's demands for better job opportunities in the real world disregard its theoretical nature. The theory is intended to explain women's acculturated behavior, not their biological imperatives.[28]

Some analysts respond to these real-world difficulties by creating new theories. They expand different male and female voices by arguing there are not just two but many different voices. Princeton University theorist Joan Scott's *Gender and the Politics of History* proposes a commonsense and superficially appealing theory that policymakers or judges might use to avoid any decisions at all about what women or men want. Scott suggests they consider individual situations one at a time. The history of feminism, she says, can be divided into two periods. In one, women strive to be treated as men's equals; in the other, women want to be treated as different from men and demand different treatment, to be protected or better. She prefers the latter; her definition of feminism insists on "differences" instead of "difference" as the very meaning of equality itself.[29]

Scott acknowledges the existence of men and women as gender categories, with cultural behavior appropriate to a given society at a particular time. She thinks, however, that the meaning of man and woman should be understood as not fixed but *relative* to specified contexts. To her, it is okay to advocate parental leave or child-care subsidies by pointing to women's ethic of care and their motherhood role as long as it is clear "women" means only some, not all, women.[30]

Other women may not express the same ethic or even be interested in motherhood and should not be denied comparable worth or have their individual rights devalued. According to Scott's theory, the judge in the *Sears* case should have understood that while some women express an ethic of care, others do not. Nor should policymakers be pure biological determinists or functionalists. They should not consider "women" but should take into account the distinct needs of "different" women when enacting child care or any other policy proposals.

Scott's theory offers little to those who want to challenge traditional job classifications because people may presume "women" fit into traditional categories, whatever the context. The burden of establishing one's own "difference" is placed on the challenger. Women do have certain group characteristics that are relevant to discrimination claims. They include a common history of exclusion from reproductive choice, employment, and economic rights on account of sex. To the extent that these grievances are suffered by women as a group, they call for group remedies.

Individual women who are not extremely privileged do not have the power or resources to effect change. As a consequence, Scott's differences theory can be used to deny a demand for any policy to help women as a group. One legal result could be that each employee would have to bring his or her own discrimination suit for a grievance rather than permitting class action suits focused on common complaints.

Even though the complaints are common, a judge could insist that each plaintiff bring suit separately so that each case might be examined for its uniqueness. Whether the courts permit such actions is one measure of their willingness to acknowledge the discrimination women experience as a group. The theory lends support to George Gilder's and Brigitte and Peter Berger's view that policy must be designed to promote individual choice without challenging customary gender roles. Insisting on policies such as child care and parental leave encourages change in traditional behavior.

Feminist law professors Mary Joe Frug and Joan C. Williams propose a more promising idea challenging directly men's traditional life patterns as well as the existing system of wage labor. They assume that in the colonial period most men could be ideal, or productive, workers because work and family were both under their control in the home. This changed during the Industrial Revolution when the ideal (male) worker left his home and his child-care responsibilities, leaving the mother at home to care for the children (and the male worker when he returned from work).[31]

Today, women try to be both ideal worker and caretaker while men largely remain free to be only ideal worker. Under such circumstances, so long as women make child care a priority, their work force marginality is the likely result. In Frug's and Williams's view, the labor system as it developed during and after the Industrial Revolution has adapted to modern conditions by exploiting employed mothers in nuclear families and impoverishing divorced women and their children through a lack of support. Frug and Williams insist that women do not really have a choice. Mothers cannot be ideal workers because in order for men to be ideal workers the mothers have to be responsible for children. Fathers assume mothers will be care-givers. Women assume that if they do not sacrifice, no one will, and men assume if they do not, someone else will. [32]

Ideal worker theorists argue that child care perpetuates the marginalization of women workers. Women cannot be ideal workers even when they have child care, parental leave, and other motherhood supports. The gender system does not change with such supports, it merely adjusts. They dismiss as preposterous Hochschild's suggestion that individual women rebel against providing all the child care. Most men and some women, they say, find it unthinkable that men should play the supportive role while women become ideal workers. Married women want to take time off or pretend they can when their children are small. They reject the burden-sharing suggested by Hochschild and others because this would mean that neither parent could be an ideal worker. Equality for women cannot be gained under current circumstances by asking that men share women's disabilities. They cite the Equal Pay Act of 1963 which compensated for past wage inequity by raising women's salaries instead of lowering men's. The ideal worker theorists ultimately join Chodorow, Gilligan, and others in encouraging change in the structure and requirements of the workplace. Changing workplace policies will perhaps make burden-sharing more effective. [33]

None of these theories solve the problem of balancing home, jobs, and family; nor do they offer women time to consider or define their individual needs. They do, however, help us to clarify what is missing from the analysis and why reform is so difficult to achieve.

Faster transformation of the workplace and restructuring of gender relations will occur when enough women decide they want change. That may sound simplistic but it is true. Just as many women feared an Equal Rights Amendment because it seemed to threaten their idea of family relations and roles, many women are frightened of changing gender roles at home to relieve the burdens about which they complain. Analysis can tell us what is required, but it cannot make us act.

The struggle for policy to help employed mothers with their family obligations has the same set of perils as the struggle for individual rights. Indeed, helping employed mothers is one way to make it possible for more women to be able to enjoy greater personal freedom. Advocating family policy may sound less strident than arguing for women's rights; it may also be more socially acceptable and even necessary under certain political circumstances.

Fundamentally, though, what is needed is an organized challenge to gender relations and patriarchy and an understanding that imposing child care responsibilities principally on one parent rather than both is a deprivation of rights. The issue of child care is really an issue of power, resources, and control among adults; it is not a battle over who is more suited for care.

Women who complain about the burden of work and child care should understand the enormity of the changes required and have the courage to be involved in the change. Mommy tracks, glass ceilings, employment discrimination, and limits on reproductive choice are only the most recent repercussions of our having defined women's rights as synonymous with women's responsibilities.

Women who retreated from the women's rights movement into family concerns in the 1980s were not so much manipulated as afraid. They were fearful of taking the next step, of demanding changes in relationships and gender roles and of moving into what they believed were uncharted waters. The way was not really unknown, however, because there was a time in our history when gender roles were more fluid and fathers successfully played a major role in child rearing.

II
Father Care, Other Care

We should not be so worried about changing our family structures to give women more freedom and opportunity. What we call the traditional family first emerged in the middle of the nineteenth century, but became fully developed only in this century. The Ozzie-and-Harriet, model middle-class family with the husband working and the wife taking care of children and home did not exist for most of our history. Upper-class and bourgeois white wives were usually assisted in caregiving by domestic servants. Even some working-class white families had African-American maids. Throughout the country until 1950, personal service was the largest census category of women employees and they mostly "lived in" until after World War II.[1]

During the seventeenth and eighteenth centuries, first in the colonies and then in the young United States, fathers had primary responsibility for child care beyond the early nursing period. They not only directed their children's education and religious worship but often decided what they would eat, played with them, and hushed them to sleep when they awakened in the night. Today's trend toward increased parenting by the father to relieve mothers from the stress of balancing jobs and child-rearing may be seen simply as a return to the patterns of old.

It appears that the customs of Native Americans made little impact on the colonists' child-care practices. When the Europeans arrived, gender roles among the Native Americans were fluid and democratic. Just like employed mothers today, Native American women did a great deal of work. They were gatherers, processors of food, and nurturers of infants. But women were also traders and exercised considerable power in kinship relations and economics. Diversity among the tribes must be emphasized. Not all Native American women shared equal power and status with men. However, a high frequency of egalitarian relationships, based on tasks performed rather than sex, existed.[2]

The Native Americans tried to insist that their women continue their prominent roles in politics, religious ritual, and trade despite the refusal of the Europeans to respect them. Europeans made agreements with males, ignoring the power and autonomy of the matrilineal clan in which women exercised considerable power. The change in the relative power relationships between Native Americans and whites as the number of Europeans increased limited opportunities for an exchange of child-rearing or other practices.[3]

The colonists, living at first in primitive conditions, maintained no clear sexual division of labor. Women worked in the households along with servants if they had them and as servants if they were indentured. Ordinary colonial white women, like Native American women, maintained and built the fire that was so important for cooking and warmth. They prepared food, sewed, and perhaps sold surplus cheeses, eggs, and bread.[4]

In some families the wife also worked in the fields alongside her husband. Indentured servants worked in households and tobacco fields. Once their indentures were up, they were free to choose marriage partners. They tended to marry and start families late. Many indentured servants were sexually abused by their masters. If they became pregnant, their term of labor could be extended as punishment for the loss of productivity.[5]

In cities, wives purchased or made household goods. If their husbands were artisans or shopkeepers they managed the business when he was away or ill. Both rural and urban white wives maintained the family's wearing apparel. They boiled laundry and routinely ironed clothing. Wealthy women had servants or slaves to perform these tasks.[6]

Africans sold as slaves to the colonists brought with them a somewhat similar cultural baggage when it came to child raising and family. In the New World, relations between enslaved black men and women and their children grew out of a complex combination of African traditions, Christian beliefs, and adjustments made to slavery. Their understanding of relationships was in many ways similar to that of the Europeans. In most African societies the family was a strong communal institution stressing the dominance of males, the importance of children, and extended kinship networks.[7]

African societies did not condemn illegitimacy, but included children born under such circumstances within the extended family circle. What the Africans found in the New World varied, depending on whether they were on a large plantation or small farm or household.[8]

In slavery, however, African men were forced to submit to the master's authority as well as to share or defer authority over their wives and children to the master. The African family had to respond immediately to a loss of power and changed circumstances.[9]

By the eighteenth century, the economic growth and success of the colonies resulted in class differentiation in the behavior and expectations of men and women. Little changed in poorer families, but in middle- and upper-class families segregation of women and their work increased. The gentlewoman's life was focused on her servants, peers, and household management. Genteel behavior meant socializing, entertaining visitors, taking tea, doing needlework, and making polite conversation.[10]

In the South, a growing gentry emerged. On Southern plantations, mistresses presided over complex households that included slaves. The gentry lived in palatial houses with wings and public spaces and slave quarters. The plantation system engendered more separation of men's and women's work and domestic roles. Under her husband's authority and supervision, the wife directed the household work of the slaves and their care of the children. When her husband died or was

away and no male relatives were nearby, the wife would also direct
the work of overseers who managed and administered the plantation.
On small plantations and farms, contact between family members and
between the slaves was more sustained and close.[11]

In the slave quarters families lived in a variety of different arrangements. There were two-parent households and families where relatives
and friends lived together. Most men and women worked side by side
in the fields, but as greater differentiation occurred with increased
settlement in the eighteenth century, male slaves were given artisan's
jobs and women slaves did household work. The separation of men
and women and the biological necessity of birth and nursing made it
more likely that children would be with their mothers than with their
fathers. Children became accustomed to a mother-child bond and their
mother's exercising authority under the overall control of the plantation
master and mistress.[12]

The European colonists brought with them in the seventeenth century
the same tradition the Africans had known. Fathers were deeply involved emotionally and personally in the lives of their children. In a
period of high infant- and childbirth-mortality rates, most women bore
a minimum of six infants, the last after the age of forty. After the
nursing stage, children came under their father's supervision. He decided what they would learn, eat, and wear. The fathers gave actual
physical care such as rocking children, walking them at night when
they were babies, or cuddling them when they travelled. They also
made decisions normally associated with male power, deciding when
their children were ready to begin work, leave home, and eventually
whom they would marry.[13]

Colonists shared a generally accepted religious belief that men were
the heads of the household as well as the opinion that women were
sinful and moral inferiors. They knew that a woman could be queen
by inheritance (Elizabeth I reigned until 1603, which was about the
time colonization began). Women in general, however, were considered
to have been naturally subordinated ever since the apple incident in
the Garden of Eden. Women and men accepted that women's sensual,
deceptive, and disruptive power made it necessary for husbands to
rule over them. Children were unable to choose the right path and

certainly women were too corrupt by nature to be trusted to show it to them. Fathers, therefore, were thought to be best suited for overseeing the children's development.[14]

Husbands and fathers exercised legal control over women and children in these colonial families, and men who failed to provide the necessities of life for their families could face legal penalties. Married women could not own property, even property they inherited from their parents. Children and wives were essentially the property of their husbands. Fathers could abide by the legal and moral imperatives, including the supervision and care for children, because they labored in close proximity to other family members. White women who worked outside their homes were considered inferior and in a class with prostitutes, vagabonds, or indentured servants who performed domestic service. The exceptions were unfortunate but deserving widows.[15]

Generally, male and female colonial children were considered economic assets. They often began work as young as age seven. At their father's direction, children tended gardens, herded animals, and cared for younger siblings. Although many white children attended some sort of school, education was generally not compulsory or tax-supported. Poor children often labored as indentured servants or apprentices by the age of ten. Boys were taught trades such as blacksmithing, coopering, and cordwaining. Girls were taught household production tasks such as spinning, weaving, soapmaking, and candlemaking. In well-off families, children usually attended boarding school. Fathers' control and responsibility for the young was an acknowledged manifestation of patriarchy. Male social and economic power included responsibility for child care.[16]

A good example of how fathers and children related in the seventeenth century can be seen in the case of Cotton Mather, the New England divine who did not even discuss his mother in his memoirs. His father, Increase Mather, kept him at home from school during the coldest winter months when he was seven or eight, but ordered him to summer school to make up the work he had missed. When Cotton or his siblings were ill at night they wakened their father for comforting, not their mother. His father sent him to Harvard when he was eleven years old. Cotton Mather's father was clearly the center of his world.[17]

The framers of the Declaration of Independence and the Constitution also grew up under the aegis of their fathers, who reared them with help from servants and slaves. John Adams, Thomas Jefferson, James Madison, and other political leaders fondly remembered their fathers' care from infancy. John Adams was closely attached to his mother but gave his father credit for molding his emotional and intellectual development. Adams loved, admired, and tried to imitate his father. It was Adams's father who decided when and where he would go to school. He taught him "wisdom, piety, benevolence and charity. . . ." The progenitor in whom Thomas Jefferson took most pride was his father, Peter Jefferson. Thomas Jefferson's earliest recollections included being physically cared for by slaves and nurtured by his father. When he was nine, his father sent him to boarding school. Jefferson boarded at school during the week, returning home for the weekends.[18]

Not only did sons remember their fathers' care, but fathers marveled at the wonders of caring for their children. James Madison's father bought two "competent" slaves to take care of his "hour-by-hour" rearing. When he was eleven years old, Madison left home to attend boarding school.[19] William Samuel Johnson, framer of the Constitution from Connecticut, was raised, with his brother, by his father, a stern and affectionate Episcopal minister who also educated the two boys. The elder Johnson was in awe that

> those little creatures from the beginning, do consider and reflect a prodigious deal more than we are commonly apt to imagine; . . . we ought to think little children to be persons of much more importance than we usually apprehend them to be; and [consider] how indulgent we should be to their inquisitive curiosity . . . ; [and] with how much candor, patience and care we ought to bear with them and instruct them.[20]

Charles Cotesworth Pinckney, a delegate to the Constitutional Convention from South Carolina, born in 1745, said that as an infant he "gained strength at the breasts of domestic slaves," but it was his father who taught him his letters by the time he could talk. His father built him a set of toys to help teach him the alphabet, which he could pronounce and write before he was two years old. Charles Pinckney senior sent young Charles and his brother to English schools to get a proper education in 1753, when Charles was eight years old. The elder Pinckney died in South Carolina in 1758 while he and his wife were visiting to tie up affairs before a permanent move to England. The boys completed their entire education in English schools while their mother, Eliza, and their sister stayed in South Carolina to manage the family's investments. [21]

The colonists cared for their children according to spiritual commands, but they were not familiar with what would be regarded today as children's developmental needs. In petitions for divorce or separation between 1692 and 1786, there was little talk of children. When children were mentioned, the child's sex or other characteristics were omitted. Few petitioners asked for custody. In these petitions, however, parents freely introduced testimony concerning their sexual conduct in the presence of the children without regard to "childhood innocence" or sensibilities. Even if the testimony was slanted, neither parents nor the public officials who heard it thought the parents' behavior was offensive or unusual. [22]

A divorce petition involving Nancy Shippen Livingston was an exception to the usual practice regarding the mention of children. Livingston showed keen parental concern when she attempted in the 1780s to obtain a divorce and child custody from Henry Livingston. Her father had forced her to marry the wealthy Livingston even though she was in love with someone else. Nancy Shippen Livingston left her husband shortly after a daughter was born, but he defeated her divorce attempts until he decided to dissolve the marriage some years later. In the meantime, aided by her sympathetic mother-in-law, she struggled to maintain a relationship with her daughter. [23]

In her diary, Livingston expressed heart-rending concern for her daughter. Her father insisted that the child be sent to her paternal grandmother. Livingston said her father thought it was in the best interest of the child whose "fortune depended on the old Lady's pleasure in that particular beg'd me to think of it and to be reconciled to it. If I know my own heart I never can." Livingston's father, exercising his decisional responsibility, finally gave the child to grandmother Livingston, who promised visitation rights. In 1797, sixteen-year-old Peggy Livingston gave up claims to the Livingston fortune and went to Philadelphia to live with her mother. She never had to face her mother's choices because she did not marry.[24]

The tradition of child-rearing directed by the father with or without the help of servants gave way gradually to the expectation that the mother would be responsible for care. Revolutionary War conditions helped to fuel the transition. The events leading up to the Revolution led to a greater separation of men's and women's activities and the beginnings of a different kind of family life.[25]

Although most people lived in rural areas, cities began to grow. Colonial men began the creation of a public arena distinctly separate from the domestic realm in the courts, in colonial legislatures, and in the political debates. Gradually men and women were inhabiting different worlds. During the Revolutionary struggle, propaganda depicted the enemy Great Britain as a corrupt and evil mother or a whore. This was so even though there were signs that woman's image as powerful but corrupt was gradually eroding; there were other symbols that depicted the colonists' cause as female purity personified. Women, as in the Bible, could be both virgins and whores.[26]

The place of wives and mothers in the new republic had to be consistent with accepted visions of women. In a well-known 1776 exchange with her husband, John Adams, Abigail Adams wrote that "if particular care and attention is not paid to the ladies, we are determined to foment a rebellion and will not hold ourselves bound by any laws in which we have no voice or representation." John Adams dismissed her plaint as a joke. He wrote to a male friend that women and children, like men without property, could not have independent judgment and that "their delicacy renders them unfit for practice and experience in the great business of life."[27]

In the new nation, bourgeois women sought a place for themselves as citizens, though not as equals to men. As mothers, they could raise their children to become good republicans. Sons would be trained in republicanism and civic virtue and daughters in supportive political domesticity. "Republican motherhood" gave women an important social and political role. The concept suggested that domestic duties were a moral training ground for government and politics. Men would manage politics in public while women managed politics in the home. Mothers would instill their male and female children with values of order, responsibility, and self-discipline.[28]

Jean-Jacques Rousseau's ideas about women's appropriate mothering role were combined with the new republican ideology of representative government. Rousseau, the French philosopher of democracy who inspired popular democrats during the French revolution, thought a citizen by definition was a male head of household. He presumed a private female world that sustained the softer domestic virtues. It was thought that female participation in politics would destroy this appropriate balance. The new ideology of republican motherhood reconciled the role of women with the new ethos.[29]

"Republican motherhood" did not change child-rearing assumptions overnight. Men continued to exercise major responsibility for children. For example, after James Madison married the widow Dolley Payne Todd in 1794, he tutored her son from her first marriage until they sent him away to school at age eleven.[30]

Another well-known republican, Aaron Burr, took great pride in supervising the education of his daughter Theodosia. He showed his friends her letters, made sure she had proper tutors, and, when she turned eleven, he had her study Greek. He also instructed her in social etiquette and the need for exercise.[31]

Catharine Beecher, born in 1800, sister of Harriet Beecher Stowe and Henry Ward Beecher, remembered her preacher father, Lyman Beecher, as being the primary nurturer in her life. Her earliest memories were of riding in his carriage in a small, specially fashioned chair as he toured his parish. Her father loved to tend his children and he was their primary source of love and authority. Her mother, Roxana, was a shy, pious woman who was indifferent to rules and money and fond of plants, embroidery, science, and metaphysics, and died when Catharine was fifteen.[32]

Rousseauian ideas and association with republican motherhood, along with economic change, began a transition in bourgeois families from father rearing, with help from nonrelatives, to mother care, with similar help from nonrelatives. This early-nineteenth-century change evolved into a well-developed concept of woman's role that persists today.

The concept defined women as being responsible for a "separate sphere" in the home while men were responsible for the public world. Under this concept, women were supposed to be interested only in husband, children, and home; this was "a cult of true womanhood." The "separate sphere" and "cult of true womanhood" ideas were nothing more than an affirmation of what we now call traditional gender roles. They created the ideas of the breadwinner father and the mother with kids and a household that included either live-in or day workers.

The cult of true womanhood was the feminine mystique that Betty Friedan blasted in her 1963 book and that "traditional" family advocates like Phyllis Schlafly and the Reverend Jerry Falwell believe is appropriate for today's mothers. It is a depiction of women that proceeds logically from defining a woman's rights in terms of her responsibilities for children and other family members.[33]

Economic change played a large role in the cult of true womanhood and the separate sphere. Manufacturing and commercial activity took male heads of households away from home to work, which made the exercise of the father's real, as opposed to rhetorical, responsibility for children well-nigh impossible.[34]

Middle-class professional fathers first began to establish workplaces away from home in the early nineteenth century. They were followed by craftsmen and factory workers. Mothers became redefined as the true purveyors of virtue with principal responsibility for the care and supervision of children. At the same time, women stopped being represented in middle-class rhetoric as devious, sexually voracious, emotionally inconstant, or physically and intellectually inferior, as they had been in the seventeenth and most of the eighteenth century.[35]

Only women, under the new dispensation, could be a source of moral values and a counterforce to the commercialism and self-interest that accompanied male economic and political activities. It is more than ironic that this cult of true womanhood among the well-to-do gained prominence in the same period that increasing numbers of poor single women left home to work.[36]

Technology, along with industrialization and ideology, also played a role in these transformations. The work of men and women gradually changed, reinforcing a shift in child-care responsibilities. Northern urban women were relieved of some household production tasks. Industrial workers spun thread, wove cloth, and preserved some foods and a new service economy took over other tasks. Unmarried women who had been in domestic service followed these tasks into the paid labor market and became part of the labor force. Industrialization in an economy with a shortage of labor and capital depended on the utilization of women and children.[37]

In New England, when textile production was industrialized in the early nineteenth century, teenaged girls from rural towns who had been performing domestic service became factory workers. Many of these white women worked not out of necessity, but because they wanted freedom and economic independence.[38]

At first, the textile industry provided these women with the high wages, status, economic independence, and respectability they sought. But by the 1840s, new Irish and German immigrants began to gain jobs not just as domestics but in the factories. Factory work became less desirable for native-born white women as immigrants offered a permanent work force of older women and children willing to work for subsistence wages.[39]

Efforts at trade organization were defeated and the mechanization of the industry turned unskilled labor into semi-skilled labor. Respectable native white women withdrew from the mills. New England-born farm girls were replaced by poor immigrants and female work lost status.[40]

Industrialization accentuated class differentiation among women and reinforced the cult of domesticity. Poorer, less-educated immigrant women were more likely to work in factories while the middle-class women enjoyed the leisure to become "ladies" and "true mothers." Idleness, once thought a sin, became a sign of social status.[41]

The child-rearing patterns for all social classes established during the Industrial Revolution became the pattern for today. Poorer women took care of the children *and* performed paid labor. Female immigrants from Ireland brought with them a tradition of "responsible mothers" who cared for the family's resources and tried to discipline "importunate fathers." They were generally older and married later in life than other European immigrants. [42]

Irish cultural history and experience in the labor force probably reinforced their responsible family roles. Irish men typically left the family for canal and railroad construction jobs while the women remained at home with the children. Poverty and the high numbers of separations created a greater need for Irish wives to continue wage earning. As young people, migrating to escape poverty, Irish women found work as servants or textile workers. Irish women were willing to perform domestic service because they saw it as well-paid, clean, and readily obtainable. [43]

German and Jewish immigrant women were rarely involved in domestic service. In these immigrant families, the husband remained the dominant head of the household and their cultural traditions ruled out having women do household work for other people if at all possible. Women earned money by working at home in the needle trades. Children in poor urban immigrant families worked either in these trades at home with their parents, or by scavenging or huckstering in the streets. [44]

To actually live the ideology of true womanhood required a certain amount of economic wherewithal. The rich could easily afford it but it also became an increasingly popular and useful status indicator for the middle class. In praise of woman's sphere, Alexis de Tocqueville expansively noted in the early 1830s:

There are people in Europe who, confounding together the different characteristics of the sexes, would make of man and woman beings not only equal but alike. They would give to both the same functions, impose on both the same duties, and grant to both the same rights; they would mix them in all things—their occupations, their pleasures, their business . . . and from so preposterous a medley of the works of nature nothing could ever result but weak men and disorderly women.

De Tocqueville noted a different situation in the United States:

They admit, that as nature has appointed such wide differences between the physical and moral constitution of man and woman, her manifest design was to give a distinct employment to their various faculties . . . American women never manage the outward concerns of the family or conduct a business, or take a part in political life; nor are they, on the other hand, ever compelled to perform the rough labor of the fields, or to make any of those laborious exertions which demand the exertion of physical strength. No families are so poor as to form an exception to this rule.[45]

This idealistic view was also promoted by Mrs. A. J. Graves, whose popular book of the 1840s, *Woman in America*, applauded the cult of true womanhood. She said that for women:

. . . *home* is her appropriate sphere of action . . . She can operate far more efficiently in promoting the great interests of humanity by supervising her own household than in any other way. Home . . . is the cradle of the human race . . . and woman is the nurse and the educator. Over infancy she has almost unlimited sway; and in maturer years she may powerfully counteract the evil influences of the world by the talisman of her strong enduring love, by her devotedness to those intrusted to her charge, and by those lessons of virtue and of wisdom which are not of the world.[46]

Catharine Beecher, writer, lecturer, and proponent of women's education for efficient domestic management, shared Mrs. Graves's views of mother's place: "The mother forms the character of the future man . . . Let the women of a country be made virtuous and intelligent, and the men will certainly be the same. The proper education of a man decides the welfare of an individual, but educate a woman and the interest of a whole family are secured." Beecher's advocacy of the mother's role contrasted sharply with her own childhood experience of effective father rearing.[47]

Graves and Beecher complained that mother's work was difficult. Graves noted that feminine delicacy prevented "true women" from performing the physical tasks of the nursery, which should be left to servants. But there was a servant problem. Native white domestics who had assisted in the skillful management of the household were being drawn into factory work. The new immigrant population lacked appropriate skills and acculturation. Beecher thought that unless they were in delicate health, mothers should do without servants. To do otherwise, she said, dishonored housework, the mother's responsibility. Women who could afford to, however, continued to have servants. Beecher devoted a chapter in her treatise on *Domestic Economy* to the "care of domestics."[48]

As the separate sphere and cult of true womanhood became established, perceptions of children and what was good for them also changed. Attitudes developed at that time, like the cult of true womanhood, persist today. Household size decreased among whites, since dependent kin were less likely to reside together as the country became more settled. With fewer family members, attention centered on the children, inducing changed perceptions of childhood. Increasingly, children were regarded as delicate persons who evolved through developmental stages in which mothering at least theoretically constituted a major ingredient.[49]

Eighteenth-century European philosophy played a key role in stimulating this change in the attitude toward childhood. For example, Jean-Jacques Rousseau's *Émile* stressed the necessity of fitting education to the special nature of the child. John Locke and Swiss educational theorist Johann Heinrich Pestalozzi focused on the unique emotional, physical, and intellectual needs of small children. The literature of William Blake and William Wordsworth emphasized childhood innocence. Because children's natural innocence needed protection and because it was felt that children needed a gradual process of maturation in their homes, the middle-class practice of sending them temporarily to be apprentices or servants when they were eight or nine years old declined. One reason for shifting principal child-rearing from fathers to mothers was the belief that children were more successfully governed by persuasion than coercion and by rewards than punishments. The fear and discipline of paternal authority was rejected in favor of special persuasive maternal talents. Even divorce petitions began routinely mentioning children as a consideration.[50]

Child-rearing literature in the nineteenth century reflected these social and economic changes. Whereas in *Émile* Rousseau wrote for fathers about raising the ideal son, the literature of the early nineteenth century addressed mothers in greater detail. Church leaders writing about childhood education in the 1820s showed confusion about who was responsible for children and the nature of childhood. But by 1833, when the Presbyterians began publishing *Mother's Magazine*, children were regarded as malleable, fathers were busy at work, and it was supposed that mothers' affectionate guidance would lead the next generation along the proper path of righteousness. Reflecting the changing perception of childhood, toys, books, and games were created specifically for children. In addition, the seventeenth-century custom of making children stand while their parents sat at the dinner table disappeared. By the 1830s, transfer of the child-rearing role to mothers was perceptible in the North, and, by the 1860s, it was seen in the South.[51]

The ideology of separate spheres could be good or bad for women, depending on their class status and preferences. Aristocratic women continued to send their children to boarding school, use wet nurses, and direct their domestic servants. Middle-class women gained power because they had real control within the household. Through the use of inventions, household tasks became easier to manage and, with fewer children, middle-class women had more time to attend to those children's needs. As household tasks became easier, standards of affluence and comfort increased.[52]

But the new rococo ornamentation of middle-class Victorian households required more cleaning than the simpler lines of the Federal style, and as a result most of these middle-class families had at least one domestic servant to help with the children and housework. Poor white women, no matter how much housework was required and whether or not they could live according to its commands, expressed satisfaction with the concept of a separate sphere.[53]

In her tale of "Emigration from New York to Michigan," Harriet Noble relates her role in building a chimney in 1825: "My husband and I were four days building it. I suppose most of my lady friends would think a woman quite out of 'her legitimate sphere' in turning mason, but I was not at all particular what kind of labor I performed, so we were only comfortable and provided with the necessaries of life. . . . Although I was obliged to stack the hay this third fall, I believe it was the last labor of the kind I ever performed."[54]

Women on the western trails did men's work but their aim was to make it possible to re-establish separate spheres. Elizabeth Geer, in her diary and letters from Oregon in 1847, told how she was left a widow with seven children after her husband became ill on the trail and died. Her three young sons went into the mines. She remarried a widower with ten children. "My boys live about 25 miles from me, so that I cannot act in the capacity of a mother to them; so you will guess it is not all sunshine with me, for you know the boys are not old enough to do without a mother. My husband is very industrious, and is as kind to me as I can ask."[55]

For women, being involved in the temperance cause or the effort to persuade men not to frequent prostitutes was regarded as appropriate, since the issues were seen as an extension of the domestic sphere and woman's interest in the family. However, at the same time that the cult of true womanhood was accepted by family proponents, some women challenged the separation of private and public spheres.[56]

The women's rights movement emerged from the abolitionist and temperance movements in the 1840s and 1850s. It wanted women to have the right to divorce, to own and manage their own property, and to have the right to vote and run for political office. Naturally, such leaders of the women's rights crusade as Susan B. Anthony and Elizabeth Cady Stanton were publicly scorned as extremists. Anthony never married, but Stanton had a complex domestic life including seven children. Anthony kept telling her to set aside domestic life for the cause, but Stanton told her in 1856, "Courage Susan, this is my last baby and she will be two years old in January . . . You and I have the prospect of a good long life. We shall not be in our prime until fifty, and after that we shall be good for twenty years at least."[57]

The cult of true womanhood, which seemed to have been idealized in most women's minds even when it was not real, was explained by Elizabeth Cady Stanton in 1861 in not-so-attractive terms:

Marriage is not all of life to a man. His resources for amusement and occupation are boundless. He has the whole world for his home. His business, his politics, his club, his friendships, with either sex, can help to fill up the void, made by an unfortunate union or separation. But to woman, as she is now educated, marriage is all and everything—her sole object in life—that for which she is taught to live—the all-engrossing subject of all her sleeping and her waking dreams.[58]

In settling child custody disputes the laws acknowledged the transition to female separate spheres and mother's responsibility for children. Family law until the early nineteenth century generally provided that, "in consequence of the obligation of the father to provide for the maintenance, and in some qualified degree, for the education of his infant children; he is entitled to the custody of their person, and to the value of their labor and services . . . while the child is under the age of fourteen years."[59]

This general understanding relaxed gradually as the cult of domesticity gained hold in the nineteenth century. By 1840, northern courts began giving custody to mothers in divorce cases. The New York court, using the prevailing standard, rejected the notion of a father's absolute right to child custody and announced instead that decisions should be based on the "best interests of the child." Because women were now understood to be caring human beings with good moral sense with a special role to play in the home, the mother was best qualified to provide the care an infant needed.[60]

In adopting a "best interests of the child" standard, the courts signaled their acceptance of the change toward emphasizing the mother's nurturant role. They also reflected an understanding that children had individual developmental needs. Women's rights advocates tried to use the cult of true womanhood to gain the passage of child custody laws biased in favor of mothers, but they failed. The courts kept control, but they minimized reliance on preconceived notions about male authority and female inadequacy. Custody could be awarded to mothers when justified by the facts.[61]

The transfer of major responsibility for child care from fathers to mothers was influenced by ideology and class. As long as father care was the rule, well-to-do men usually asked for and received custody of children in divorce cases. As divorce increased among the middle and working classes in the middle of the nineteenth century the cult of true womanhood began to influence the outcome of the cases. Women who filed for divorce were considered the innocent party and would thus be awarded custody and alimony. However, when courts decided that a woman had exhibited immoral behavior, such as adultery, she would always be at risk of losing custody. Whether white mothers became identified as the principal child-rearers because fathers were absent as they went out to work, or for ideological reasons, by the 1860s the pattern was set.[62]

It was a different story for poor and working-class white wives. The experiences of these women certainly contrasted with the ideology of the cult of true womanhood. Even when they did piece work at home they had to balance child care and domestic chores as well as paid labor. The experience of African-American parents during the same time provides an even starker contrast to the reigning ethos. The child-care experiences of African-Americans remained consistent from slavery until after the beginning of the civil rights movement. African-American women became defined as caretakers of other people's children as well as their own.[63]

Black women and children, already largely separated from adult male relatives including fathers, were threatened with greater family separation at the end of the eighteenth century during the migration into the Mississippi Lands and after the invention of the cotton gin. The slave trade ended in 1807, but the further southwest expansion increased the demand for slaves.[64]

Planters sought to increase the number of slave births to take advantage of the market and children were sold as quickly as they were old enough to work. During this period, the slave system became even more closed. Attacks on slavery by Northern abolitionists resulted in concentrated Southern responses that tried to justify the existing system of labor and family management. Southern men justified the perpetuation of patriarchy. They viewed slavery as entirely efficient and morally just.[65]

In the South, the nineteenth-century separation of public and private space, with males and females constituting separate spheres, was not a product of urban commerce or industrialization but of the need to reinforce hierarchy within a slave system and to justify the old ways to maintain order. Long after the rest of the country legalized divorce and shifted child custody rules to favor mothers the South lagged behind. Women were placed on a pedestal and the myth of the Southern pure woman was perpetuated.[66]

Furthermore, the demands of the slave society required men not to accept the need for change or loosen the reins on anyone, including their own wives and children. There was little separation between work and home in the South. In the towns, middle-class women experienced more separation but the majority of Southern women lived on rural farms where everyone worked. Generally, the plantation mistress occupied herself with overseeing a garden, a dairy, the food processing, the manufacture of clothing, and the health of blacks and whites alike. She also oversaw the management of the child care-givers, who were typically slave women and children.[67]

Black women understood that their role was to care for their own children while the father was absent and to be the care-givers for white children. There was essentially no feminine mystique or cult of true womanhood or woman's sphere for female slaves. Slaves were seen as resources from whom the greatest amount of labor could be extracted while protecting their capacity to produce additional laborers. They might gain some security against sale and separation when they bore and nurtured children. Under the supervision of the white mistress, slave women weeded, hoed, plowed, harvested, and a few worked as household servants.[68]

Contrary to myth, slaves did not regard household work as superior to working in the fields because in the absence of machinery and modern appliances, it could involve heavy labor. Also, being a house servant meant being on the job around the clock and being more subject to abuse and scrutiny by the mistress and master.[69]

One ex-slave poignantly described his mother's backbreaking work as a household servant in Person County, North Carolina. For about twenty years, she cooked for twenty-two to twenty-five people, including masters and slaves. Each morning, she milked fourteen cows, set a child to churning milk, and prepared the white family's breakfast. At noon, she fixed warm bread and milk for the slaves. Then there were beds to be made and housecleaning. After this, she cooked the white family's dinner. Next she prepared corn bread or potatoes and any meat left from the master's dinner or one herring apiece for the slaves to eat at night. By early night it was time to again milk the cows. Of course, she also did the laundry for the master's family and for her husband and seven children.[70]

Slave women performed cooking, cleaning, and sewing for their own families at the beginning or end of the work day. One South Carolina slave remembered: "My mammy, she work in de field all day and piece and quilt all night. . . . I never see how my mammy stand such hard work. She stand up for her chillen though. De old overseer he hate my mammy, cause she fought him for beatin' her chillen."[71]

One household slave returned to her family's cabin so late at night and so tired she could hardly stand. But "she would find one boy with his knee out, a patch wanting here, and a stitch there, and she would sit down by her lightwood fire, and sew and sleep alternately, often til the light began to streak in the east; and then lying down, she would catch a nap and hasten to the toil of the day."[72]

Slave husbands hunted, fished, collected firewood, made shoes, carved ax handles and butter paddles for their families. Even men who lived elsewhere and came for occasional visits performed such tasks. In relating to whites, black men were generally required to be submissive, but in the slave quarters, black men exercised dominance. One ex-slave reported:

I loved my father. He was such a good man. He was a good carpenter and could do anything. My mother just rejoiced in him. Whenever he sat down to talk she just sat and looked and listened. She would never cross him for anything. If they went to church together she always waited for him to interpret what the preacher had said or what he thought was the will of God. I was small but I noticed all these things.[73]

The slaves experienced another phenomenon with which we are familiar today, the first example of institutionalized nonparental child care in the United States, the communal care of slave children. Lacking standards except the will of the master, the care was primitive to say the least, but consistent with the status of the children. Plantation owners might register the births of black children as they did foals, except that they named the horses' sires but not the slaves' fathers. On a large plantation, there could be as many as one thousand children ranging in age from one-month-old babies to four- and five-year-olds. All the young children were put in a nurse house until they were old enough to work. The children ate from a big tray on the floor or from a pig trough using oyster shells as utensils. An ex-slave said, "Chillun slop dat milk jus' like pigs." Another woman reported that on her plantation the children had no supper, "only a little piece of bread or something of that kind in the morning. Our dishes consisted of one wooden bowl, and oyster shells were our spoons." On small plantations where there was no nurse house, mothers were sometimes forced to leave their babies alone all day when they went to the fields. One ex-slave reported that she would hang her baby in a basket with some boiled flour water for nourishment until she returned. "It cry all day an' I cry all day, an' he died, 'cause he cry so," she said.[74]

Free Negro families tried to emulate the cults of true womanhood and woman's sphere that were the prevailing ethos. Like working-class whites, most often they succeeded only rhetorically. In the comparatively small number of free Negro families, many women were wage earners. Wives worked to add to family funds and ran their own businesses. Black women's responsibilities had increased due to the high mortality rate among black men.

Some wealthy Southern free Negro families owned slaves and plantations. In these families, just as in similarly situated white families, the separate sphere prevailed. Female children learned to be ladies: to read, to display proper etiquette, and to ride horses. In rural areas, however, there were few free Negro families and the black women led isolated lives.[75]

Southern urban free Negroes ran small cook shops and grocery stores that catered to slaves. They also operated beauty and barbershops, boardinghouses, and pastry shops that catered to whites only. In poor and female-headed families, the courts apprenticed free Negro children at the request of plantation owners without their parents' consent long after the practice was abandoned for white children.[76]

In the North, free Negroes worked as domestic servants caring for the children and households of white families or performed other low-paid labor. A few African-American men were able to operate lucrative catering establishments, become teachers and lawyers, or run newspapers. But many were destitute because racism prevented them from finding jobs. The African-American woman's role was already being modified by racial restrictions as well as her need to perform financially productive labor.[77]

The plight of free Negro women and children in the North was described by a prominent white female abolitionist in the 1830s this way: "No matter how worthy, they cannot gain admittance into or receive assistance from any of the charities of this city. In Philadelphia, they are cast out of our Widow's Asylum and their children are refused admittance to the House of Refuge, the Orphan's House and the Infant School connected with the Alms House, though into these are gathered the very offscouring of our population."[78]

Native American women and children too were negatively affected by the growth of the colonies and expansion in the nineteenth century. The Five Civilized Tribes were moved from the southeast to the Oklahoma Territory. Research on the Cherokees shows some of the results. The Cherokees, who had matrilineal descent and lived matrifocally in the mother's home, changed their practices. Men were pressed to give up land which had been traditionally "owned by the women and farmed by them." Prominent Cherokee men who had assimilated signed it away.

By the 1820s, across the country, only white men could vote and patriarchy was imposed. The cult of true womanhood meant a loss of power for women and Native Americans felt the pressure to adopt the white man's way of subordinating women. Native American men emulating the white man tried to keep "their women & children at home & in comfortable circumstances."[79]

By the middle of the nineteenth century, responsibility for children had shifted from fathers to mothers. There is no evidence that children fared better or worse as a result of the change. As the Civil War neared, the history of father care receded in memory and the "tradition" of mother care replaced it.

III
Mother Care, Other Care

By the time the first shots of the Civil War were fired, a war that pitted brother against brother and father against son, the male child-care tradition had given way to one dominated by women. The war, the nation's bloodiest, had a devastating effect on families. Brides were widowed, children were orphaned, mothers and wives were left behind to cope with the overwhelming problems generated by the conflict.

Before the war, women understood family life to include female deference to men. With the men on the front lines, women volunteered as nurses, raised money to help finance the war effort, and began to run the farms, businesses, and plantations. In the cities, women replaced male clerks in stores, in the federal government, and in other occupations. Middle-class women who might have become school-teachers became clerks instead, as these jobs called for a well-educated English-speaking work force.[1]

There were also new employment opportunities for women whose wage-earning husbands had entered the military, leaving them desperately in need of income. In addition to clerical jobs, single women moved into factory jobs and married women did piece work for low pay at home, manufacturing shirts and underwear, for example.[2]

65

The war also produced a new activism on the part of women. In the South, women participated in bread riots occasioned by food shortages and in the North, Irish women joined their men in anti-draft riots. Female cooks and nurses routinely traveled with the army, without disruption of prevailing values, and over four hundred women were discovered posing as soldiers.[3]

The widely publicized wartime employment of women gave private employers the chance to consider using "respectable" women as clerical employees. Many women, wives as well as widows, held on to these jobs after the war despite societal norms to the contrary. They assiduously hid their married status for fear that other employees would complain or that they would be fired. In the mid-1870s, a married woman working in the Treasury Department was accused of violating the tenets of domestic virtue: "She had an infant at home about one-year-old which requires the care of a mother . . . All cares of her house including the washing and ironing etc., are imposed on her husband's mother, an old lady 65 years old." After the war, some federal departments prohibited the employment of more than one member of a family.[4]

For African-Americans, the Civil War meant freedom by degrees and new gender roles. Some slaves left the plantations as soon as they heard that the Yankees were coming. On the Allston rice plantation in South Carolina, Stephen, the valet, defected with his wife and children. The mistress, Allston's widow, complained that Stephen's leaving created "Obstanetry in Some people" meaning the other slaves. She moved Stephen's parents and in-laws into confinement as hostages as a warning to the other slaves. Other mistresses worried about losing their property to the Union soldiers. As the troops moved near, a Tennessee mistress ordered a slave woman named Jule to tell the soldiers that if they found the trunk of money or silver plate it belonged to her. Jule refused: "I can't lie over that; you bo't that silver plate when you sole my three children."[5]

The end of the war and the abolition of slavery resulted in some gains by African-Americans and placed black women theoretically in the same position as white women. They could own property, marry, and move about more freely. But, like white women, they could not vote and were subordinate to their men. Still, black women participated in the political mobilization of ex-slaves during Reconstruction. They attended rallies and urged the men to be active.[6]

Some black men favored political rights for women. William Whipper unsuccessfully introduced a woman suffrage resolution at the South Carolina Constitutional Convention. He told his fellow delegates: "I acknowledge the superiority of women. There are large numbers of the sex who have an intelligence more than equal to our own . . ." Whipper expected to be voted down, but he knew that the cause of woman suffrage would "continue to be agitated, until it must ultimately triumph." The Republican Party saw voting as necessary for women to hold the political gains made as a result of the war. But the idea of women voting without regard to race was too challenging to the existing mores to be high on any male agenda.[7]

The Fourteenth Amendment assured full citizenship rights for African-Americans and other citizens, but it did not give women the right to vote. This engendered a split in the women's rights movement, with one branch led by Susan B. Anthony and Elizabeth Cady Stanton, and including Sojourner Truth, demanding the priority of voting in a woman-suffrage movement. Other women, such as Frances Ellen Harper, Lucy Stone, and Julia Ward Howe, conceded that the rights of black men took priority in the short term and stayed with the Republican Party cause. The party of Abraham Lincoln had organized in response to slavery, and won a war to save the Union, whose cause included the emancipation of and military service for African-Americans. They knew that given the political climate, an amendment providing for female suffrage was improbable. However, in the struggle for suffrage for African-American men, black and white women partook of the prevailing ethos preserving public space for men and the private sphere for women.[8]

The woman suffrage cause gained ground slowly, but another crusade quickly provided an outlet for the activism of large numbers of white women while reinforcing the ethos of women's devotion to children, husbands, and housework. A revitalized temperance movement became the avenue which allowed respectable well-to-do women to spend their leisure time doing good without challenging existing mores. The temperance movement erupted in the early 1870s in small towns in Ohio and Michigan as a protest against saloons and male consumption of "demon rum." While the sources of their discontent can be debated and questions raised about whether unrest over their continued exclusion from the political process played a role, the fact is that thousands of women took to the street to close down saloons. They started at churches where they would sign pledges of abstinence and pray before going out to march into saloons, demanding that the men leave, and asking owners to close. Working with temperance men, these were "conservative" women who had not been part of the women's rights or suffragists' cause.[9]

The postwar temperance movement, like its antebellum predecessor, saw itself as protecting home and family from the violence and immorality associated with inebriation. The Women's Christian Temperance Union (WCTU) was organized in 1874 to give focus to the movement. It was exclusively a women's association, with no male members, and it quickly grew, attracting more women than the suffrage groups.[10]

Frances Willard, president of the WCTU from 1879 to 1899, emphasized the cult of womanhood, female purity, and virtue to advance the movement's goals, and used the slogan "Womanliness first, afterwards what you will." The WCTU promoted voting for the purpose of "Home Protection." Through WCTU activities, women of the leisure class could exercise citizenship duties "For God, Home and Native Land," as an extension of the domestic sphere. The WCTU and other nineteenth-century reform campaigns, including the Populist Party, like today's groups such as Mothers Against Drunk Driving, allowed women to be moral guardians and to act in the public arena while focusing on their role as mothers.[11]

Despite the ravages of war and women's participation in moral reform, the ideal of separate gender roles and the elevation of white womanhood remained unscathed throughout the country. In the South, white women who had found it necessary to do domestic labor during the war when the slaves left, complained that it was demeaning and arduous. They resented the demands on their time and they were anxious to have their servants back.[12]

As Emma Holmes of Camden, South Carolina explained: "I am very weary, standing up washing all the breakfast and dinner china, bowls, kettles, pots . . . and churning, washing stockings, etc., a most miscellaneous set of duties, leaving no time for reading or exercise." A Florida mistress, noting how tired she was asked, "will all the days of the year be like this one?" She wondered, "what are we going to do without the Negroes?"[13]

African-Americans wanted to share the ideals of domesticity and separate spheres practiced by the master and mistress. They tried to consolidate their families immediately after Emancipation. For the first time, ex-slave fathers and mothers had the legal authority to exercise responsibility and authority for their children. When parents found their children, from whom they had been separated, they often had an especially hard time extricating them from whites who claimed them as apprentices on their plantations.[14]

Most former slaves traveled far and wide searching, usually unsuccessfully, for their relatives. If they were lucky and found them, there were usually poignant reunion scenes such as this one: "Not until the woman at the door removed her hat and the bundle she carried on her head did a young Tennessee freedwoman see the scar on her face and know that she was looking at her mother whom she had not seen since childhood."[15]

Another woman found a daughter who had been sold as an infant in a Virginia refugee camp: "See how they've done her bad," the mother told anyone who would listen. "See how they've cut her up. From her head to her feet she is scarred just as you see her face." One of the positive results of the war was the knowledge that such separations would no longer be possible. One ex-slave said he was joyful knowing that he would not wake up one morning to find his "mammy or some of the rest of my family done been sold."[16]

After organizing their families, African-Americans established the separate sphere ideal with wives and daughters of able-bodied men trying to avoid the labor force. "When I married my wife," a Tennessee freedman told his employer, "I married her to wait on me and she had got all she can do right here for me and the children." Whites complained about black women "playing the lady." But most black women were quite willing to work to help support their families if they could avoid the abuses they had known during slavery.[17]

A decision not to work was almost impossible, in any case. Planters needed labor and blacks needed money for subsistence. Moreover, southern legislatures enacted Black Code laws to insure the role of blacks as a labor force. For example, there were strict vagrancy laws imposing heavy fines that were designed to force all blacks to work whether they wanted to or not. The federal government's Freedmen's Bureau enforced contracts between blacks and their employers to help facilitate the transition from slavery to full citizenship. The contracts, however, proved unpopular with blacks and whites. With their detailed requirements, they reminded blacks of slavery, and the whites had little cash available to pay the laborers.[18]

Most blacks engaged in sharecropping, a system whereby a landowner furnished food and supplies to a small farmer or laborer before harvest in exchange for the first lien on harvested crops. This became the prevailing way to solve the employment problem for black and poor white farm laborers. The system was plagued from the beginning, however, by greed, overcharges, and debt. Owners sometimes claimed perpetual indebtedness, thus reducing the worker to peonage.[19]

Black women worked as domestics and, along with their husbands and children, in the fields at planting and harvesting time. Despite economic deprivation, most African-American families established after Emancipation were patriarchal. Women were primarily responsible for housework and the feeding, clothing, and nurturing of children. Like other working women, African-American women aimed for the happy housewife model projected by middle- and upper-class women. Though no longer slaves, black women were required to balance husbands, housework, and jobs, including the care of their own and others' children. Black women, like white women, saw an expansion of their domestic responsibilities along with newly granted rights.[20]

The United States was transformed after the Civil War from a largely agrarian society to a business civilization with a powerful manufacturing economy. In 1886, midway in the course of this transformation, Andrew Carnegie wrote proudly that: "The old nations of the earth creep at a snail's pace; the Republic thunders past with the rush of the express."

The expansion began as early as 1840 but was accelerated by the catalytic effect of the war on the Northern economy. It was fueled in part by invention and technology that created new industries and revolutionized old ones. These included the coming of electricity after Edison's invention of incandescent lighting in 1879 and new patents for the manufacture of steel. European immigration and greater employment of women helped to create a supply of cheap and plentiful labor.[21]

Immigrants brought cultural expectations about work and familial relationships which in most cases were patriarchal and fit in with the reigning ideal. Many of these new immigrants were from Italy, Russia, Poland, Greece, Turkey, and the Austro-Hungarian empire instead of the British Isles or Germany, where many of the first settlers and earlier immigrants had originated. Many were Roman Catholic, but they were Greek Orthodox and Jewish as well.[22]

The Italians and other Eastern Europeans tended to come alone and most planned to return home at some point, whereas Russian and Eastern European Jews came in family groups. Young Irish and Scandinavian women came alone. Many of them were illiterate, often from rural villages and unfamiliar with urban society. They moved into the slums of industrial cities and established enclaves.[23]

Some had immigrated to escape persecution and poverty, but when they entered the mines, mills, and factories they were given the most distasteful tasks. The immigrant labor force made it possible for native Americans and second-generation immigrants to move into white-collar jobs and become middle-class.[24]

The northern cities also began attracting African-Americans in large numbers in the late nineteenth century to join those who had established communities before the war. Blacks began migrating north in the wake of the collapse of Reconstruction and increased violence by white hate groups such as the Ku Klux Klan. An upsurge of lynching and the attraction of northern economic opportunity accelerated the migration at the end of the century. Blacks joined immigrants in the search for middle-class respectability. But, like other newcomers, southern African-Americans experienced the pains of adjustment to the urbanized and increasingly industrialized America.[25]

In the North, just as in the South, women and children made up a large percentage of the labor force. Neither blacks nor poor immigrants had the job opportunities available to second-generation white women because of racial and ethnic discrimination. Until the late nineteenth century, private clerks and secretaries were usually men on a career ladder that often led to managerial jobs. Women were low-level copyists or clerks in federal offices and some private businesses during the Civil War and afterwards. After the typewriter came into general use in the 1880s, clerical and secretarial jobs, usually in settings more pleasant than factories, became the domain of white women. White men moved onto distinctly managerial career ladders.[26]

The poorer native white women, immigrant women, and black women took jobs in commercial laundries and other service establishments. In some immigrant families, doing piecework at home allowed parents to care for the children. Some took in boarders to augment the family income. Employment choices were influenced by economics and opportunity. Southern and Eastern European immigrant women preferred manufacturing jobs to domestic service, according to Elizabeth Pleck, author of "A Mother's Wages: Income Earning Among Married Italian and Black Women." Jews and Italians predominated in the garment industry, in which Jewish women labored in factories owned by Jews if possible, and Italian women did piecework at home. Polish and Slavic women worked in food-processing plants in the Midwest and in the textile mills in New England and the South, as did poor white southern women. In textile mills such as those in Fall River, Massachusetts, and rug weaving mills in Philadelphia, women made up about a third of the work force.[27]

In some cases, mothers as well as fathers had to do industrial work away from home. School-aged poor immigrant children either did paid work at home, in factories, or mines, or attended public or parochial school. Some mothers left small children unattended at home, feeding them narcotic cordials as pacifiers. Infants and toddlers would sometimes burn to death from coal fires. Relying on old-world kinship networks, poor or widowed mothers gave their children to relatives when they could not care for them. Others left their children in orphanages or reform schools.[28]

Rose Schneiderman, a women's trade union organizer, described her childhood in an immigrant family on New York's Lower East Side in the late 1880s and 1890s as typical. Schneiderman's parents brought her to the States when she was five years old. Her father worked as a tailor and the family lived in two rooms on Eldridge Street. In Russia both parents had earned money, but in New York only her father worked. Schneiderman had two younger brothers. Rose had to drop out of school when she was nine after her father became ill and died. Her mother was pregnant and went to work soon after the baby was born, earning about eight dollars a week.[29]

Rose became "the house worker, preparing the meals and looking after the other children." Her mother left home at 7:30 A.M. and didn't return until 6:30 P.M. When an aunt started taking care of her little sister and her brothers started going to the Hebrew Asylum, "a splendid institution [that] turns out good men," Rose said she returned to school. But soon Rose had to quit school again to help support the family. She obtained a job as a cash girl at two stores and then "got a place in the factory of Hein and Fox" making cap linings, and was paid by the piece. The employees, who earned only five dollars a week, had to buy their sewing machines, which cost forty-five dollars. They were allowed to buy the machines on an installment plan.[30]

Black women, with the fewest job choices, most often labored in housecleaning jobs or laundry, which they did in their own homes if possible. When they did get a job in the mills, it was usually as sweepers or scrubbers, but not as machine operatives. When African-American mothers were compelled to go out to work, they left their children alone or with "babytenders," who either kept them in their homes or came by to check on them while the mother was away.[31]

Black women were much more likely than immigrant mothers to work outside of the home even though some immigrants, the Italians, for example, had more adult relatives to serve as caretakers. Black men, who wanted to replicate the separate sphere ideal, resisted their wives' working, despite the family's often dire financial needs.[32]

Well-to-do women joined male social reformers who took up the cause of improving the slums and tenements and the cities during this period. A declining birth rate meant that many of these women had more free time. The size of the average family decreased by 50 percent from the beginning of the nineteenth century to the end, which meant that women who did not have jobs could devote themselves to their own children and other activities. The availability of bakeries and laundries, improved household technology, indoor plumbing, cookstoves, and refrigerators made housework easier for women who could afford the modern conveniences or for their servants.[33]

Magazines such as *Ladies' Home Journal* (started in 1883) and *Good Housekeeping* (1885) published articles aimed at helping married women manage their sphere. The message from these magazines was that women could be good housewives, have lots of time to devote to mothering, which was the biological and ideological ideal, and still be eager consumers of all the advertised delights.[34]

Bourgeois and upper-class women involved themselves in a number of activities for self-development that were consistent with the true womanhood ideal. Some focused on higher education, which flourished at women's colleges designed for the most part to educate women to be good wives, to be able to make conversation with their husbands, and to promote the education of their sons and daughters. It was the custom for middle-class women to attend boarding school and college, and then to marry. Female professional employment also increased, but in fields understood to be an extension of women's separate sphere: teaching and nursing.[35]

The WCTU continued to serve some women's cravings for useful and appropriate social activity. Other women found their satisfaction in settlement houses, clubhouses, women's clubs, and the Young Women's Christian Association (YWCA), founded in 1867. But the focus of most women remained on motherhood and the home. For mothers who were employed, any child-care problems had to be resolved within the confines of conventional wisdom, which said child care was a mother's responsibility. Interest in extraparental child care coincided with interest in alleviating the plight of poor children.[36]

Social reformers saw institutional care in nurseries and kindergartens as a way to relieve children of the effects of crime, poverty, and vice in the slums. Their interests were moral, political, and practical. Some well-meaning upper-class women adopted nurseries and kindergartens as their charity work. These women, along with professional social workers, took up the cause of helping children in order to reach the children's families. They organized fundraisers, supervised the staff and programs, and were proud of helping to save immigrant families from disruption and bad influences.[37]

One solution was to adapt and expand old methods for a different purpose. "Child saving," the creation of publicly financed "homes" in some northern states, was in the 1840s a way of responding to public concern about lost and abandoned children. It was an institutional solution to prevent children from becoming purveyors of crime, ignorance, and vice. In 1853, Charles Loring Brace started the Children's Aid Society in New York, which indentured poor white abandoned or orphaned urban children or placed them with foster families in rural areas. The society also established industrial schools for the children through private and public donations. By 1892, 84,318 children, most of them boys, had been sent away from urban blight by the society.[38]

The institutionalization and placing-out of neglected children came under attack from reformers in the wake of growing evidence of mismanagement and the careless placement of children. There were stories of pauperism, criminality, and "enslavement" of children sent westward. The mounting numbers of poor urban families further undermined the wisdom of these approaches. After all, in many cases, these were not abandoned children in a strict sense, but children with at least one parent. A better solution, some said, would have been to help the working mother function according to her appropriate child-rearing role. Instead of sending potentially "bad" children away, reformers focused on preventing the child from ever being stamped with the intemperance and immorality that they thought was bred in the slums.[39]

The reformers and mother-care enthusiasts decided that the needs of children could be met by day nurseries for infants and kindergartens for preschoolers. Nurseries or infant schools for children from one month to three years old began in England in the early 1800s for the children of poor and working mothers. Utopian Socialist Robert Owen established such a school in 1816 in Scotland to relieve working mothers of the care of their infants during the day. The school employed female teachers and provided an unheard-of mixture of play and rudimentary instruction. Exercise, music, and dance were included. Others picked up Owen's ideas and used them in the London slums, where American reformers heard about them. In America, the movement existed primarily in northeastern cities on a very small scale before the Civil War.[40]

An infant school was organized in New York City in 1827 by Joanna Bethune for children from eighteen months to six years of age. This was soon followed by infant schools in Philadelphia, Boston, and New Haven. In addition to Owen's care and instruction, religious education was added to "save" the children's souls. Moral regeneration, according to Republican tenets, would be engendered by the movement. In 1828, the Boston Infant School opened "to relieve mothers of part of their domestic cares" when they had to work. These institutions were to help mothers unable to remain in the domestic sphere by shielding their children from bad and immoral influences.[41]

During this same period, day nurseries modeled after the French crèche were also established in the United States. These institutions, too, were devoted primarily to the physical care of the young children of working mothers. In 1854, New York Hospital established its "Nursery for the Children of Poor Women," providing care for the children of wet nurses and for infants of working mothers. In 1863, Miss Biddle opened a day nursery for the children of Philadelphia.[42]

Well-to-do mothers supported nurseries and the use of kindergartens for the children of poor women as well as for their own children. Using John Locke's ideas concerning the flexibility of infants' minds and Johann Pestalozzi's concepts about the ability of children to learn by observation, description, and naming, educational reformer Amos Bronson Alcott opened a school in Boston in 1830. To these earlier concepts, Alcott added his efforts to probe children's inner spiritual beings. His concern was educational experimentation, not social reform. Assisted by Salem schoolteacher Elizabeth Palmer Peabody, Alcott opened his school in Boston's Masonic Temple, catering to the children of some of the city's most respected families. Alcott was forced to close his school when his teachings on human reproduction aroused controversy.[43]

Peabody, however, was instrumental in helping German emigrés in

1848 to bring the kindergarten movement to the United States. These emigrés had studied the ideas of German reformer Friedrich Froebel. After attending Pestalozzi's institute, Froebel developed his own approach to the education of young children. Froebel said children had great mental acuity from the ages of four to six. The problem, he argued, was that their lives were restricted in those years, limited by the cradle, the nursery, and the family. Nor were they old enough for the passive obedience school required. His solution was the kindergarten. In a controlled atmosphere, children relating to their peers and led by a specially trained teacher would develop to their fullest abilities. Kindergarten would be a place of physical beauty, of colors and light, where everything was scaled to the child.[44]

Children would be taught reading and writing, drawing, block-building, and other learning techniques. A simple, easily managed system of child care, with women trained in Froebel's principles of child-rearing and early education, would restore the appropriate dignity to women's sacred role. The idea was to support mother's role by educating her child. The first kindergarten for English-speaking children opened in Boston in 1860. The kindergarten was designed primarily for preschool education of children from ages three to six.[45]

Support for the German kindergarten gradually grew among affluent women intent upon finding a better way to educate and care for their children. Catharine Beecher endorsed the idea in 1872. Five kindergarten displays by manufacturers at the Centennial of 1876 in Philadelphia brought the kindergarten message home to millions. Pure Froebelians complained that toy manufacturers, intent on selling balls, blocks, and other items, commercialized Froebel's message but the publicity encouraged the movement.[46]

In keeping with the late-nineteenth-century emphasis on helping employed poor mothers, Froebelians began establishing free kindergartens. By day children were cared for and educated while at night their mothers were trained in supportive techniques. Between 1880 and 1890, more than one hundred free kindergarten associations were formed in large and small American cities.[47]

For almost two decades, Boston's charitable kindergarten work was financed by the wealthy Mrs. Pauline Agassiz Shaw. At the urging of

Elizabeth Peabody, she opened two kindergartens; within five years she supported thirty-one free schools at an annual cost of $200,000. In California, Jane Stanford and Phoebe Apperson Hearst, the railroad and mining fortune heirs respectively, were major kindergarten patrons. In Chicago, Mrs. Potter Palmer and Mrs. George Armour led the cause. By 1890, there were 143,720 children attending kindergartens in the United States. There were 223 free kindergartens with a combined enrollment of 14,987 children. Advocates began a successful campaign to have kindergartens operated in the public schools.[48]

Social settlements adopted kindergartens for older children and nurseries for infants as part of their mission. Jane Addams's Hull House opened a kindergarten in 1891, providing an example of the cooperative spirit between the movements run by professional social workers and do-gooders. Unlike kindergarten advocates, Jane Addams and her fellow social workers saw working with children as only one part of settlement work for the whole neighborhood. In addition, women of the settlement-house movement did not view their work as preparation for domestic responsibility and married life but as careers.[49]

Day nurseries and kindergartens for the poor operated twelve hours a day, every day but Saturday. They took in children from two weeks to six years old. Some provided emergency night care when a mother was sick; others allowed a child to be dropped off for a few hours; and some hired a visiting nurse to assist mothers when children were ill.[50]

Most of these day nurseries and kindergartens had "mothers' clubs" which women were required to attend in exchange for free child care. The clubs which met in the evening had a social and educational purpose. Lectures on hygiene and child care would be followed by tea and cookies. The operators of these facilities, used mostly by immigrants, were not always charitable themselves, sometimes expressing contempt for the parents. As one worker asserted, their "slum babies would all be better off in nurseries" than at home. There were no records kept comparing children in the nurseries with those left with baby-sitters or at home.[51]

The supply of child-care facilities was a constant concern for African-American mothers, since most of them worked and because many of the day nurseries and kindergartens barred black children. Ida B. Wells, a pioneer crusader against racial subordination, and one of the founders of the National Association for the Advancement of Colored People (NAACP), noted that Chicago's Armour Institute (later the Illinois Institute of Technology) served black children but there was a long waiting list.[52]

A young African-American woman who had graduated from the Chicago Kindergarten College came to the local Ida B. Wells Club to ask for help in establishing a kindergarten in her neighborhood. Another young woman member of the club had completed the same training years before but could not get a job in a kindergarten and was a dressmaker. Employing these two women, the club established a kindergarten in Bethel African Methodist Episcopal Church in 1897 with the strong support of the pastor, even though some members feared this might cause the exclusion of black children from the kindergarten at Armour.[53]

In 1898, Anna Evans Murray, who headed the kindergarten committee of the Colored Women's League in Washington, D.C., led a successful lobbying effort to get a $12,000 federal appropriation to establish kindergarten classes in the District's public schools. The New York Colored Mission, founded in 1865 as the African Sabbath School Association, the most important settlement house for blacks in the city, provided a medical mission and other social services including a nursery. There were black-organized missions in other cities, including Indianapolis and Philadelphia, which also offered nurseries.[54]

Despite the child-care movement in several northern cities, by 1897 there were only 175 infant nurseries in the entire country, according to the Census Bureau reports. The few that existed were subject to criticism. In the early days, many charity organizations opposed day nurseries or kindergartens for the children of employed mothers on the grounds that orphan asylums and county children's homes were sufficient. Some thought that the churches could better handle the problem. Others believed that the provision of day care weakened family ties, undermined the role of husband as breadwinner, encouraged women to abandon child-rearing for work outside the home, or made the mother lazy by caring for her children.[55]

Social workers accepted the idea that day nurseries were a temporary solution. The real answer, they argued, was to heal the family. Thus, they made sure the women were truly needy and not just working for luxuries. They were avid supporters of a "family wage" for men. They believed nurseries could close when men became economically able to support their families and mothers returned to their rightful place in the home.[56]

Some reformers also tried to impose their ideas about family on Native American policy. After the Civil War, they wanted Native Americans in the west to adopt the cult of domesticity and separate spheres as white settlement expanded to embrace them. Most refused and western Native American cultures, like their eastern counterparts earlier, began to dissolve with the pressures of increased white expansion and its interference with subsistence agriculture and hunting. By 1870, the goal of the national Native American policy became to civilize and assimilate the Native Americans and to have them abandon their own cultures. As a consequence, they were expected to embrace the tenets of separate spheres, the cult of true womanhood, and Republican motherhood like everyone else.[57]

The Women's National Association led the effort to impose domestic virtue on Native Americans. Communal living, either in freedom or on the reservations, was to be abandoned and middle-class values adopted. The reformers particularly abhorred the sexual division of labor that resulted in women doing all of the work, tending crops, raising children, cooking, curing hides, and making tools and clothes while men did nothing but hunt. These reformers did not understand that for Native American women these responsibilities reinforced their economic independence.[58]

The federal government stopped making treaties with Native Americans in 1871 in order to demolish tribal authority and permit agreements with individual Native Americans. By 1887, the Dawes Act comprehensively summarized the policy being implemented. Native Americans would have individual allotments of land, although the reservation system was to be left intact. Children would be sent to boarding schools off the reservation to hasten their assimilation. White church groups were given money to establish religious schools in aid of the effort.[59]

The Native American wars continued, but Native American control of land was reduced with Dawes. Individual Native Americans were duped into selling their allotments. The assimilation policy, however, did not work. Some Native Americans wandered across the descriptive line that separated the races and moved into towns but Native American children left the boarding schools and tribes continued to practice their religion underground. The policy failed, but the combined shocks of change and warfare reduced the numbers of Native Americans. Many fell victim to diseases like smallpox and alcoholism.[60]

In the late nineteenth century, women reformers became concerned about another threat to the motherhood ideal as more and more white women entered the workplace. The typical woman worker was young and single, however; married women workers remained a very small group. Between 1880 and 1900, the numbers of employed women grew from 2.4 million to 4.8 million. One out of three single women was self-supporting and living away from home.[61]

The expectation that all women would eventually be mothers dominated discussion of their life-styles. Public concern was expressed over whether their participation in the labor force would render them unfit for their assigned roles. Charity workers, reformers, and clergymen wondered whether young women should leave the work force and return home before they became too independent to be satisfied with a proper marriage and domestic life. They were also concerned that young single women remain moral and not threaten to undermine the family by their personal behavior. These social do-gooders did not want to see young women going about unchaperoned or dressed immodestly or engaged in sexual liaisons. This was especially seen as a problem in areas of the country where females outnumbered males, such as the northeast.[62]

The practice of single working women living as boarders with private families was thought to present too many opportunities for mischief-making. The idea was to keep women "moral" until marriage, fit for motherhood, and avoiding interference with other people's marriages.[63]

Grace M. Dodge, a young heiress, founded a working girls' club in New York City in 1885, and set up similar clubs later in Brooklyn, Philadelphia, and Boston. Girls fourteen years old and older were eligible to join. They could use the club's piano and writing supplies as well as the comfortably furnished library. They could also attend frequent lectures, and sewing and embroidery classes. Through Dodge and other wealthy benefactors, the young women had use of two summer houses on Long Island for a fee of $3.00 per week. The clubs brought working-class and well-to-do women together, but many workers did not join—they were too tired or did not have spare time. Furthermore, the women who started the clubs were concerned primarily with imbuing their members with good work habits and genteel notions of femininity. Members published essays with titles like "What Constitutes an Ideal Womanhood and How to Attain It" and "Purity and Modesty: Two Words of Value."[64]

Reformers also voiced concern for the physical health of these potential mothers. Traveler's Aid Services, the YWCA boarding homes, and recreational programs were established to guard against waywardness. Reformers also worked for legislation to limit women's hours, provide minimum wages so they could afford nutritious food and decent lodgings, and improve the working conditions of female employees. They wanted to ensure the health of the mother for the welfare of the species.[65]

As a British physician put it in an 1873 report cited by concerned Americans, infants suffered under the present system: "Mothers nursed the infant in the morning and then left it to be bottle-fed or stuffed with indigestible food." The working mother returned at noon "overheated and exhausted. Her milk is unfit for the child's nourishment." The child sometimes suffered from "spasmodic diarrhea, often complicated with convulsions ending in death."[66]

In the 1890s, there were declining birthrates among native whites and increased immigration of families who had higher birthrates. One physician wrote that the birthrate was declining in "our most intelligent communities." There were more journal articles on the subject such as, "Medical and Sociological Interpretations of the Decline of the Birth Rate," and the "Dangers and Duty of the Hour."[67]

Middle- and upper-class children became so valuable, emotionally, to their parents that they were termed "priceless." This attitude led courts to increase damage awards for accidental injury done to children beyond estimates of their potential contributions as workers. Poor children, however, remained valuable to the society at large only in terms of their economic contribution to the family.[68]

The late-nineteenth-century emphasis on scientific method and industrialization influenced the direction of child care. The need for a scientific approach to child-raising began to win acceptance among upper- and middle-class women. The scientific approach had an additional appeal for mothers beyond its supposed benefits for their children. It seemed to demonstrate that women, too, were scientific and modern. Charlotte Perkins Gilman, in 1898, suggested giving women more freedom while ensuring the care of children. Gilman proposed apartments or houses conjoined with central cooking, day nurseries, and professional house cleaners because economic independence for women necessarily involved a change in the home and family relation. Gilman did not see this as a change in the mother-child relationship: "Mother, in the sense of bearer and rearer of noble children, she will be, as the closest and dearest, the one most honored and best loved." But a woman could not be "nursery-governess" and be nothing else. Most women did not want to change their duties according to Gilman's formulation but they did want to be good mothers. They began to search for professional reinforcement of their duties. Child study and motherhood groups spread rapidly among the middle and upper classes leading to the National Congress of Mothers in 1897.[69]

Working women's problem of balancing jobs and children remained difficult. They strained to follow the tenets of true motherhood and domestic purity. Writing at the turn of the century, Ida B. Wells recorded her own problems in this regard. She was a newspaper editor, organizer of black women's civic clubs, and leading crusader against lynching. Along with her husband, Ferdinand L. Barnett, a Chicago lawyer, she ran an influential newspaper, and raised two children from his first marriage and four of their own. After the birth of her first infant, she recalled: ". . . all this public work was given up and I retired to the privacy of my home to give my attention to the training of my children." She described herself as glorying in the "profession" of motherhood.[70]

"I wonder if women who shirk their duties in that respect truly realize that they have not only deprived humanity of their contribution to perpetuity, but they have robbed themselves of one of the most glorious advantages in the development of their own womanhood," she said.

In fact, Wells did not withdraw from all public work. "Even though I was quite content to be left within the four walls of my home, it seems that the needs of the work were so great that again I had to venture forth," she wrote. Wells began rounds of lecturing, taking her nursing baby, then six months old, with her. The groups of women that invited her provided a nurse to care for the baby while she spoke and engaged in other public activities. Every lynching or organizational meeting attracted Wells to the public sphere. At the founding meeting of the Afro-American Council in 1898, her "second baby was just being weaned and I could safely leave him with his grandmother." She reported that Susan B. Anthony told her that her circumstances made for "a divided duty."[71]

Ida B. Wells resolved her problem of "divided duty" in the manner expected of any woman of her times, including social reformers. She gave up the newspaper and professed to devote herself to homemaking until her youngest child was eight years old. In reality she continued her activism, albeit sporadically, until her children were in school. Wells thought of herself, however, as fitting the standard definition of women: They were either mothers or prospective mothers.

IV

Reinforcing the Mother-Care Tradition, 1900–1930

In the early twentieth century, women expanded their employment and public roles and enjoyed greater sexual freedom than ever before. The mother-care tradition survived, reinforced rather than subverted, under these changing conditions.

The turn of the century was an occasion for celebration around the world. Expositions and congresses projected a future when human aspirations would be realized through the wonders of technology. Social awareness seemed also to quicken. The reform spirit intensified as Americans tried to make order out of the transformations that attended the industrial age.

Progressive reformers worked to cure social ills, from impure food and drugs to substandard housing for urban immigrants. They addressed the labor strife, corporate abuses, and environmental waste that came with industrialization and the production of unprecedented amounts of goods and services that stimulated a culture of consumption.

Women experienced liberties in many areas of their lives. Middle-class and working women went boldly about unchaperoned on city streets and bobbed their hair. Single women worked in offices and shops and started working as sales clerks in the new so-called temples of commerce, the department stores. Affluent women wandered about the stores alone or with their friends, utilizing the refreshment rooms, cloakrooms, and sometimes even reading rooms and libraries that unaccompanied women could not previously have visited without damage to their reputations.

Affluent woman not only indulged in the culture of consumption and high style; many of them, such as Mary White Ovington and Josephine Shaw, a socially prominent Massachusetts widow who founded the National Consumers League, became progressive reformers.

Political and social changes stimulated challenges to the assumptions about gender roles that had held steady through the upsurge of immigration in the 1880s. Middle-class women found it more possible to have a family, economic independence, and self-development through a career. Continued changes in family life at the beginning of the century increased the possibility of such endeavors.

The size of the average household continued to shrink. By 1900, indigenous white Americans had an average of 3.5 children. The birthrate for foreign-born women and black women was slightly higher. The continuing decrease in the birthrate for native-born white women, due in part to their access to birth control devices, exacerbated concerns about race preservation. President Theodore Roosevelt and other politicians continued the late-nineteenth-century complaints about the prospect of "race suicide." Native white male and female advocates of the race suicide theory implemented various birth control efforts aimed at reducing the poor and immigrant "inferiors" and redressing the balance. Men blamed native white women for abandoning the role of mother and insisted they produce more children. Recently, Ben Wattenberg, in *The Birth Dearth* (1987), and others have expressed similar concerns about the likelihood of the United States becoming a nation with a majority of nonwhites.[1]

The nativism efforts did not prevent the continued decline in the birthrate among white women over the next decade. The lower birthrate generally meant that most mothers had to spend less time engaged in household tasks and the care of children. By 1900, additional technological improvements, including gaslight and electrical illumination, and oil- or gas-fired furnaces lessened household chores. In rural areas, farm implements and appliances freed women and men from many tasks, making time available for truck gardening or other remunerative work. But each new appliance generated more work for women as cleanliness standards rose with each innovation. Because the new technology was expensive, the more affluent acquired it first while the poor did without.[2]

The nineteenth-century ideal of "true womanhood" was replaced by the "new woman." The so-called new woman was college educated, frequently unmarried, and self-supporting. In 1890 one college-aged woman in fifty continued her education. Female college attendance tripled between 1890 and 1910 and doubled again during the next ten years. Many women emerged from the women's colleges as committed to careers as to marriage. This generation married late and bore fewer children and some did not marry at all. They were the reformers like Jane Addams and Florence Kelley of the National Consumers League. They were interested in purifying society rather than in being mothers who simply stayed at home.[3]

During the Progressive period, many well-to-do college-educated women, with experience in charity organizations, found work in new public sector health and welfare programs. Although the number of professionally trained women grew substantially as World War I resulted in more employment opportunities, most of these women remained in female-dominated "social housekeeping" jobs. By and large, they became social workers, nurses, classroom teachers, and staff librarians. Experts in fields like home economics sought to professionalize women's domestic work for the family's greater good.[4]

Participation in the labor force by college-trained married women rose six times faster between 1900 and 1930 than participation by single women. These women also thought careers in which wage-earning wives helped with the family's finances would be fulfilling. Although this was still a small minority of working wives, the idea that middle-class wives should have more active public lives became popular. They organized volunteer organizations, increased their professional activities and pioneered new fields.[5] Aviator Amelia Earhart daringly flew across the Atlantic in 1928, becoming an appropriate symbol of the times. The highest level of women's share of professional employment was reached in the 1920s and declined in the 1930s until a resurgence in the 1960s and 1970s. For example, the opening of medical schools and hospitals for women in the late nineteenth century led to the education of more women doctors. But the schools established quotas for females after World War I, which led to a decline in the numbers and percentage of women practitioners.[6]

Free sexual expression, symbolized by the flapper, only seemed to accelerate the trends. Psychologists and sociologists decided that femininity was the most important aspect of a woman. She could be employed but not in every field. She should avoid masculine "coarsening" fields, such as business management.[7]

Meanwhile, "traditional" motherhood roles remained but some aspects of the marital relationship were modified. Social scientists spoke of a new ideal, the "companionate marriage," in which young people should be friends and even lovers before they married. Whereas feminists had earlier decried bourgeois marriage, marriage along these lines became women's ideal. A perfect feminist was a woman in a happy, emotionally fulfilling companionate marriage with children. But the companionate marriage left standing sexual hierarchy at home as well as in the public arena.[8]

Mothers remained responsible for children but they were no longer insulated within the family circle. Mothers encouraged children to enjoy greater latitude in expressing their feelings and increased interaction with their peers. The wife became the dominant figure in the home. The husband was a reliable "good provider" who could repair things. Men's lodges and civic clubs enjoyed popularity and masculine humor deprecated family responsibilities and being concerned about children and the home. Men who found domestic activity frivolous and boring were the ideal.[9]

Professional home economists contributed to the new "traditional" attitudes. By their own activities they underscored the belief that women could have employment, but they magnified the complications of housework to justify their field of expertise. Before 1890, most middle-class households engaged live-in servants who helped with child care among their other duties. New technology, gas, electricity, plumbing, and refrigeration, the automatic washing machine and the factory system which produced processed and canned foods came into use, making it possible to reduce the number of servants. Furthermore, as new job opportunities opened to women, fewer servants were available. By 1920, instead of young immigrants or native-born whites who "lived in," servants tended to be older black day workers.[10]

The decline of live-in domestic servants brought several changes. First of all, the housewife ended up doing much of the work herself. Not only were housework and homes redesigned, but Congress funded two thousand home demonstration agents to train housewives in proper budgeting, child-rearing, and homemaking. For the first time, Congress appropriated funds for teaching vocational home economics courses in secondary schools.[11]

All of this reinforced the assumption that women were responsible for the care and feeding of men and children. Occasionally, the idea of wages for housework surfaced, but husbands legally owned their wives' domestic labor and were obligated to support them. This rule meant that wages for housework would have the husband paying himself.[12]

Prevailing opinion saw women, employed or not, as "professional" wives and mothers, utilizing the wealth of information published by experts to help them in their tasks. *Parents* magazine, founded in 1926, reflected this emphasis. Advertisements and social science converged. It was all right to be a feminist. Careers were wonderful, but feminism required, by definition, knowledgeable motherhood. Women's rights advocates liked the "scientific" discovery that motherhood required training and was not just done by instinct, but they did not like its continued characterization as women's work.[13]

Mother was still in her separate sphere. It was her duty to nurture and create new people for the country's future. This emphasis, which was reminiscent of the republican motherhood ideal, was necessarily the domain of the well-to-do and consumed the energies of some women, including the bourgeois mothers who organized the National Congress of Mothers (NCM) in 1897. At their annual meetings, NCM members heard from experts such as G. Stanley Hall, whose view of the proper approach to scientific motherhood included an active role for the mother in observing and reporting on her child's behavior. As younger experts entered the field, however, they expressed disinterest in the mother's unscientific observations. They wanted mothers to follow their instructions and to raise children scientifically. The mothers could receive their marching orders by sending for the federal government's twenty-five-cent pamphlet, *Infant Care*, first published in 1914, the best-selling publication of the Government Printing Office by 1918– 1919.[14]

The approach to child-rearing soon found an ally in the new science of behaviorism. John B. Watson, one of the first generation of psychologists who began their academic careers studying rats in mazes, formulated the theory. He was interested only in observable phenomena and believed that objective behavior could be modified through a system of rewards and punishments.[15]

The type of mothering celebrated by the National Congress of Mothers, which had been absorbed by the National Congress of Parents and Teachers (later the Parent-Teacher Association), was labeled misguided, since it relied on emotion and instinct. Training a child, Watson thought, was like training any other animal. Children should be handled with firm discipline, taught stoicism, independence, and immunity to emotional elements. This procedure would train the child to perform successfully in the industrial world. The twentieth century had begun with middle-class white mothers organizing to use the help of science in raising their children, but behaviorism minimized the role of mothers. Watson even went so far as to opine that children might be better off trained in controlled environments rather than in the family home.[16]

The Laura Spelman Rockefeller Foundation turned its attention to the problem of training poor families to raise children by using the scientific method. The foundation spent over seven million dollars between 1923 and 1929 training a battery of experts to reach out to uneducated and isolated mothers. Institutes and research stations were established across the country offering standardized, controlled child-raising techniques. Experts shared information at Rockefeller-sponsored conferences. The idea was to train home economists and teachers to be parent-educators while they carried out their principal duties.[17]

Although the federal government began sponsoring mass parenting education in 1914, the Rockefeller Foundation deserves credit for the rapid "professionalization" of the child-raising business in the 1920s. The financial crash of 1929 stifled the growth of the movement, but by then the experts and structures were in place. Physicians, home economists, and the government freely dispersed advice on child-rearing in books, pamphlets, and in popular women's magazines.[18]

Public discussions of sexual freedom and professional mothers' standards of behavior and child-raising presented a life-style that was far beyond the reality of poor women's existence. Few employed women, less than 4 percent, had careers. A disproportionate percentage of female wage workers were nonwhite. Most married women did not work, but those who did were largely employed in domestic service, manufacturing, and agriculture as low-paid wage workers.[19]

Articles that described professional women who kept their husbands happy while they balanced career and children with help from domestic servants became a staple of women's magazines. They had titles like "From Pram to Office" and "The Home Plus Job Woman." These stories had little to do with the lives of poor women except that poor women were the domestics who provided the help and had few choices. The career women described in these articles did not threaten established gender roles, but reinforced them. They were employed but they were also responsible for child care and housework.[20]

The increased employment of poor married women also reinforced rather than undermined the mother-care tradition. Poor women—native whites, immigrants, and blacks—worked in commercial laundries and other service establishments. Some took in boarders to augment the family income. And yet, only 25 percent of women in the United States were in the labor force in the early twentieth century. Between 1900 and 1940, the percentage changed little, but there were changes in the mix of jobs, and in the age, class, and marital status of female workers. According to the U.S. Census Bureau, in 1900 only 15 percent of employed women were married and just 6 percent of the married female population did paid work, compared to 41 percent of single women.[21]

The proportion of married women doing wage work doubled between 1900 and 1930, even though by 1940 less than 15 percent of married women were in the labor force. Poor married women who worked tended to leave their jobs when their children were old enough to work to make up the lost income. Compulsory school attendance and child-labor regulations changed poor women's job participation patterns. They began to return to work after the children entered school, in effect raising the average age of the female labor force.[22]

Although they had difficulty emulating this pattern because of poverty and prejudice, African-Americans, Hispanics, and Asian-Americans in this period shared with poor whites an adherence to the motherhood ideal. Subjected to invidious discrimination, they began with agricultural or domestic jobs and gradually found low-skilled jobs in factories. Hispanics and African-Americans, unlike Asians and European immigrants, did not move as quickly into higher-status jobs. For each of these groups, family life was not easy to maintain in the face of these odds. For blacks, two-earner households were a legacy of slavery and Jim Crow; for Hispanics and Asians, female-headed households were a byproduct of male migration for jobs and of immigration rules. In these minority families, women had three shifts; they worked in field and factory alongside men, they performed household and child-rearing tasks, and they did paid domestic work, often taking care of other people's children.[23]

Newspapers, reformers, government agencies, and private foundations launched investigations to determine whether wage work interfered with mothering in poor families. For the most part, poor white immigrant families were studied. The investigators wanted to detail the work habits, moral behavior, and family life of the workers. A number of studies resulted, including a twenty-nine-volume Senate report on "Woman and Child Wage Earners" covering the years between 1910 and 1914. Most of the investigators found fault with married women for working. They did not seem to understand that the women being studied were working not out of greed or the desire for expensive goods, but because of acute economic distress. Even when working, these women regarded themselves as primarily wives and mothers.[24]

As the number of women workers increased, concern about the health of mothers and future mothers led to increases in what was called protective legislation specifically designed for women workers. Maximum hours and minimum wages became increasingly the rule. The first law limiting work hours was adopted in Ohio in 1852, but widespread attention to maximum hours did not come until the end of the nineteenth and the beginning of the twentieth century. In 1908, the Supreme Court in *Muller* v. *Oregon* broadly endorsed protective legislation, giving impetus to the practice. Curt Muller was convicted of violating an Oregon maximum hours statute when an overseer in his Portland laundry required a female employee, Mrs. Elmer Gotcher, to work more than ten hours on September 4, 1905. The Supreme Court upheld the state law, explaining that ". . . as healthy mothers are essential to vigorous offspring, the physical well-being of woman becomes an object of public interest and care in order to preserve the strength and vigor of the race."[25]

The early protective laws were much like the present-day fetal protection policy of Johnson Controls Inc., a Wisconsin battery manufacturing company, which excluded women from jobs involving exposure to lead. Occupational exposure to lead which is used in making batteries entails some health risks, including harm to fetuses. Johnson first had a policy of informed consent for women who were in jobs which might involve lead exposure. In 1982 they shifted to a policy of exclusion of any pregnant woman or any woman capable of bearing children; this meant excluding all women except those who could medically document their inability to become pregnant. Workers sued the company. Among those bringing suit were Mary Craig, who had chosen sterilization to avoid losing her job; Elsie Nason, a fifty-year-old divorcee who had lost pay when she was transferred out of a job involving lead exposure; and Donald Penney, who had been denied a request for a leave of absence to lower his lead level because he wanted to become a father.[26]

The Supreme Court ruled that Johnson's policy was sex discrimination and discrimination on the grounds of pregnancy. Fertile women could help make batteries as well as anyone else. Also, despite evidence in the record about the debilitating effect of lead exposure on the male reproductive system, the company was only concerned about the unborn offspring of female workers. Justice Harry Blackmun concluded that "Decisions about the welfare of future children must be left to the parents who conceive, bear, support, and raise them rather than to the employers who hire those parents."[27]

Between 1909 and 1917, nineteen states enacted protective laws restricting women's workday. Manufacturing establishments, mercantile factories, laundries, and telephone companies came under regulation early in this century. By 1924, only five states lacked some form of restriction. (Domestic service and agriculture remained unregulated, however, leaving African-American women largely uncovered by the hour and wage laws.) Women who needed to work longer hours and for more pay were hurt by the new regulations. It helped those who had other earnings available to them, however.[28]

During World War I, women gained a number of so-called men's jobs as industry expanded to meet war needs and required additional workers to replace men called up for military service. Women in the federal civil service took men's jobs but at lower pay. They also began working in the chemical, automobile, iron, and steel industries. Women doing menial labor prospered during the war by moving up as more favored groups took jobs formerly held by men. A number of black women who had been domestics were able to get jobs in industry.[29]

White women who occupied clerical posts in banks were promoted to positions as tellers, department managers, and junior officers. Most of the women who took advantage of the opportunities caused by the war were already in the work force. Unfortunately the boom for working women was short-lived. After the war, few working women were able to hold on to the new jobs they had gained.[30]

During World War I, the government set up a Women in Industry Service to collect information and to track the inclusion of women in the war industries. Women reformers demanded that the service be continued after the war to provide special representation for women's concerns. They persuaded Congress in 1919 to establish it as the

Women's Bureau in the Department of Labor. The bureau was first headed by Mary Anderson, a former shoe worker from Chicago. Anderson had been a leader in trying to gain protection for women employees through the Women's Trade Union League established in 1903 by middle-class reformers in Boston. The Women's Bureau and trade unionists continued to remind the public that women worked because they must, not because they wanted to challenge gender roles. They emphasized that men who were not being paid a decent wage could not support their families.[31]

The great unmet need for employed poor mothers was help with their child-care responsibilities. This obvious need went unmet in large part because any services beyond reliance on families challenged the mother-care tradition. There were no publicly funded day nurseries until the New Deal. The number of existing charity-operated institutions did not grow much at all as a result of greater employment of married women. Many of those that were available could not afford the educational services recommended by experts and only provided custodial care.[32]

From 1912 to 1917, the Day Nursery Association of New York printed in its annual report a series of articles designed to help member institutions to improve the quality of child care. There were articles on the training of nursemaids, the need for emergency night shelters, the value of different methods of instruction, medical examinations, and fire safety measures. The National Federation of Day Nurseries promulgated similar measures in its monthly bulletins and also kept count of nurseries that operated day and evening shifts.[33]

The available institutions were clustered geographically. Of the 166 day nurseries for infants and preschoolers recorded by the federation in 1904, 113 were in Massachusetts, New Jersey, New York, and Pennsylvania. By 1912, the federation could find only 500 nurseries in the entire country and most were still concentrated in the northeast. The for-profit institutions, observers reported, exhibited the most unsavory conditions, but the charity-operated facilities were also unsanitary. Also, there were too few attendants and, in some cases, a total lack of supervision. The general societal attitude remained what it had been since the shift in the nineteenth century towards mothers taking primary responsibility for children—that reforms should be directed toward mother care and the home.[34]

The first White House Conference on Care of Dependent Children was called by President Theodore Roosevelt in 1909. It opened a long campaign for the passage of widow's pension laws in the states to allow some poor mothers to stay home and raise their children in genteel poverty. Enshrining the gradual transformations that had taken place in family life in the United States, the final conference resolution stated: "Home life is the highest and finest product of civilization. It is the great molding force of mind and character. Children should not be deprived of it except for urgent and compelling reasons." This sentiment guaranteed widow's pensions and more. Missouri enacted a pensions law in 1911, and in the next two years eighteen states enacted similar laws. The conference also recommended the establishment of the Children's Bureau in the Department of Labor as the principal federal government advocate for children and the traditional family. The bureau was later moved within the federal bureaucracy and remains today in the Department of Health and Human Services.[35]

Without adequate day-care service, employed mothers managed as best they could. In Chicago in 1918, an Irish mother with two children worked in a meat-packing company pasting labels for eight and a half hours a day. The eldest child attended school but was sent to a nursery for lunch and after school. The preschooler was in the nursery all day. To keep her home "immaculately clean and in perfect order," this woman had to work until late at night and Saturday until 5 P.M. She did without conveniences. She cleaned one of her family's four rooms each night. She washed on Saturday, baked on Sunday, and ironed on Monday evenings.[36]

Just as today's employed mothers generally try to provide care for infants and toddlers in the home, female workers in the early twentieth century would engage relatives or lodgers who would be given room and board in exchange for helping with child care. Some simply left the children home alone or, in a few cases, with their fathers who were willing to "help out." Some of these fathers were craftsmen who worked at home and watched young children as best they could while they worked. Other men worked the night shift and slept during the day while their wives worked.[37]

Many women who had child-care problems were female heads of households. Well over 30 percent of widowed and divorced women were employed between 1900 and 1930. Women without husbands had to work because they had no savings and husbands who died left medical bills or, if disabled, were usually not covered by insurance. Many poor mothers without husbands would leave their children at orphanages for long or short periods.[38]

Infants were often left in the care of other children. A Children's Bureau investigator traveling around the country in 1918 reported that in manufacturing town after town, she found "half-grown children playing about . . ." paying no attention to the babies they were caring for. She saw ". . . babies sleeping everywhere but in their proper places, heads hanging grotesquely from go-carts, [baby carriages] and half empty nursing bottles covered with flies . . . lying about." Working-class mothers believed they should be at home, but could not be there because of poverty. Child care was their responsibility even when they were married. In addition to working, it was usually the mothers who arranged for child care, talked to teachers, policemen, and charity workers about their children when necessary, and sewed and cleaned and cooked.[39]

Despite the increased need for nonparental child-care services, day care was no more available by the 1920s than it was earlier. The urban black migrant population, despite greater needs, was never the main target of efforts to assist working mothers. Immigration restrictions reduced the number of needy Eastern and Southern Europeans coming into the country; they had been the major focus of charitable efforts. States began to focus on the poverty and dependence of female-headed families. They enacted widow's pensions or aid-to-dependent-children laws which encouraged poor mothers to stay at home; by 1935, only two states lacked them. Strict eligibility standards, however, excluded many mothers, and still larger numbers of children were institutionalized or placed in foster homes when parents were disabled or completely destitute. Social service agencies screened and monitored foster parents who might keep children for short periods and in some cases adopt them.[40]

In many cases, black women were explicitly excluded from pensions because of race. A 1931 Children's Bureau study of eighteen states found that 96 percent of the mothers receiving assistance were white, even in locations where nearly half of the population was black. Furthermore, during the Depression many states that legislated grants simply stopped providing them altogether because of financial distress.[41]

Widow's pensions did not obviate the need for child-care services. Many of the women who used such facilities were "unwidowed," married women whose husbands were ill, unemployed, or did not make sufficient incomes or abandoned or divorced mothers whose only income was their own work. Some widows with pensions worked because the pensions were inadequate. Groups that had been organizing day-care centers sometimes abandoned widows (and their children) because they received pensions. From the White House to local communities, the ethic that mothers should be encouraged to stay at home was strong.[42]

Throughout the 1920s, jobs in the remaining nurseries attracted professional workers, especially schoolteachers and social workers, but instead of making care facilities more available to working mothers, these professionals constricted services. In 1919, for the first time, day-care institutions became a topic of discussion at the National Conference of Social Work. These middle-class professionals, whose goal was to improve society and not merely to care for children of working mothers, adhered to the conclusions of the 1908 White House Conference. Like many reformers today, they wanted child-care services to be focused on keeping the family together, not just on caring for children.[43]

In policy statements consistent with this emphasis, the Children's Bureau kept characterizing the need for child-care services as a minor problem and mothers' pensions as the solution. The 1920 report of the bureau noted: "The rapid growth of the mothers' pension movement is indicative of the belief, generally held, that home life and a mother's care are of paramount importance . . ."[44]

The bureau emphasized that during economic good times men expected to make enough money to support their families and their wives could stay at home. The expectation that employers would pay men wages high enough to support a family won widespread public acceptance during the early 1900s. These attitudes reinforced the traditional motherhood role of women. Wives only worked to supplement their families' income. Unmarried working women would not benefit from this approach because they were paid less. The very idea that wives were wage workers was inimical to the social ideal of family and motherhood. [45]

The activities of the women's rights movement between 1900 and 1930 also ended up reinforcing the motherhood tradition. A reunited women's movement achieved the Nineteenth Amendment, gaining women's suffrage by 1920, in part by abandoning the strategy of using the vote to make far-reaching changes in the role of women. As part of their winning strategy, women pointed to the lack of change in women's roles in nine western states where women had gained the vote in 1912, and the continuing male control of the society. They suggested that female voting would fulfill the American tradition of representative government without negative effects and with the positive influence of validating the political system. [46]

The suffrage campaign proceeded during the same period in which paid work became increasingly important to women. The campaign won passage of the amendment with the support of a broad cross-section of women, but politicians soon realized there was no women's vote on feminist-defined "women's issues." Rather, women voted like their husbands or fathers as Democrats or Republicans. The Sheppard-Towner Act of 1921 demonstrated the lack of a feminist voting bloc. The act established child health and maternity programs for the needy. Politicians enacted it into law because they perceived that feminists wanted it, but just eight years later the law failed to win extension because women's votes did not matter. If there was no organized women's vote on specific issues there was no reason for a politician to concern himself with supporting their policy choices. [47]

The legislative agenda proposed by feminists largely failed because of divisions within the movement, which resulted in women's failure to vote en bloc on issues of importance to them. To Alice Paul and her National Women's Party, an Equal Rights Amendment (ERA), introduced in Congress in 1923, seemed the logical next step. But to the majority of women who had worked for the right to vote, equal treatment outside of the voting booth was not an issue.[48]

For those former suffragists now in organizations such as the League of Women Voters and the National Consumer's League, women's suffrage was a way of securing legislation that would treat women advantageously, not equally. The ERA proposal seemed particularly pernicious. The Nineteenth Amendment, after all, had been won finally with a strategy that accepted women's "traditional" roles and their differentiation from men.[49]

Alice Paul's agenda conflicted sharply with the desire of the Women's Bureau and "social feminists" to concentrate on the continuing movement for protective legislation for employed women. This conflict ostensibly involved differences over issues of women's work, but there were fundamental differences over gender roles and how to achieve equality for women.[50]

Labor union leaders, for their own reasons, agreed with those "social feminist" reformers who favored protective legislation. They took the position, by and large, that women should be discouraged from wage work because their place was at home. This was consistent with the idea that men should be paid a family wage. Wartime labor demands and a wave of organizing in the clothing trades brought large numbers of industrially employed women into trade unions by 1920. Returning veterans took some jobs from the women who had worked during the war in "male jobs"; nonetheless women still held thousands of unionized jobs. In 1920, 6.6 percent of wage-earning women were in trade unions, nearly half of them in the garment industry and another quarter in printing. About 8 percent of organized workers were female.[51]

Trade unionists and social reformers had spent over thirty years on issues such as the family wage, hours, and working conditions by the time the ERA was introduced. Paul not only created consternation among the social reformers, but she made enemies of the male-dominated labor unions which supported protective legislation. Labor unions, like reformers, argued that women's capacity for future motherhood should be protected in the interest of the "race." Union leaders also knew protective legislation would shelter male workers from female competition. A few working women appreciated these protective measures, but most single and poor women worried about how such measures limited their earning opportunities.[52]

This protective legislation dispute, like most of the employment issues that drew the feminists' attention, almost exclusively concerned white women. Black, Hispanic, and Asian women worked mostly as domestic servants or in industrial or agricultural pursuits with which neither unions nor protective labor legislation were concerned. Even when these women were in industries where such measures did apply, the jobs they held did not fall into protected categories. Although their labor force participation rates were much higher than those of white women, minority women were not part of the discussion.[53]

Alice Paul's insistence that all laws should be applied equally to men and women was a very unpopular idea to social reformers and unions who wanted protective legislation. But Paul recognized that protective legislation for women only would continue to define women's opportunities by childbearing and allow sex discrimination in the workplace. Paul lost the argument at the time, but as white women entered the workplace in growing numbers, they found themselves in occupationally segregated low-wage jobs just as Paul had predicted. The dispute between Paul and the protectionists was centered on long-term consequences versus the alleviation of immediate problems. The protectionists wanted to reduce the physical burdens that laundresses, factory workers, store clerks, and other women workers were suffering. Paul wanted to make it possible for women to enter any job freely and to join with men in demanding better working conditions for both sexes. Paul's goal was a lot harder to achieve than suffrage because it required a change in assumptions about "traditional" gender roles. Protective legislation only reinforced the tradition.[54]

The social and economic changes of the early twentieth century severely tested the mother-care tradition. Science, ideology, and the national interest, however, converged in reinforcing the motherhood ideal.

V

Extending the
Mother-Care Tradition,
1930–1960

The nineteen thirties, forties, and fifties are remembered now through the movies: Judy Garland as Dorothy in *The Wizard of Oz* (1939) singing "Somewhere Over the Rainbow" and Scarlett O'Hara (Vivien Leigh) in *Gone With the Wind* (also 1939) consoling herself with "tomorrow is another day."

Those films mark the end of the Depression—the decade in which the "modern woman" arose. Eleanor Roosevelt, who helped her husband run the country, was a national symbol, but the typical American "modern woman" —the ideal mother—was her husband's partner who shared the burdens of raising a family in hard times.

But then came the "Good War." Husbands, fathers, and sons—and a few daughters—marched off to defeat fascism worldwide. Mother and sister went into the factories and yards to build planes, ships, and munitions. And Humphrey Bogart told Ingrid Bergman to get on the plane with Paul Henreid, choosing duty over love.

The war lasted almost six years, brought the first use of the atomic bomb, and cost untold damage and millions of lives, including 322,188 American lives out of a total of 1.1 million American casualties. On the home front, however, economic times were very good. Rationing made meat and stockings difficult to find, but at least now there was money to buy them. When Johnny came marching home after VE-Day and VJ-Day, his job was waiting for him. Women were then told by advertisers that their new job was to raise a family—and, incidentally, to be consumers. New products flooded the market as American factories began producing in the peace-time economy.

Child-raising became Americans' patriotic duty during the Cold War of the 1950s. In the propaganda of the decade, American women were reminded they were obviously better off than their counterparts in the Soviet Union. American women cared for their children and husbands; Soviet women worked and sent their children to day care. American women shopped in overflowing supermarkets; Soviet women stood in line for bread. The reality of American women's lives in these decades meant more mothers balancing jobs and children.[1]

During the Depression new laws and regulations had limited married women's employment, which created problems for those who needed to work. In certain fields, such as teaching, banking, and government, women were restricted to low-level service jobs. Opponents of married women's employment had long insisted that working wives neglected their family responsibilities. These critics now argued that working wives also interfered with the wage-earning opportunities of men, who had to support families. The most concerted effort to keep women out of the workplace came from the Congress and President Hoover's administration.[2]

After the Civil War, when large numbers of women had been hired to replace men who had left for battle, some federal departments decided they would employ only one family member. This was not a government-wide policy and was implemented sporadically. The 1932 Economy Act mandated that only one person in a family could remain employed in the entire federal government in the event of a layoff. As a consequence, most "persons" fired were wives and daughters. Many state governments adopted the same policy. Women civil servants protested the policy vigorously, but they were unable to have the clause removed until 1937. Public opinion polls indicated that most Americans were absolutely opposed to the employment of married women. Even after the law was changed, states continued such policies, despite the opposition of the U.S. Women's Bureau. Bureau Chief Mary Anderson argued that women's jobs paid so little that they would be unsuitable for men. She wanted women to be allowed at least to keep the jobs they already held.[3]

Despite the barriers, wives who needed income found ways to remain employed. Some women used outright deception and pretended they were not married. The proportion of working women who were married increased from 29 percent to 35.5 percent during the 1930s. Single white native-born women obtained employment in greater numbers and proportions than African-American and foreign-born women. Immigration restrictions reduced the numbers of foreign-born women, beginning in 1923. Racial exclusion and discrimination, even in jobs that were available, affected the rates for black women and men.[4]

In the 1930s, women's employment in clerical and sales pursuits grew at the expense of white-collar professional jobs. Some of that statistical growth was due to the fact that once women became the primary employees in some professions, the U.S. Census Bureau reclassified the jobs as clerical. The post–World War II pattern for women's occupational categories was set by 1940. Single or married white women predominated in white-collar low-level clerical and semiprofessional work. Racial minorities held even lower-level and less desirable jobs.[5]

By 1940, almost four-fifths of working women were white and native born. They remained on the job longer, leaving the labor force not after marriage, but after the birth of their first child. Married women were no more than 20 percent of the total employed women in any age group. During the same period, 17 percent of all married women were in the labor force. The overwhelming effect of the Depression years for advantaged white women was a retreat from combining rewarding careers with families. Women could have jobs and families but they would no longer be "careerists."[6]

Poor women's struggle to remain economically afloat while caring for children was made more difficult by economic hard times. New Deal legislation designed to benefit workers, such as the National Industrial Relations Act (NIRA), did not benefit many women. Domestics were exempt from Social Security as well as the wages and hours provisions of the NIRA codes because they were "not in interstate commerce." Women and children in the sweatshop sewing trades were also excluded from the NIRA codes.[7]

During the Depression, when married women's work was thought to take jobs away from family men, there was a general assault on custodial child-care services. The New Deal enacted the Aid to Dependent Children (ADC) program, which today is commonly called welfare. This legislation gave federal sanction to the housekeeping-mother approach to the care of children. Instead of providing jobs or encouraging mothers to seek employment, ADC assumed that mothers should stay home to avoid competition with male workers. Male and female social reformers shared the view that mothers would be supported in order to provide important care for children. Mother care for the children might prevent juvenile delinquency. For a woman who really wanted a job, the program offered paltry benefits instead of work.[8]

For working women, shortages in child-care services remained a serious problem. In 1930, most day-care institutions served only white and poor immigrant children. They did not serve poor black children. African-Americans managed to establish a few centers with their own resources. At the 1930 White House Conference on Child Health and Protection, black sociologist Dr. Ira De Reid, research director of the National Urban League, reported on the enormous problems of African-American children. He emphasized that in the entire country, there were less than forty day nurseries for black children.[9]

Underscoring the negative attitudes toward day-care institutions, the Association of Day Nurseries dissolved in 1931. They succumbed to attacks that day care undermined the family. The association acknowledged that day nurseries should be a last resort after care by the mother, relatives, or foster care by women in their own homes.[10]

New Deal recovery and rehabilitation agencies funded day-care centers essentially to create work for the unemployed, not to help employed mothers. Some children, who otherwise would not have had care, received the benefits of what was essentially a Works Progress Administration (WPA) jobs program. Usually located in school buildings, the centers employed teachers, nurses, nutritionists, cooks, and janitors. They operated from about 9 A.M. to midafternoon. Mothers had to follow their child's progress and participate in parent education classes. Parents used the centers to provide food and educational services that they could not afford for their children and to baby-sit while they sought work. If the wife or her husband found a job, they could no longer use the services.[11]

During World War II, women workers responded to the wartime emergency. They increased their participation in the labor force by taking nontraditional jobs. The new jobs led to increased wages. There was even some upward mobility as white women's employment in business increased. Large numbers of black women moved from domestic service and agricultural fieldwork to manufacturing jobs that paid higher wages. Women found, however, that equal pay and assignments to top jobs remained elusive.[12]

The millions of mothers who entered the work force during the war were immediately affected by the shortage of child-care services. Governmental response to the increased need for services was dictated by financial considerations and the belief that a mother's primary duty was to care for her children. In 1941, the Children's Bureau organized a White House conference on the problems of child care for working mothers. At the conference, Katherine Lenroot, head of the Children's Bureau, stated that "mothers who remain at home to provide for children are providing an essential patriotic service." The War Manpower Commission, in 1942, directed that "no women responsible for the care of young children should be encouraged or compelled to seek employment which deprives their children of essential care until all sources of supply are exhausted."[13]

The same year, the federal government decided that New Deal–funded nurseries were no longer needed as a source of employment. Some of the nurseries were first transformed into centers for the care of children of defense workers. The next year, most of them were closed because they were located in areas where there were no defense plants.[14]

To relieve some of the pressures on defense industry workers, the Roosevelt administration reluctantly ruled that the Lanham Act, passed by Congress for the construction of wartime facilities, could be used for day-care operations for war workers. Some of the programs funded by the act were formerly WPA day nurseries. Unfortunately, the application procedures under the Lanham Act were so arduous that it was difficult to use the funds for the purpose. By the end of the war, however, about fifty million dollars had been spent on construction and operation of day-care facilities. The federal government established 3,102 day-care centers serving about 105,000 children of defense workers. State governments and some industries also opened day-care centers. Operated by local school systems, these centers provided limited educational services.[15]

During the war, the birthrate began an upward trend rising to its highest level in two decades. Day-care facilities remained inadequate for the nearly 1.5 million mothers with children under the age of ten who joined the work force. Many children, left alone by working parents, became known as "latchkey" children, a term still used today, because they carried the house key with them.[16]

The Women's Bureau noted repeatedly that day-care provisions during the war were inadequate. Even when provided, they were not conveniently located near black neighborhoods or African-American children were denied admission. African-American women migrating to work in the defense industry often lived outside black residential areas and beyond traditional kinship networks. Finding care-givers was well-nigh impossible for them. Many children were left alone.[17]

The Office of War Propaganda described the new workers as older women who no longer had heavy maternal responsibilities. They were working to help out during the war. Their children were in school, so only limited child-care services were needed. Magazine stories, newspapers, the radio, and movies made Rosie the Riveter a war heroine. The office's Magazine Bureau met regularly with editors from such popular periodicals as *Ladies' Home Journal* and *McCall's* and suggested specific stories to writers. Some stories portrayed women as happy in nontraditional occupations. Others, aimed at married women, showed how to do housework in a shorter period of time and portrayed day-care centers favorably.[18]

One magazine story depicted two debutantes who took an aircraft factory job to help with the war effort. The magazine indicated that everything possible was done to see that the women workers were happy and productive. The debutantes established a child-care center at the factory that became a model for factory workers around the country. Another story described the romance that developed between a shell-shocked veteran and the director of a child-care center. He even helped her with her work during his recovery.[19]

Some of the real World War II day-care programs, like earlier ones, left much to be desired by any standard. There were few, if any, qualifications required for care-givers, and few building regulations. Child-care facilities were overcrowded, expensive, and often lacked outdoor play space. The deficiencies in the programs explain, perhaps, why a 1943 Gallup poll reported that 56 percent of mothers would not use government day-care centers, even if they were provided free. Tragedies at the centers only increased the public's suspicion of them. In Auburn, Maine, in 1945, sixteen babies and preschoolers burned to death in a fire at a nursery for children of women war workers.[20]

Children from three months to five years of age boarded in the Auburn nursery during the week and went home with their mothers for the weekend. The nursery was located in an old farm building. Although it was constructed of wood, the local fire chief said the building met all laws related to structure and exits.[21]

The Auburn fire led to warnings by social welfare experts about maintaining standards. The public, of course, deplored the fire deaths, but most responses emphasized the dangers of custodial child care and yearned for the end of the war and the restoration of families.[22]

When questioned about day-care conditions and demands, Howard W. Hopkirk, executive director of the Child Welfare League, tried to stimulate demands for better child-care services. He noted, "wives of servicemen increasingly are compelled to rely upon the cheapest available nursery care while they are at work." Hopkirk saw problems resulting from "the demand for women workers on night shifts; small incomes of the families of servicemen; the need for more foster homes, which have been proved to be the best facility for the care of infants; and the failure of the country to budget enough for child welfare." At the Auburn facility, he noted, four women were in charge of twenty-one children when the ratios should have been no more than one worker for every three children.[23]

Dr. Leona Baumgarten, director of the Bureau of Child Hygiene in New York City, said the Auburn tragedy pointed up ". . . the need for parents to be very careful where they leave their children." They should at least require a permit from the health department and remember that, "young children can't help themselves."[24]

When the war ended, the Child Welfare League worked to prevent a total cut-off of Lanham Act funds. They argued against a lapse in day care. Indeed, the league argued that more funds should be made available for day and foster care for the needy. Increasing services for black children was part of the League's postwar agenda. Abigail F. Brownell's report on the subject noted, again "the increased need of Negro children and that the services provided them are few and far between." Brownell found also that child care could easily be racially integrated. There was "less resistance to eliminating discrimination in regard to children than to adults, less in regard to babies than school-age children and less in regard to school-age children than to adolescents."[25]

Despite arguments in favor of day-care funding after the war, Lanham Act funds were discontinued. Attempts by proponents, including the Children's Bureau and the Child Welfare League, to gain federal funding received little public notice. Some people argued that Lanham funds should be cut off because large numbers of women had left the work force and returned to the home.[26]

Women had worked productively in all types of jobs and industries during the war, which made opponents of women's employment even more determined that they should return to the woman's place. Some women relinquished "men's jobs" because of family commitments; others shared the prevailing ideology that they *should* return to the home; and unions favored male veterans, who were returning from the war. Management took the lead in purging women from nontraditional jobs. Employers regarded the wartime experience as a necessary evil. Since union efforts and litigation had narrowed the wage gap, there was less financial advantage in hiring women.[27]

Higher and higher local standards were placed on the remaining publicly funded day-care centers in the postwar period; consequently, the number of facilities shrank. Opponents of nonparental care took little notice of the continuing needs of poor employed mothers. They also ignored the large numbers of poor black, Asian, and Latino women hired to help with other parents' children while rearing their own. Institutional day care became a marginal child welfare issue, and centers provided space to only a small number of the children who needed it. Even the term "day care" largely disappeared from public discussion by the late 1940s and did not appear again until the 1960s. The press most often used the term "baby-sitting" to refer to nonmother care.[28]

The child-care needs of employed Hispanics and Asian-Americans remained similar to those of other poor and African-American families, despite differences in culture and time of arrival in the United States.[29]

Mexican-Americans have been the largest group of Hispanic immigrants and residents in the United States, and their patterns of employment have reflected the subordination they have faced. In the southwest, whites traditionally employed Mexican-American women as domestic workers. In the west, employers relied on Mexican-American women's labor in cannery factories. The women also used self-employment schemes including sewing, laundry, and taking in boarders to augment their incomes.[30]

By 1930, 25 percent of Mexican and Mexican-American women wage earners in the southwest worked in industry. This figure was comparable to the number of European immigrants in the east who worked outside the home. Two-thirds of the women workers were single, without children. The one-third of Mexican-American women workers who were married and had children had to arrange child care. In Mexican culture, admitting that a wife had to accept employment undermined a husband's self-respect, so working wives also had to persuade their husbands that their paid work was only temporary. "Temporary," however, might actually turn out to mean long periods of time. From the 1880s to World War II, domestic service remained the largest field of employment for Mexican-American women, closely followed by agriculture.[31]

Family and motherhood discussions and the economic stresses of the 1930s undermined the efforts of women struggling for individual women's rights. During this time, social reformers and social workers gathered in Washington to help the New Deal. They were warmly received by First Lady Eleanor Roosevelt. For the first time, women were appointed to policy-making posts in larger numbers. As Secretary of Labor, Frances Perkins was the first female cabinet member.[32]

But New Deal programs were designed to help the family, not to change gender roles. Helping the family meant ADC and not day care. In this political climate, the National Woman's Party (NWP) struggled to gain an Equal Rights Amendment and tried to heal the breach over protective legislation. Alice Paul hailed the National Industrial Relations Act (NIRA) codes of conduct and the Fair Labor Standards Act because they eliminated the need for women to insist on protective legislation. Under these regulations, the same standards were used for women and men. But the Women's Bureau disagreed, arguing that women still needed wage and hour guidelines in jobs not covered by NIRA and the Fair Labor Standards Act. The Bureau continued to rationalize that women were physically and emotionally different from men; that women rightfully fulfilled different family roles, could not compete equally with men in the economic sphere, and needed special legislation based on sex.[33]

Although the conflict over protective legislation remained, the NWP and business and professional women's organizations continued to oppose wage differentials and other discriminations against working women generally. They did not attack the race problem but they did not retreat behind class lines, abandoning the cause of women factory workers and clerks just because their members were mainly professionals.[34]

In the atmosphere of reduced support for women's advancement beyond "traditional" bounds, the NWP, almost alone, criticized the changing currents. People inside the administration, including Eleanor Roosevelt, emphasized women's right to work without discrimination. A distinct feminist critique of the particular effect of the Depression on women, however, never emerged. The public overwhelmingly supported the idea of traditional family roles and opposed married women's employment.[35]

For mothers seeking information about how to care for children, the expert advice changed again in the 1930s. Permissiveness, rather than the strict discipline that John Watson and the behaviorists had recommended, came back into fashion. The experts argued that the child's spontaneous impulses were good and true. In the 1930s, as a result of the popularization of Sigmund Freud, who criticized the undue repression of Victorian children, child experts were recommending greater freedom for children. [36]

The theories of John Dewey and Maria Montessori, emphasizing children's curiosity and independence, fueled the new attitude. Arnold Gesell recommended flexible schedules and tolerance of children's phases such as thumb sucking. According to successive generations of infant care bulletins published by the federal government, children developed from fierce animals in 1914 to mellow and temperate creatures in 1942. What the baby wanted, it must need and should get, according to this line of thinking. The child was the expert. [37]

Coincidentally, the mammy figure in *Gone With the Wind* was the perfect example of the kind of uncomplicated, unchallenging love children needed from parents and their child-care helpers. Psychoanalysts agreed with the child-raising experts. Mother love was biologically natural to women. The ideal mother would find not duty but passionate fulfillment in child care. Because only the nonworking mother fit the ideal, mothers were urged to quit their jobs and succumb to the impulses they were fighting. Bad mothers, those who did not fit the ideal, would be betrayed by their children's pathological, cranky behavior. [38]

As soon as mothers attuned themselves to administer proper doses of attention and love to their children, the experts added a slight twist to the rules. Dr. David Levy said in 1943 that mothers had the problem of maternal overprotection. When a mother immersed herself too deeply in child nurturing, Levy said, there were detrimental effects, particularly with boys. In World War II, when psychological testing showed some men unfit for service, their problems were attributed to overprotective mothers. Such mothers took advantage of the country's "megaloid mom worship" according to Philip Wylie's 1955 *Generation of Vipers*. Mom was not really the sweet unselfish server of her family but a power-hungry oppressor who was bad for children. If not taken in hand, Mother would undermine completely the power of Father, Wylie said.[39]

The experts' ideas about what mothers should and should not do could be most successfully implemented by housewives whose husbands provided well. But working wives and female heads of households could hardly stick to the advice. With the paucity of institutional services, these women struggled to find care of any kind for their children. Poor working mothers' arrangements for child care involved a great reliance on school, grandparents, and other family members. But mothers were responsible for arranging care even when the family was father-headed. When children went to school, after-school and lunch arrangements had to be made; meals were rarely offered at school.[40]

Many wives had help with household work. In the south, white women, even low-paid textile workers, often had black domestics who did the housework and provided some of the child care. African-American women in the north often sent their children back "home" to the south when school was out to be taken care of by other relatives.[41]

The end of piecework under the NIRA made it harder to combine employment and child care, particularly for Jewish and Italian women who relied on the needle trades. The NIRA was designed to stimulate industrial employment by prohibiting unfair competition, and requiring fair wages. The policy meant that these mothers now had to wait until all of their children were in school to go out to work.[42]

When poor children were old enough they often worked after school. As the children of immigrants became acculturated to American ways, they resented the old-world pattern of turning over all wages to the family. This placed even greater pressure on wives to work.[43]

The question of a woman's primary responsibility for the home and child care was seldom raised in the 1930s, or even during World War II. Women only "helped out" in the workplace while the men were away during the war. After the war, women were expected to return home as soon as possible. They wanted this, men wanted it, and it was considered good for children. When the men returned from the war, nonparental child care received even less public attention. Poor women and minority group mothers were displaced from better-paying wartime jobs. They had an even harder time finding the day care they still needed. Although growing numbers of white married, divorced, and widowed women worked, there was little public discussion of women's labor force participation.[44]

After the war and until 1947 divorces surged. Thereafter, making and keeping families became all the rage for the middle class. Suburban homemaking and raising a family became a new ideal for women. Poor white women, even when they had to work, also emulated the goal of having a husband support them while they managed the home. Poor women of color who were accustomed to balancing jobs and children also wished for the ideal.[45]

Marriage rates soared for all Americans in the 1940s and the 1950s, bettering all demographic records. By 1960, 70 percent of all women were married by the age of twenty-four, compared to just 42 percent in 1940. People married at younger ages, had more children, and had those children at an earlier age. A million more children a year were born in the 1960s than in the 1930s. When asked the ideal size for a family, three-quarters of the women surveyed in 1960 answered that it was three or more children. In 1941, women had expressed a desire for no more than two children. But by 1946, most people responded no to a Gallup poll asking whether the country needed a Baby Bonus Plan modeled after a British policy to encourage having children. No one needed incentives to have children. A generation battered by the Depression and by sacrificing for the war had decided to seek refuge in children and the home.[46]

Women's magazines, the media, and public opinion polls all assumed that women wanted careers as wives and mothers. College graduation rates for women fell and the number of women entering the professions slackened. Women declined from 47 percent of all college graduates in 1920 to 31 percent in 1950. The percentage of women seeking graduate degrees was lower in the 1950s than in the previous two decades. Experts, journalists, and opinion leaders all emphasized the importance of marriage and family life. During the postwar economic boom, the suburbanization of America began, spurred by low-interest home mortgages and a growing federal highway system that made commuting long distances easy. It was more possible for people to acquire the house, car, and consumer goods that the media suggested made a happy family.[47]

Suburban living brought isolation and transience but, for some, networks with neighbors replaced the old family bonds. The commuting husband rushed home to his family and rushed back to his job. Husband and wife became partners in the marriage but with different duties.[48]

The upper-class companionate marriage of the 1920s became the 1950s ideal marriage for a much larger group of people, especially for the broad middle-income group of Americans. As television became the dominant medium in the 1950s, shows projected images of "typical" families, the working-class "Honeymooners" or the middle-class "Leave It to Beaver" and "Father Knows Best." The working-class husband, as Jackie Gleason portrayed him, was a bumbling clumsy fool; a dreamer but loveable anyway. The wife was a scatterbrain but with solid common sense. Middle-class mothers were shown baking cookies and taking care of the children while fathers gave wise counsel mixed with permissiveness to their wives and children.[49]

Children growing up in these families in the fifties lived a child-centered life. The early 1900s were replicated, with Dr. Benjamin Spock replacing Hall and scientific motherhood. Spock's book on child-rearing became the best-selling book of its time. Like Gesell had done earlier, Spock told parents to eliminate the rigidities of child-rearing and give babies more autonomy. Although Spock was later criticized for being too permissive, he did, in fact, emphasize the importance of discipline. However, he said that parents should use love, reason, and parental example instead of physical punishment, intimidation, or behavioral approaches. He expressed traditional views about how little boys and little girls should behave and particularly emphasized the mother-child bond.[50]

Mothers were told that they could have an especially harmful or beneficial effect on their children's development. John Bowlby's 1950 study of war orphans, child inmates of hospitals, and those who had been boarded in rural areas to protect them from air raids kindled discussions of the evils of maternal deprivation. Bowlby concluded that a child required a continuous relationship with one person, a mother or mother surrogate. Both mother and child would be happier that way. Furthermore, he claimed that nothing was so pernicious or nonfunctional as families in which mothers were employed full time.[51]

Mothers were supposed to protect the child's physical and mental health; they were to avoid taking out their hostilities on the child. Erik Erikson and other psychologists linked mother's behavior to mental health problems; homosexuality, identity diffusion, and an inability to mature were blamed on the mother.[52]

Boys' sexual identity development was of particular concern since they were raised by women. Consequently, fathers were instructed to take a major, though constrained, role in child-raising. A father should play sports with the boys and compliment girls on their hairdos or the cookies they baked. He might also occasionally help out with the dishes or the baby's formula, but not too often, since that would induce role confusion in the children.[53]

According to these formulations, children brought stability and fulfillment to mothers and fathers. Fatherhood became a way of expressing authority and manliness and making sure that the children, especially the boys, became proper adults. In increasing numbers, fathers took courses on marriage. *Life* magazine, in 1954, hailed the "New American Domesticated Male." *American Home Magazine* asked in 1950, "Are You a Dud as a Dad?" None of this meant that men were to take on women's primary child-care role. They were still the good providers while the wife was the manager of the "scientific home," which included birth control and the spacing of children. Dad would bring his masculine influence to enforce discipline when he arrived home, as in, "Wait until your father comes home."[54]

Why Johnny Can't Read by Rudolph Franz Flesch detailed the deficiencies of American children's education in 1955 and, two years later, the Soviet Union launched *Sputnik*, their first space satellite. These events helped to impose an additional burden on Mother. She became "educator." Mothers in upwardly mobile families were expected to teach the children from earliest infancy. Love was important, but they were also supposed to use mobiles and toys and other objects to stimulate the child's sensory apparatus. Mother would see to it that older children played with tinker toys and chemistry sets. She also chauffeured the kids after school to dancing, art, and music lessons, individual tutoring and other enrichments.[55]

But all was not well with some members of the happy family. Marital separations became more frequent even if there were fewer divorces. Evidence of alcohol, drug, and barbiturate abuse by housewives surfaced, as well as wife swapping and even prostitution. Women who had enjoyed freedom and independence and work during the war resented the confinement of their suburban existence. More work was done at home but less was acknowledged. Fathers complained that their only job was to bring in the money. Commuting did not help those men who found their work unchallenging and who displaced their problems on the job onto their families.[56]

Blue-collar males who tried to provide their families with the ingredients of the ideal but could not, experienced new stress as they tried to maintain traditional roles. This was especially a problem for men who experienced high unemployment rates or intermittent employment. Incipient humanistic psychology gave men a rationale for challenging their breadwinner role. The new theories said that human beings continued to grow and change throughout life. They did not need to respond to any particular expectations if those expectations made them uncomfortable.[57]

During the 1950s, large numbers of women worked outside of the home for remuneration and as volunteers. They engaged in volunteer activities at schools, hospitals, libraries, and in politics. But the suburban life-style and the acquisition of consumer goods required money. The end of child labor, compulsory education, and the expectation that children would attend college added additional financial pressures.[58]

The two-income family became more commonplace as women increasingly took paid work and the pattern became a greater topic of discussion. In 1940, wives earned wages in only 21.6 percent of families. By 1960, 30.5 percent of wives worked. Some of them worked part-time and many were young women without children. Others were mature women, forty-five years old or older, with grown children.[59]

Even in the 1950s, the proportion of women with small children who sought paid employment increased by one-third. The proportion of women with children under six seeking paid employment increased by one-quarter. Unlike wartime, when women had moved into nontraditional high-paying jobs, women worked mainly in occupationally segregated jobs where they made less money than men. As a result, median earnings for employed women, relative to those of men, declined. By 1960, about one-third of all working (mostly white) women held clerical jobs. The number of domestics declined, and poorer and minority-group women gained blue-collar "service jobs" as health care aides and technicians, beauticians, waitresses, and office cleaners. By 1960, nearly 80 percent of women worked in jobs in which most of the other workers were female.[60]

The 1950s were also the era of Margaret Mead. Although the decade was dominated by an emphasis on mothers at home and children, there *were* female achievers in the workplace. Most of the achievers did not regard themselves as feminists. There was Senator Margaret Chase Smith of Maine, who was placed in nomination for vice president by the Republicans in 1952; the philosopher Hannah Arendt; environmentalist Rachel Carson; Oveta Culp Hobby, Secretary of the U.S. Department of Health, Education and Welfare (HEW); Rosa Parks of the NAACP and Montgomery bus boycott fame; and older women such as Eleanor Roosevelt, who traveled the world as U.N. ambassador, and her good friend Mary McLeod Bethune, a college president, who had been one of a group of black advisers to President Franklin Roosevelt. There were journalists such as May Craig and Doris Fleeson and novelists and critics such as Mary McCarthy and Diana Trilling. Freda Kerchwey, remarkably, was editor and publisher of *The Nation* until 1955.[61]

These well-known women worked in a variety of fields; they were activists and crusaders; some received their education for later leadership as part of the small group of women graduating from college. Some of these women maintained successful relationships with their husbands and children in households with servants. Still, most women continued to see husbands and children as their major priorities.[62]

There were still feminists, or women's rights activists, huddled in the National Woman's Party and in some local organizations, eclipsed by the trends of the times. The National American Women's Suffrage

Association had become the League of Women Voters, focusing entirely on voter education. Feminists made some progress in the battle for women's rights. Both parties supported a proposed Equal Rights Amendment, as did President Harry Truman. But some prominent women, Eleanor Roosevelt among them, still opposed it as inimical to protective legislation. Both major political parties in 1952 and 1956 supported the idea of equal pay for women, as did President Eisenhower in his 1956 State of the Union message. Citing increased employment but continued discrimination against working women, the Women's Bureau in 1954 withdrew its long-time opposition to the ERA without endorsing it.[63]

In the 1950s, two million mothers with preschool-age children were employed, yet most did not use institutional child care. There were few facilities available and institutional care had become associated in the eyes of middle-class parents with poor dysfunctional families. The Children's Bureau continued to research and publish studies on day-care regulation but with little public notice. Employed mothers existed but the idea of using institutions to care for their children was contrary to reigning ideals.[64]

The federal government did not develop new child-care facilities during the Korean War (1950–53) because it did not require the massive mobilization needed for World War II. The 1952 Democratic Party platform advocated day-care facilities for mothers in defense work but Eisenhower won the election and ended the war. If women went into defense work, policy makers reasoned, they should rely on private organizations or on local governments to provide help. One of the major private organizations, the National Conference of Catholic Charities, took the position that mothers should be encouraged to stay at home with their children. By 1958, most children continued to be cared for by relatives and neighbors; only 2 percent of children of working mothers under twelve years of age were in day care or nursery school. Day care remained an institutional resource for poor women or nonfunctional families.[65]

Soon, however, the Republican Party included a new approach to addressing child-care needs along with its proposed new tax code. In his campaign for the presidency, Dwight Eisenhower promised to reduce taxes in order to generate a business expansion, despite a projected $5.5-billion deficit. The GOP-controlled Congress revised the entire tax code in the landmark Internal Revenue Act of 1954. One part of the package that became law was a deduction for child-care expenses resulting from employment. Under the old 1936 code, a taxpayer could not deduct child-care expenses incurred because of employment.[66]

A Board of Tax Appeals decision in 1939 denied a deduction to a two-earner family on the grounds that the wife's functions as "custodian of the home and protector of the children," made child-care expenses of a personal, not a business, nature. Even if the wife chose to have someone else perform her functions, that did not "deprive" the work of "its personal character. . . . We are told that the working wife is a new phenomenon," the court noted. "But if that is true it becomes all the more necessary to apply accepted principles to the novel facts." No deduction could be taken for satisfying personal preferences of taxpayers, the court ruled.[67]

But by 1953 the working wife was no longer quite so "novel" and millions of working mothers needed more help with care. Party politics helped to influence the Republicans to enact a child-care provision. Democrats objected to the tax code proposals as benefiting the rich when the Republicans refused to raise dependency exemptions but reduced the capital gains tax. Some members of Congress thought the child-care deduction and a few other smaller deductions were put in to rebut this criticism, but denounced them as only "a pittance." House Minority Whip John McCormack (D., Mass.) described the bill as "trickling down policy," saying that in his experience, "very little has trickled down to the people."[68]

As enacted, the child-care provision permitted a $600 deduction for actual child-care expenses paid by a working widow, widower, a divorced person, or a working mother, amounting to $12.50 a week, as long as its purpose was to permit the taxpayer to hold gainful employment. The deduction was allowed for children under twelve years of age, or for mentally or physically handicapped dependents.[69]

During congressional hearings on the bill, witnesses and members acknowledged the reality of employed mothers as a growing concern. The needs of working widows of servicemen killed in World War II and Korea and of families in which returning servicemen had low-wage jobs figured prominently in the discussion. Most members of Congress were willing to allow a deduction for the impecunious who worked from necessity; they did not want to allow mothers who took paid work for what they regarded as frivolous reasons to have a deduction. [70]

Labor unions, betraying their disinclination to support an increase of women in the labor force who would compete with men for jobs, were not enthusiastic about the proposal. The Congress of Industrial Organizations (CIO) reluctantly supported a deduction, pointing out that they had been trying to "raise the earning power of all those who are employed. Nevertheless, many women feel compelled to supplement their husband's earnings in order that family income may be sufficient to provide proper food, clothing, housing, and other necessities." But the American Federation of Labor (AFL) preferred to increase the dependency exemption because the various child-care deduction bills "would permit wholesale evasion and abuse and be very difficult to enforce." [71]

Most of the witnesses and members of Congress insisted repeatedly that they did not want to encourage mothers to work. But other witnesses focused on women who were needed in the work force or who were already working. Democratic congresswoman Leonor Sullivan of Missouri noted that women worked "because they have to, but under our present economic system we need these women workers." Julia Thompson of the American Nurses Association believed the deduction would help to relieve the rampant nursing shortage. Twenty percent of active registered nurses had children under eighteen. Considering that it cost about $40 per week for child-care in large metropolitan areas, she wanted the proposed deduction increased from $600 to $2000. [72]

When President Eisenhower signed the new tax bill, including the child-care deduction, in August 1954, he made clear his view that this new policy departure was the Republican way to deal with the child-care issue. He insisted it provided mainly for widows and widowers and wives whose husbands were incapacitated. The New Deal and World War II child-care policies were designed to keep mothers at home. The Republicans' new direction had similar overall objectives. Tax policy acknowledged the reality of employment without undermining the family. A tax credit could be given to the working poor to bring day care into the home, but anything other than mother care remained a matter of necessity, not preference.[73]

VI

Challenging the Mother-Care Tradition, 1960–1980

The greatest challenge to the preference for mother care and the idealized traditional family came in the 1960s and 1970s. Reformers demanded gender role changes and government aid for day care but mother care remained the dominant tradition.

The 1960s began with great optimism and ended in confusion. John Kennedy's election in 1960 promised a new spirit of change in public life. Change did come, although not as expected. Promising to get the country moving again, Kennedy drew up an ambitious New Frontier program to improve the quality of life. A conservative coalition in Congress stalled Kennedy's plans and they were left hopelessly immobilized when his presidency was tragically cut short by his assassination on November 22, 1963.

Beset by intimidation and violence, the civil rights movement continued to grow in this period. Those who joined the movement forced changes in race relations that had been too long in coming. A feminist movement devoted to gaining equality of rights and opportunities for women burgeoned, involving many women who had been active in the civil rights movement, where they learned useful strategy and tactics.

Under Kennedy's successor, Lyndon Johnson, Congress implemented and extended the Kennedy social agenda, and for a time it seemed that the federal government would commit large resources to the renovation of American society. The growing protest against the war in Vietnam decidedly interfered with the achievement of Johnson's Great Society objectives, and by 1968 the country began sliding into a state of constant crisis as the public lost confidence in the president's leadership.

Bemused and discomfited by racial uprisings in cities and the alienation of the young, the country, in a search for order, elected Republican Richard Nixon as president in 1968 and 1972. But Nixon, projected as the embodiment of hard work and restorer of middle-class values, became a lawbreaker and was forced to resign the presidency in the wake of the Watergate scandal. Gerald Ford and Jimmy Carter tried to regain the public's respect for the office, but they were beset by domestic problems that included high interest rates and inflation, as well as by reaction against the pace and direction of social change.

A search for practical and politically palatable positions on women's rights, the problems of employed women, and the care of children remained items on each president's agenda. When Kennedy took office, he confronted increasing numbers of working women and a Democratic Party position on employed women that was more attuned to the early 1950s than the 1960s.

Republicans supported the Equal Rights Amendment and were responsible for a child-care tax deduction. The Democrats' position on women's rights and employed women, however, seemed to be dictated by organized labor. Esther Peterson, CIO legislative representative, expressed labor's preference for different, protective treatment for women rather than equal treatment. The Democratic party platform supported the extension of protective legislation and opposed the Equal Rights Amendment. After Kennedy's election, Peterson was named assistant secretary and director of the Women's Bureau in the Department of Labor, which was headed by labor lawyer Arthur Goldberg.[1]

In 1960, 36 percent of the nation's women were employed. Sixty percent of the working women were married and 27 percent were mothers with preschool children. In order to prove the administration's interest, counteract pressure for an equal rights amendment to the Constitution, and indicate that women were already making progress, Peterson proposed a device routinely used by Presidents for such purposes, a study commission. In December 1961, Kennedy appointed a Commission on the Status of Women with Eleanor Roosevelt as the chair.[2]

After Roosevelt's death in November 1962, Peterson gained control of the commission's work. The President's Report on the Status of Women, issued in 1963, was predictable, given organized labor's influence. It presented an optimistic view of women performing their traditional roles in the home as well as new roles in the workplace, making them a great resource for the country. The commission thought an equal rights constitutional amendment was not needed for women and that protective legislation should be extended. It said that child-care facilities and the child-care tax deduction should be increased, but new choices for women did "not imply neglect of their education for responsibilities in the home." There was no call for changes in the sexual division of those responsibilities.[3]

Although the commission played a consciousness-raising role, in general its work on the status of women was out of touch with the social and cultural trends of the early 1960s. The birth control pill came into use in the 1960s and the birthrate began falling until it reached zero population growth in the 1970s. The average number of children per family fell from 3.8 in 1960 to less than 2 by 1980. Individuals justified childlessness as socially responsible because of the world population explosion or the threat of nuclear war, which would so shorten everyone's life that it was not worth having children in the first place.[4]

Usually, however, when pressed, young marrieds confessed that children would interfere with their single life-styles. Romantic relationships became regarded as rational exchanges easily started and ended, with each person responsible solely for his or her own feelings and expectations. By 1963, the new sexual freedom became "cool" in the cities. While the Commission on the Status of Women reiterated a commitment to traditional values, Helen Gurley Brown popularized the fun and benefits of the new life-style in *Sex and the Single Girl*. In the popular media, housewives soon became as unpopular as they had previously been celebrated.[5]

When Betty Friedan summed up the discontent of white middle-class and affluent women in 1963 as "the problem that has no name," she found an immediate positive response. In a period of civil rights reform in which many women were activists and attitudes about family were changing, Friedan's book resonated deeply with the prevailing mood. Friedan said the dissatisfaction of women was not caused by "material advantages" and it ". . . may not even be felt by women preoccupied with desperate problems of hunger, poverty, or illness." The main problem was the denial of woman's opportunity to fulfill her own identity and needs, as she herself defined them. For too long, anatomy had been destiny. Friedan, reflecting the growing numbers of employed wives, proposed careers as remedies for what ailed women who stayed home. Friedan provided the justification for wives who were already working and encouraged the developing trend.[6]

In *The Feminine Mystique*, Friedan explained not only women's discontent, but also that of men. She shared the prevailing male contempt for homemaking, regarding it as decidedly overrated. Husbands suffered from the housewife's thwarted emotional and intellectual growth. The old hostility against domineering "mom" and aggressive career girls dimmed, in this view, before hostility toward the dependent wife who exaggerated the importance of housework as a career while her husband supported her.[7]

Friedan thought the rising divorce rate showed the hostility of men toward the millstones around their necks. Before men abandoned traditional family commitments in droves, they had to also be willing to abandon the male privilege and authority they bought by being the good provider. Men would have to decide if the traditional masculine role was worth the obligation of being the breadwinner. Not all men were willing to go this far, but large numbers did as indicated by the increasing divorces, female-headed households, and fathers who did not even pay child support in the 1960s and 1970s.[8]

But Friedan and other leaders of what became an organized women's movement did not concern themselves immediately with this half of her book. They were more interested in enlivening the lives of women. After a prohibition against sex discrimination was added to the race discrimination employment ban in the Civil Rights Act of 1964, the National Organization for Women (NOW) was founded to ensure enforcement of the anti-gender discrimination provisions.[9]

Friedan and other founders and members of NOW, reflecting their liberal roots, focused on change within the system. They thought that legislation could create equality. Women's liberation groups, growing out of the peace, civil rights, and student movements, focused instead on consciousness-raising, female-male differences, and in some cases the need to change the entire economic and social structure of the country. They included such groups as the Redstockings, founded by Shulamith Firestone and Ellen Willis in 1969, and The Feminists, originally known as the October 17th Movement, a splinter group formed from NOW in 1968 by Ti-Grace Atkinson.[10]

These were the movement radicals who wanted to change the system. Both camps agreed on some issues, including an end to job discrimination in pay and work opportunities; elimination of the assumption that women should do all of the housework and be principally responsible for raising children; the repeal of laws restricting access to abortion and birth control in order to provide freedom of choice; and the end of physical violence against women.[11]

The influence of the women's movement began to show in a number of ways. Married women began to say they took jobs for personal growth, not because of economic necessity, and working women sought better opportunities. Religious women fought for nontraditional roles, including the ministry. Whereas many women once said they only wanted to marry, polls indicated that increasingly women also wanted to work. By 1970, 41 percent of women were employed, and ten years later, 51 percent of all women were employed, with well over 60 percent of women workers married and/or mothers of preschool children. The women's movement made it possible for some women to enter professional and blue-collar fields from which they had once been excluded.[12]

Day care was on the agenda of women's rights activists from the beginning. NOW's 1966 statement of purpose asserted the need for an equitable sharing of the responsibilities of home, children, and employment. The 1968 NOW Bill of Rights demanded the establishment of child-care facilities on "the same basis as parks, libraries and public schools, adequate to the needs of children from the pre-school years through adolescence, as a community resource . . ." Feminists in major cities and university towns were the first to set up day-care centers. Some established cooperatives, where parents were required to volunteer. For example, in the late 1960s, in Iowa City, home of the University of Iowa, the radical-feminist-organized day-care center stressed a nonsexist environment. Boys and girls were taught to both hammer and cook.[13]

In the African-American community, the growing women's liberation movement became another source of contention. During a period of increased breakdown in the traditional white family in the 1960s and 1970s, the disruption of black families was even more severe. Black families became increasingly female-headed and poor. Daniel Patrick Moynihan's 1965 report on the weaknesses of the black family blamed black women for being too matriarchal. Black women, who had always been more likely to be employed, found that if they tried to address their subordination by calling for women's liberation, it created dissension within the black community. These concerns were the object of heated discussion that took a variety of forms.[14]

A black woman writer, Toni Cade (now Toni Cade Bambara), explained the difficulty. Black women's "concerns, priorities and methods" were not the same as those of the feminist "experts," such as Friedan, Cade said. Black women wanted to be free and equal but on their own terms. "The job then regarding roles is to submerge all breezy definitions of manhood/womanhood . . . until realistic definitions emerge through a commitment to Blackhood," according to Cade.[15]

Controversy over whether the women's movement was relevant to African-Americans led *Ebony*, the most widely circulated black magazine, to publish an article by Helen H. King denigrating feminism as a divisive white women's movement, in which black participation undermined black men. The article generated numerous heated responses.

Most of the published respondents said it was ridiculous to assume black women needed to resist their own empowerment for fear of reinforcing weakness among black men. One writer said: "Only by uniting with each other and our black men as equal human beings will we have the strength for the liberation struggles that face us. This unity is key to our victory."[16]

Another woman wrote that the problem was that "male-run magazines such as *Ebony* are strongly against the women's movement. This thought is summed up in a quote from Ashley Montague about women taking care of babies: Any interference with this is very dangerous. Yeah, dangerous to men who are afraid someday they might have to do a little diaper changing." Other writers acknowledged that "women's lib" was a threat to black unity but they agreed with one who said: "Women's lib has some interesting points. Equal pay for equal work and more child care centers would be very helpful. Black women have always been liberated, in a sense. Black women have had to work to support husbands, children and family."[17]

In response to the women's movement and the civil rights movement, the federal government established a goal of removing barriers to equal opportunity for women and minorities. Congress, in Title VII of the Civil Rights Act of 1964, had prohibited sex as well as race discrimination in employment, including all job classifications, assignments, promotion, and training. Executive orders and regulations supplemented these provisions, in particular Revised Order No. 4, which in 1971 detailed affirmative action guidelines for federal contractors. In addition, court decisions upheld the use of these provisions and accelerated the pace of change.[18]

In this new climate of a revived women's movement, the National Women's Party and NOW resuscitated the Equal Rights Amendment. The amendment was reintroduced by its principal sponsors, Representative Martha Griffiths of Michigan and Senators Birch Bayh of Indiana and Marlow Cook of Kentucky. By 1970, presidents Johnson and Nixon had endorsed it, and even a few of the unions and the Women's Bureau supported it.[19]

After lengthy testimony and debate, Congress passed the Equal Rights Amendment in 1972 and sent it to the states for ratification. The amendment, based on the language of the Fourteenth Amendment, which had been enacted to outlaw race discrimination after the Civil

War, provided that no state or the federal government could deny equality of rights on account of sex. The Congress could enforce the amendment by appropriate legislation.

On another front, several states passed abortion reform laws, while the Supreme Court in *Roe* v. *Wade* (1973) upheld a woman's right to reproductive choice, in consultation with her physician.[20]

Title IX of the 1972 education amendments prohibited sex discrimination in educational institutions receiving federal funds. Two years later, the Women's Educational Equity Act authorized grants and contracts to promote equity at all levels of education, from preschools through adult and vocational programs. The education amendments of 1976 gave further impetus to efforts to end sex bias in vocational educational programs.[21]

In the 1970s, Congress extended Title VII protection to employees of educational institutions and state and local government employees. Title VII also prohibited discrimination on the basis of pregnancy. In response, employers treated pregnancy variously as a temporary disability or as a special condition requiring paid leave, unpaid leave, or termination. In 1976, the Supreme Court supported this flexible approach when it decided that an employer had the right to exclude pregnancy-related disabilities from its disability benefits plan. In 1978, Congress took a more commonsense view and said that a healthy pregnant woman is to be treated just like any other healthy employee. When a woman becomes medically disabled as a result of the pregnancy, she must be treated like any employee who becomes medically disabled.[22]

Federal government guidelines and regulations said that after maternity leave, women were to be reinstated in jobs at the same or similar levels as the ones they had held before. In addition, the Equal Employment Opportunity Commission (EEOC) took the position in 1979 that if an employer allowed nonmedical leave which was not job related, it must also give leave for child-care purposes. If a state law permitted child-care leave, then a woman had a right to it beyond the period of pregnancy; if not, there was no federal requirement in this regard. A state could also mandate that quitting a job for want of child

care precluded collecting unemployment compensation without violating federal requirements.[23]

Because EEOC guidelines required only that an employer grant
child-care leave on the same basis as other nonmedical leave, it remained generally unpaid. The needs of single parents and low-income,
two-earner families who could not afford unpaid leaves were not addressed. Furthermore, in most two-earner families, the largest portion
of income came from the husband. This meant that if anyone took
leave it would most likely be the wife. As established, child-care laws
and policies were unevenly enforced and inadequately extended. Nonetheless, they provided one measure of the environment for improving
women's rights as women increasingly entered educational institutions
and the workplace.[24]

Through the 1970s, the inadequacy of child-care services as a con-
straint on women's opportunities gained increasing public attention.
Poor female-headed households were a new focus of public concern.
Many of these families, mostly white in actual numbers, but dispro-
portionately black by percentage, were on welfare. A desire to reduce
welfare rolls by providing jobs and day care influenced responses to
the child-care problem as much as the women's liberation movement did.[25]

Sociologist Jessie Bernard predicted in *The Future of Marriage*
(1972) that while day care had been "advocated on the basis that of
course child care is exclusively a woman's job, increasingly the idea
is gaining currency that the husband has a shared role." But men were
slow to become more involved in child care and housework. Women
remained principally responsible for these tasks, as well as for their
jobs or education. Writers began to describe "role overload," a phenomenon that supposedly discouraged women from taking higher-
paying jobs because they required more time and energy.[26]

In extensive studies of white working-class families, Lillian Rubin
found that "when it comes to the division of labor in the family, it's
still quite traditional. He does man's work and she does woman's work."
If the husband did any household work at all, it was just helping her
out. The ever-growing group of divorced, widowed, or never-married

women with children exhibited even more severe stress overload.[27]

While the women's movement worked to gain rights for individual women, scholars complained that most public policy focused on women as individuals and not as family members, wives, and mothers. Some women's advocates joined in criticizing government policymakers for not understanding that equal opportunity depended on the availability of child care. Federal guidelines for affirmative action merely mentioned child care. Order No. 4 advised federal contractors to "encourage child care, housing and transportation programs appropriately designed to improve the employment opportunities for minorities and women." These admonitions had no visible effect.[28]

Moreover, the effort to expand government's role in day care moved slowly. In 1960, the Children's Bureau and the Women's Bureau held the first national conference on day care since 1941. Although the conferees mentioned the increasing number of women in the work force as a rationale for child care, most of the discussion concerned welfare dependency and the need for child care so that mothers in the AFDC (Aid to Families with Dependent Children) program could work.[29]

Just before his inauguration, John F. Kennedy had expressed approval of day-care centers for welfare mothers in a letter to Elinor Guggenheimer, one of the conference organizers. As president, Kennedy got Congress to pass a bill funding day-care centers for AFDC mothers, but only five million dollars was appropriated the first year and ten million dollars each year thereafter.[30]

By May of 1963, Dr. Ellen Winston, the federal commissioner for welfare, noted that there were eighteen thousand child-care facilities in the entire nation but about fifteen million children in need. "Already we have more latchkey children running in our streets than we had during World War II." President Kennedy and Congress emphasized repeatedly the welfare reduction goal, insisting that day care would not be provided for anyone else for any reason. They drew no requirements for what work welfare mothers would perform; they just wanted them off the federal dole.[31]

The work of scholars in the child development field gave a push to efforts to expand day care for poor children and to make it educational instead of custodial. J. McVicker Hunt, professor of sociology at the

University of Illinois, published findings in 1961 which showed that children could benefit from well-thought-out stimulation and that the day-care experience could result in increased intelligence.[32]

University of Chicago Professor Benjamin Bloom's 1964 work on *Stability and Change in Human Characteristics* concluded that stimulation would increase verbal performance and that there were differential effects; the impact on young children could be "dramatic" whether the environment was negative or positive. Bloom based his conclusions on a series of longitudinal studies of children which measured their intelligence at birth and ten years later. Children developed rapidly in the early years and much slower thereafter, Bloom said. This meant, Bloom suggested, "new responsibilities on the home, the school and society." Middle-class parents generally sent their children to nursery schools to promote their children's emotional growth, but nursery schools clearly could also be used for cognitive growth and could benefit poor children in this way. Increasingly, in the 1950s and 1960s, researchers published studies showing that enriched experiences at an early age improved human intelligence. Child care might therefore play an educational role for poor children.[33]

Head Start was created in the 1960s to improve the learning skills of poor children, but the experts' research findings on human development was not the major impetus. The federally funded program arose primarily from the civil rights movement, the war on poverty, and the concerns of President Kennedy and his family. One of the president's sisters, Rosemary, suffered from mental retardation, and as a result, he and his family had had a longtime interest in early child development. The family had been in contact with Dr. Robert F. Cooke, professor of pediatrics at The Johns Hopkins School of Medicine. Dr. Cooke encouraged the Kennedys to better understand child development. When Cooke was asked to put together a panel of experts on education and social services to make some proposals, the work of Bloom and other child development experts was included. These forces came together in the institution of Head Start, which proved instantly popular, but was not enacted into law until after Kennedy's death.[34]

Head Start would provide health, education, and social services for preschool youngsters, would sidestep educational officials and governmental regulation, and would emphasize community participation. It even survived a 1969 Westinghouse study that concluded it was largely ineffective because the education gains did not persist once the children left the program. In response to the Westinghouse study, Congress authorized a small follow-through program and then similar supportive services in a Title I program to help maintain the gains when the children entered elementary school. Later longitudinal studies attested to the long-term effects on children through the high school years. Being involved in the program enriched the lives of poor mothers as well as their children. Head Start never received enough funding to serve more than 20 percent of the eligible poor children in this period. It remains in existence today as the most talked-about model of preschool developmental education for the poor.[35]

Needless to say, neither scholars nor politicians approved of some of the community-based child-care approaches implemented during the 1960s and 1970s. There were, for example, the programs established by the Black Panther Party for Self-Defense, which had been organized by Eldridge Cleaver, Huey P. Newton, and Bobby Seale, young California militants who found the nonviolent civil rights movement too weak and ineffective. They set up free food, day-care, and training centers for black children in Oakland and other California cities.[36]

The Panthers became nationally prominent when Huey Newton, who had led a group of gun-carrying demonstrators, was convicted on a charge of manslaughter in the death of an Oakland policeman. Soon chapters spread to major cities across the country. Their manifesto was full employment, decent housing, African-American control of the black community, and an end to repression and police brutality. Day-care schools were part of the Panthers' campaign to help the community and to educate the young in revolutionary consciousness.[37]

The Panthers were declared subversives by the Federal Bureau of Investigation, which made a successful effort to eliminate them as an effective organization. By 1973, the Panther leaders were all either dead, in jail, reformed, or in exile, and the organization was shut down but it left a legacy of community-based action. The Lords, a militant New York Puerto Rican group with a Panther-style manifesto, pressed churches in Spanish Harlem to provide free breakfasts and day-care centers for neighborhood children.[38]

The community-based approach was not the only one that drew fire. Radical feminist child-care cooperatives were criticized because they emphasized ending sex role stereotypes. Radical feminists, including novelist Rita Mae Brown, author of *Rubyfruit Jungle* and other works, and Charlotte Bunch, a theorist of radical feminism, organized a collective called the Furies, which jointly edited the magazine *Quest*. The radicals were attacked for advocating an end to the sexual programming of children, the end to assumptions that families needed to be nuclear, and the establishment of communal child-care facilities under the control of "woman-identified women."[39]

Politicans still limited their interest in day care mainly to stressing the need to make it possible for poor women and those on the welfare rolls to work. There was little acknowledgment that other families might have working parents or that there were divorced working women who needed good care. By May 1965, Women's Bureau Director Mary Dublin Keyserling was speaking generally on the provision of day care for every child, but focused on working mothers. When Congress enacted the Work Incentive Program (WIN) in 1967, it required AFDC mothers to obtain jobs or lose benefits. There would be some government-financed care, but welfare mothers were encouraged to form labor pools to staff day-care centers for their children and other welfare recipients if nothing else was available.[40]

When the government officials responsible for WIN began writing regulations, those wanting the cheapest care engaged in a hard-fought war with those wanting developmental care along the lines suggested by Bloom and others, as reflected in Head Start requirements. The final regulations included a series of vaguely worded admonitions to encourage but not require adequate staffing ratios and other components of good care. Even so, the rules lay dormant and unenforced, as the Nixon administration moved on to debate the administration's ill-fated welfare reform, the Family Assistance Plan (FAP), promoted by Nixon adviser Daniel Patrick Moynihan, a Democrat.[41]

FAP expanded WIN's punitive approach. It included a broadened work requirement for welfare mothers, requiring more day care, but the intention was custodial and little attention was paid to the educational and nutritional needs of poor children. Nonetheless, the day care would have been controlled by federal officials in the reorganized Office of Child Development, which contained the Children's Bureau and other child-related agencies and which was run by Yale child developmental psychologist Edward Zigler.[42]

Zigler came to Washington in May 1970 with high hopes. He revised the unenforced day-care regulations and promoted a plan for a "child development associate" to be the new type of care-giver. It was hoped that the use of child development associates would make it possible to significantly expand day care at a reasonable cost. After several months of classroom instruction, care-givers would receive in-service training. They would be paid less than teachers and would work in groups under the overall supervision of a master teacher, who might not, however, be actually present. Zigler put demonstration training programs into place and made it clear he wanted these standards to be required in federally funded child-care programs. He fought to get his ideas approved by his superiors in the administration, but made little headway.[43]

The Family Assistance Plan, battered by those who thought it did too little on the one hand and those who thought it did too much on the other, failed to pass in Congress. Its failure was both ideological and a budgetary matter. Paying benefits above the poverty level to families on the rolls, paying for training so that welfare recipients could leave the program, and paying for day care for their children would have constrained even the booming Vietnam War–fueled economy, much less its demobilized inflation-ridden successor.[44]

Even if FAP had been adopted, the problems with child care and work would not have been eradicated. New York City Human Resources Director Mitchell Ginsburg stated flatly in 1969 that there would be no "dramatic" results because of the difficulty in providing job training, finding day-care facilities, and meeting health and safety requirements for centers. Despite the problems of FAP, publicity about neglected children and the inspiration of Head Start stirred interest in enacting a national child-care program.[45]

Elinor Guggenheimer and other longtime child-care advocates attempted to distinguish day care from social services. Guggenheimer testified before the New York City Commission on Human Rights in September 1970 that "the day care center is an educational program to provide care in order to fill a family need . . . the day we can divorce day care and child services from social services is the day we can begin to look at them the way they ought to be looked at." The idea that day care was for "slum babies" or for the children of impoverished employed mothers was finally attacked head-on. Guggenheimer argued that day care was for everyone and should be more appropriately placed in the category of education rather than social services. [46]

The Human Rights Commission seemed to have trouble understanding Guggenheimer's distinction, but her views were in accord with the views of child development experts. Senator Walter Mondale (D., Minn.) and Representative John Brademas (D., Ind.) led the Congress to pass a Comprehensive Child Development Act in 1971 along the lines of Guggenheimer's position. The Child Development Act was designed to meet the growing day-care demand and to remake day care into a developmental service available to every child that needed it. The legislation included proposals for a wealth of medical, nutritional, and educational services for children from infancy to fourteen years of age. Welfare mothers, the working poor, and the middle class could receive the services. Any family above the poverty line would pay on a sliding scale. Like Head Start, the program would be controlled by local governmental bodies and nongovernmental groups, not states. Community action agencies, Head Start agencies, labor unions, Indian tribes, and public and private educational agencies could receive funding. [47]

Although initially appearing receptive, President Nixon vetoed the child-care bill in December 1971, saying it would "commit the vast moral authority of the national government to the side of communal approaches to child-rearing over and against the family-centered approach." [48]

Nixon preferred the FAP program for welfare mothers, believing, apparently, that those families would not be undermined by day care. Nixon was reportedly interested in a "crime-prevention" plan presented to him by his personal physician, Dr. Arnold Hutschnecker, which included day care for three- to five-year-old slum children. Hutsch-necker's plan also called for psychological testing to identify troubled youth, therapy, and rehabilitative camps for the most severely disturbed, as crime prevention measures.[49]

Although Nixon said he opposed the Mondale-Brademas child-care bill because of its costs, he used his veto message to curry favor with the right wing of his party. A series of exchanges between the president and various staff members, including Charles Colson, Chief of Staff H. R. Haldeman, and speechwriter Pat Buchanan confirm this conclusion. Colson and Buchanan were concerned about conservative challenges to the president during the Republican primaries leading up to the 1972 election. They recognized that Nixon's ascension to the presidency came in part because of his embodiment of traditional values after the fast-moving social changes of the 1960s. Mondale and the social reformers might not be able to imagine how anyone could be against helping children but Nixon's advisers saw that the president's constituency might regard the legislation as undermining the traditional family. They persuaded Nixon that the language of his child-care veto message should be conservative enough to prevent anyone's getting to the right of him on the issue. Colson told Nixon that if the message came down very hard against child care as a matter of principle "it may be precisely what we need to buy ourselves maneuvering room with the right wing."[50]

Colson and Buchanan got their way, despite the differing point of view of Elliot Richardson, secretary of the Department of Health, Education and Welfare. Nixon cautioned there would be "a lot of heat from the left so I should get all the support I could for our point of view." When Pat Buchanan sent "the draft veto message as requested" to Haldeman, he had made it strong. "Since we are certain to get our lumps from the opposition even with a milquetoast veto, we ought to reap the rewards of an unequivocal one," Buchanan wrote. He asked that it be gone over "with a finetooth comb" since the "other side is going to crawl all over this." Buchanan got almost half of his draft into Nixon's message. Nixon denounced the bill as a "most radical piece of social legislation." He said it violated good public policy which should "enhance rather than diminish both parental authority and parental involvement with children, particularly in those decisive early years when social attitudes and conscience are formed, and religious and moral principles are first inculcated."[51]

In their concern about the Republican right wing, Colson, Buchanan, and Nixon perpetuated the myth that the "traditional" mother-care model was the only one Americans had ever used to define family roles. The president's statement echoed the 1909 White House Conference on Family's resolution that "home life is the highest and finest product of civilization." With more than a little hyperbole, Nixon called what had become traditional home life the "keystone of our civilization." That aspect was not, however, attacked because everyone, including women who were making proposals to deal with the burdens of employed mothers, shared assumptions about the history of American families. Although politicians wanted to help women meet their child-care needs, they accepted the "unassailable" truth that women were the child-rearers. Feminists urged fathers to share but most mothers accepted the principal child-care responsibility; fathers preferred it; and children seemed no worse or better off for it.[52]

Proponents of comprehensive day-care legislation continued to run afoul of women's preferences. Even though more and more married women entered and stayed in the work force, they consistently shaped their employment around their families' needs through temporary or part-time work. In 1965, only 2.3 percent of children under twelve were in day-care centers. By 1971, less than 8 percent of white working women placed their children in day-care centers and almost twice as many black working women did. Child-care advocates continued to argue that there were not enough centers, but preference polls indicated that regardless of the number or quality of such centers, most parents did not want custodial nonrelative care. They believed that centers were for poor people or would interfere with child development. Even the small number of group care centers located at work sites attracted only small percentages of working mothers. Only those who could not have a neighbor or relative take care of their children used the centers as a last resort.[53]

Nixon's veto of the December 1971 Comprehensive Child Care Bill dimmed the prospects for a national child-care program in the near future. In retrospect, a confluence of favorable circumstances had fueled congressional passage of the legislation, including Nixon's own emphasis on child care in his earlier reform proposals. An effective coalition of labor and public interest groups had converged on a receptive Congress to win passage of the 1971 bill. The coalition included forces interested in child care, cognitive development, civil rights, and community change. It believed that millions of mothers would be willing and able to make a free choice between being at home and working if child care became widely available.[54]

Marian Wright Edelman of the Children's Defense Fund (CDF) played a major role in getting the child-care bill through Congress. She stressed child development as an instrument of community change. She organized and kept together a coalition of diverse interests from labor unionists to mayors, scholars to civil rights groups. Unions wanted to organize the large anticipated numbers of child-care workers and needed care-givers for their women members. Mayors and community groups liked the bill because it bypassed the states, which had generally been ungenerous toward helping largely minority populations and which in the South had had a history of racial discrimination. Edelman made it clear from the beginning that ". . . those concerned with equal opportunity and civil rights will oppose giving any control of this child legislation to the States." Although the coalition could not overcome Nixon's veto, a strong foundation had been laid.[55]

In the federal government, a disappointed Edward Zigler, unable to gain approval even of his day-care standards, soon went back to Yale. The administration expressed interest in a minimum-cost approach to day care. Zigler's proposals, designed to fit his view of the requirements for the most effective development of the child, were costly from their perspective although less costly than the existing regulations. Zigler was attacked by advocacy groups, including the CDF, because his rules decreased the number of staff required for each child from the regulations approved after the WIN legislation passed in 1967. The earlier regulations had better ratios and even though they were not enforced, the CDF preferred to keep them on the books and hope for enforcement someday.[56]

The Republican Party decided to hedge its bets on the issue in the presidential campaign. Nixon and his advisers believed that taking a traditional position was more popular but the Democrats were supporting day care.

In the 1972 presidential campaign, both parties supported the objective of quality day-care services. The Republican National Convention Resolutions Committee called for public and private voluntary comprehensive and quality day-care services. The Republicans proposed that day care be federally assisted and locally controlled, with a requirement that those participating pay according to ability.[57] Democratic presidential candidate George McGovern called for earmarking funds for day-care centers paid from general-purpose revenue-sharing funds, already being allocated to the states.

After he was reelected, Nixon continued his opposition to child-care bills on ideological, qualitative, and financial grounds. The Day Care and Child Development Council of America asked its honorary chairwoman, Mrs. Richard Nixon, to explain her husband's opposition to comprehensive child care. She resigned from the post instead.[58]

Demands by the poor for more child-care services in the face of budget cuts, weak quality standards, and targeted approaches to funding resulted in public demonstrations. In April 1974, mothers and children rallied in New York, Detroit, and other cities against proposals to reduce the number of poor children that could attend the few federally sponsored centers without paying. Three hundred women garment workers and their children marched through Chinatown in New York to the Chinatown Planning Council to protest proposed cuts in child-care services. The council's day-care centers provided care for 700 children but about 3,000 more mothers needed similar services. Even though the protests continued, President Gerald Ford was unmoved and told the leaders of women's organizations that he had "serious reservations" about the desirability of creating a program of government-financed child-care centers. He was worried about the budgetary consequences but also about alienating party conservatives who still thought day care undermined the mother's role.[59]

The child-care coalition and congressional supporters were slow to understand that their proposals were simply in conflict with prevailing conservative attitudes despite their laudable attempts to help children and families. Hostility to child-care legislation on the grounds that it would "Sovietize the family" erupted when Mondale and Brademas introduced the Child and Family Services Bill of 1975. The bill would have subsidized developmental child care for nonwelfare families. In the thousands of letters to Congress and the president, critics claimed the act would injure the American family. Mondale, as a cosponsor of the bill, finally got the point. He admitted the proposal would go nowhere because of the violent opposition. Lobbyists and academics soon understood also. They realized that considerable groundwork would have to be laid before a comprehensive bill could advance again.[60]

President Ford's National Commission on Observance of International Women's Year took up child development again in January 1976. The commission reported that the shortage of day care left an estimated 6,000,000 children in need and that only 900,000 places were available. The commission advocated nationally financed day care. Audrey Rowe Colom, chair of the commission and the National Women's Political Caucus, said "a child's right and society's obligation to avoid the cost of neglect" meant a universal voluntary child development program was needed. The care would be available to everyone but only if parents chose to participate. Colom knew that conservatives would argue that such a program would mandate federal government intrusion in family matters, but "these programs ought to be available upon request so that it is clear that they are not mandatory. If someone wants and needs these services they should be available to them." The commission noted that fathers needed help, too. They added: "Young widowers with children, as well as single fathers who are increasingly gaining custody of their children in divorce proceedings, are primarily responsible for arranging child care and coping with the tensions when the care available is inadequate."[61]

In April, despite the commission's recommendations, President Ford vetoed the first $125-million Social Services bill for upgrading facilities to meet federal standards. He based his opposition on the grounds that "the states should have the responsibility and the right to establish and enforce their own standards." Congress failed to override his veto and the resulting compromise suspended the mandated staffing ratios, leaving the states to decide whether to use money for day care. They could develop their own standards. Having forced the Congress to remove the objectionable requirement, President Ford signed the legislation into law in September 1976, leaving a national day-care policy issue for the next president.[62]

Women's organizations were deeply involved in the struggle for the Equal Rights Amendment when Jimmy Carter became president in 1977, but child care was still a major concern. NOW and other organizations wanted to show the public that they advocated policies to help women in discharging their family responsibilities *and* gaining equal rights. One-half of women with children under eighteen years old had entered the work force; 40 percent of women with preschoolers worked; and over five million children under age thirteen spent thirty or more hours per week in the care of someone other than their parents or teachers. Of almost five million preschoolers, 13 percent attended day-care centers or nurseries; 23 percent were cared for by nonrelatives away from home, but the vast majority were cared for by relatives at home or in a relative's home.[63]

NOW, the National Women's Political Caucus (NWPC), and other women's groups concerned about antidiscrimination enforcement, the ERA, and child care, among other domestic budget priorities, were increasingly disaffected during the Carter years. President Carter and his wife, Rosalynn, supported the ERA but did not do much for it in the states. The president opposed reproductive choice and exhibited a moralistic and fundamentalist view toward the family. He was also fiscally conservative and supported little new funding for social programs, especially those that particularly concerned women's groups. The administration made several false starts on the child-care issue and after four years had only a weak record of accomplishments to show for its efforts. It took the administration four years to issue day-care regulations that were then never enforced because of Reagan's election in 1980.[64]

During his campaign, Carter had taken his running mate's suggestion and appointed Joseph Califano as a special adviser to help develop a pro-family policy. Califano presented some sketchy proposals and, when he became secretary of the Department of Health, Education and Welfare (HEW), began working to achieve a policy. But campaign promises do not policy make. Anything called family policy raised the same disputes about gender roles as the acrimonious ERA debate. A prime example of the Carter administration's failure was the White House Conference on Family that was promised for 1979 but doomed from the start. Plans for the conference were well under way when Catholic church officials criticized it because they wanted the definition of family to be an intact nuclear family. Califano appointed a divorced woman as executive director of the conference. Under criticism, he had her "resign" before actually undertaking the work, and then he reassigned her. The well-publicized controversy, however, overshadowed any good that might have come from the conference and defeated any effort to have the president appear in a positive light on the child-care issue.[65]

The president did not want to support child-care legislation even though Mondale was his vice president. National day care would be too expensive, but more importantly he understood that basic differences existed among voters over whether the federal government should or should not have a role in private family matters. What neither Carter nor his critics in the women's movement seemed to understand was that his traditional views concerning gender roles and a mother's responsibility were inconsistent with greater freedom and opportunity for women.

When Senator Alan Cranston invited administration testimony on his comprehensive child-care bill, he expected White House support since Vice President Mondale was a longtime advocate. Arabella Martinez, a new HEW assistant secretary, was picked to deliver the disappointing news to Cranston. The administration would not depart from the Nixon-Ford policies. Whatever the administration's family policy was supposed to be, it did not include federally financed day care.

Cranston's bill avoided the Mondale-Brademas bill's politically damaging feature of bypassing the states and it deleted previously mandated family services, including social, medical, and prenatal care. Finally, Cranston's proposal was much less costly: a first-year authorization of $90 million, not the 1971 proposal of $1.2 billion. But Martinez's testimony showed that the Democratic president had no more interest in federally financed day care than his Republican predecessor. President Carter was neither religiously, ideologically, nor politically interested in attacking accepted gender roles or contradicting the position that Nixon and Ford had advanced. Cranston quickly retreated.[66]

The administration then proposed that a child care component be included in welfare reform proposals. But, like Nixon and Moynihan's FAP before it, the proposal died after a lot of work, with the recognition that no guaranteed cost savings would result. Reformers had hoped that the Carter administration, coming as it did after eight years of Republican ascendancy, would use the presidency to lead the public toward more positive change on rights issues and social policy in general.

The president saw his election as a response to Watergate and was by temperament a fiscal conservative and a social conservative except on race issues. He believed the public was closer to his views than those of the social reformers. The administration's ineptness in dealing with issues including day care and the White House Conference on Families made matters worse by feeding the fires of right-wing opposition.

The 1960s had begun in hope, and much change in women's opportunities had occurred. The scant progress on child care and related issues by the end of the Carter years did not inspire confidence that more change would come soon. Keeping the coalition of labor, civil rights and child advocates, the women's movement, and child development experts together after the defeats in the 1970s would be a difficult task.

There were increasing numbers of employed mothers, poor female-headed households, divorces, and much demographic movement. The need for child care was greater for many women, but new statistics did not seem to help. For many women, by 1980, the struggle for equality had led to greater employment diversity and more necessity for paid work despite serious problems with child care.

NOW, as well as the radical feminists, found that the promotion of nonparental child care ran headlong into conventional wisdom about the importance of mother care for children. It was one thing to encourage middle-class women to get a job; it was quite another to challenge societal expectations of gender roles.

To the extent that women's rights to greater autonomy and freedom meant sharing responsibilities for children with fathers and a redefinition of women's roles, the resurgent women's movement was frightened away from that objective by the political disappointments of the 1970s.

Women who were anti–day care liked the idea of father as head of the family, mother as nurturer and manager of the family, and children as their future. Father was not wanted as nurturer and manager and women certainly did not want to be thought of as providers even if they were.[67] These women most certainly did not want their children to be cared for in day-care facilities where they might be abused at worst or develop different belief systems from their parents at best. The very sophisticated direct mail and media tactics used by Phyllis Schlafly and others kept anti–day care women mobilized and reinforced their activism.

Presidential rhetoric about undermining the family made advocating change harder. The public relations and policy failures in Congress and the White House reflected public attitudes and reinforced hostility to change. Child-care advocates could not yet overcome the public's preference for mother care and their idealized vision of the traditional family to gain the government policy they sought.

VII
The Mother-Care Tradition
Renewed, 1980–1988

By 1980, more change in gender roles—or at least a little bit of government help in policy, leadership, or money for women with jobs and children—was long overdue. Ronald Reagan's election symbolized exactly the opposite—more hard times for those who challenged the mother-care tradition. It also meant dismal prospects for reformers who insisted that the rights of women should be defined as more than just their family responsibilities.

Reagan, whether because of age and experiences or political ideology, could be counted upon to reinforce traditional gender roles. Long before his presidency he was fond of joking that "If it wasn't for women us men would still be walking around in skin suits carrying clubs," or "As Will Rogers once said, if women go around trying to be more and more equal to men, someday they won't know any more than men do."[1]

These quips fit in perfectly with the political ideology he reflected during his presidency. The 1980 election confirmed that conservatism had become the dominant mood in the 1970s. The public expressed doubts about government solutions to poverty and other domestic problems. Instead, the majority favored tax cuts, wanted prayer in the schools, less sex in the movies, and expressed a sense that the United States had declined as a world power and needed to reassert itself.

If the 1970s were the "me" decade, the 1980s were the work and the greed decade. The hallmark of Reagan's domestic policy, "Government is not the solution to our problems, government is the problem," meant that those who sought government help on any domestic problem, including sex discrimination or the lack of child care, were in trouble.

Political feminism had focused on the issues of individual rights, freedom, family, sexuality, and reproduction, the latter considered the key to women's liberation. With a different twist, the revived political right incorporated these same issues as part of its agenda in the 1980s.

A return to traditional American family values became an overriding theme of the Reaganites. The New Right pro-life, pro–traditional family constituency was a major part of the Reagan coalition. The Reverend Jerry Falwell's Moral Majority, with its newspaper and daily radio time, conservative-funded think tanks such as the Heritage Foundation, and public relations firms, formed a public opinion network that was expanded to dominate the television talk shows and the print media during the Reagan era.

Many people who felt confused and alienated by increasing divorce, crime, drugs, racial tensions, and other societal problems felt reassured by the moral certainty of the pro-family proponents. Discussions of the need to return the family to the idealized version depicted in Norman Rockwell paintings and in television situation comedies comforted those who resisted change in child care and gender roles.

Under such circumstances, efforts to preserve women's right to reproductive choice and to gain greater economic equity and more personal autonomy were derailed. Child-care policy would have to be reconciled with concern for the traditional family before it could be enacted.

Contradictions, however, were everywhere, beginning with Reagan himself. As governor of California, he had signed into law fourteen bills concerning rape, child care, sex discrimination in employment, credit, property and insurance, and a strong pro-choice bill. This was all before 1976 and the mobilization of the right against the women's movement.[2]

In the home, kitchens had food processors and other gadgets for a revival of interest in cooking but they also had microwaves for eating on the run. Maintaining the yuppie life-style, with its growing materialism, made two-income households mandatory. Meanwhile, middle-class women were being told to focus on family. The increased number of employed mothers could not escape general public notice. Fifty percent of American women were gainfully employed and the typical woman worker was a mother. Nearly two-thirds of all women workers were married; participation rates for white women in the work force had nearly reached those of African-American women. As the numbers of employed white females skyrocketed, increased public attention was paid to women's work patterns and to the household burdens of the employed wife, attention which had been lacking when poor, African-American, and immigrant workers composed the majority of the female labor force. Women were more likely to be poor than men, and women's earnings were about 65 percent of men's since occupational segregation remained the rule. This was particularly a problem for women over thirty, those most likely to be divorced with children.[3]

Although women were moving into new career fields, about 80 percent of women workers were still employed in traditionally female occupations: sales, clerking, teaching, nursing, and other low-paid professions. The stress of paid employment became a "front burner" issue, but the apotheosis of the "traditional family" and traditional gender roles barred effective solutions. The exaltation of motherhood and the traditional family that had caused the ultimate defeat of the Comprehensive Child Care Act in 1971 and had defeated child-care policy in the 1970s became a greater problem for these concerns in the 1980s. The emphasis on motherhood and the traditional family confused the agendas of women's rights organizations such as NOW, the National Women's Political Caucus, the Women's Legal Defense Fund (WLDF), and the National Women's Law Center. In 1980, leaders in the women's movement, including NOW president Eleanor Smeal, were increasingly frustrated by the rightward tilt of the electorate.[4]

The 1980 presidential election campaign could be seen as a referendum on women's rights, the transformation of gender roles, and the issue of responsibility for children and family. The election results underscored a rejection of change despite the emerging demographic realities of labor force participation. The Republican Party convention rejected a concern for the rights of individual women by repudiating its forty-year-old pro-ERA plank. During the convention, Republican women, including Representative Margaret Heckler of Massachusetts and Helen Milliken, wife of Michigan's governor William Milliken, led a losing fight to get the plank reinserted in the platform in spite of Reagan's opposition. In the final days of battle, former National Republican Party chairwoman Mary Louise Smith of Iowa, a feminist, called for reconciliation by saying she felt "comfortable" with the compromise language achieved. The compromise stated: "We acknowledge the legitimate efforts of those who support or oppose ratification of the Equal Rights Amendment." This was the best Smith could get. Essentially, Phyllis Schlafly had won. Her wing of the party, the Moral Majority, pro-family social conservatives who stood for traditional motherhood roles, prevailed.[5]

Although thirty-five states had ratified the ERA by 1980, proponents were losing the battle to obtain the required three additional ratifications. Opponents argued throughout the struggle that ERA supporters wanted to change women's "natural" roles, to force housewives to be employed, to contribute half of the family's support, and to reduce women's preferred protected position under state domestic relations laws and labor codes. Women, the conservatives asserted, did not want equality, they wanted men to be responsible for their support.[6]

Accusations that the women's movement was antifamily became more strident. Those who wanted to focus on the necessity for subsidized child care to allow women to enjoy greater autonomy and expanded rights faced mounting opposition.

Betty Friedan's *The Second Stage* appeared near the conclusion of the ERA fight. Friedan accused women's rights proponents of polarizing the movement into pro- and anti-family camps. Friedan said feminists should modify their goals to include men and children, and recognize that men and women wanted interdependence, not the traditional provider/dependent roles. This conclusion was at odds with most people's adherence to traditional roles despite women's movement efforts to encourage change. As a leading feminist, Friedan's criticism sustained Phyllis Schlafly's charge that the women's movement was anti-family. [7]

When the Equal Rights Amendment died in July 1982, as its ratification deadline passed, blame-casting was widespread. Gloria Steinem thought the movement had waited too long to focus single-mindedly on the ERA. Eleanor Smeal thought she might have spent too much time on details before embarking on new tactics and that proponents were too complacent after Congress passed the Amendment. "The movement never realized the depth of opposition," Smeal said. Some analysts blamed the defeat on radical "bra burners" and lesbians who should have been expelled from the movement. Others cited a confusion of goals and conflict between the national and local leaders of the movement on strategy or the tactics of the insurance industry, which wanted to maintain discriminatory rates. [8]

One obvious answer was unmentioned by those who wanted the ERA so much. Amending the Constitution requires an overwhelming consensus in three-fourths of the states, not just a majority. The absence of a supportive consensus for ERA reflected fundamental opposition to changing gender roles. Opponents successfully reinforced the idea that ERA supporters would demand changes, such as abortion rights or women in combat or even subsidized day care, and that Congress would have to enact them to ensure equality of rights for women. Even if the majority of women were paid workers, employment was not regarded as their major priority. Polls showed that ERA opponents were more likely to be opposed to day-care centers and preferred to have their children cared for by relatives or friends or at home. [9]

Also, opponents believed something fundamental was threatened by the ERA—woman's place, man's place, and even child's place, the ideal even if not the reality. They knew that their lives did not exactly replicate the halcyon Rockwell paintings but it was a goal toward which they worked. It was myth, but it was familiar and good. Furthermore, as Phyllis Schlafly put it, the "ERA was the men's liberation movement." Equal rights might have sounded wonderful to feminists, but she argued that equality might make women more vulnerable to ill treatment from which their feminine inequality now protected them.[10]

The ERA might have sounded harmless: "Equality of rights shall not be abridged by the United States or any state on account of sex," but it was so vague that it could mean anything. Also, "Congress shall have the power to enforce it by appropriate legislation" could mean anything. To Catholics it could mean ordaining women and ending single-sex schools; to Orthodox Jews it could mean ending a sharp division of roles between the sexes. Requiring independence, self-support, and sharing meant feminists were putting all women at risk, having to compete with men even when they did not want to or would rather have men take care of them. Increased divorce rates, female-headed households, and employed women were the reality, but the illusion that homemakers were being well supported by breadwinner-husbands in nuclear families prevailed in the discussion.[11]

Defeat assaulted the consciousness of women's movement leaders and the role that the pro-family emphasis had played in the defeat took on great significance. Schlafly, under the banner of "You Can't Fool Mother Nature," had insisted that no claim to rights overrode a woman's primary duty to be a mother and a wife. The well-executed strategy, which amounted essentially to defining women's rights as women's responsibilities, had been effective. "Traditional family values" would be the turf on which any 1980s battle would be fought.[12]

In this environment, Judy Goldsmith, the new president of NOW, and Kathy Wilson, chair of the National Women's Political Caucus (NWPC), and other women's rights organization leaders reevaluated their goals. They would respond to the criticism that they were anti-family by making their first priority legislation to gain child care, parental leave, and other support for employed mothers. This, they hoped, would expand the possibility for the enjoyment of greater personal autonomy and economic choices to more women. They would continue also to work for political change and support litigation and legislative strategies on sex discrimination issues.[13]

The ERA was reintroduced in November 1983, but did not gain even a two-thirds vote in the House of Representatives. The vote was 278–147, six short of the required majority. Maintaining traditional gender roles and family values, not equal rights for women, remained the focus of congressional and public debates.

Women's groups were able to get Congress to pass legislation to help women so long as it clearly reinforced traditional roles. They succeeded in getting a child-support provision that helped states find scofflaw fathers and deduct child support payments from their wages. This legislation would help the 40 percent of the 8.2 million female heads of households with children who received no support or only partial support from fathers. Representative Barbara Kennelly, Democrat of Connecticut, the only woman on the House Ways and Means Committee, and Senators David Durenberger, Republican of Minnesota, and Bill Bradley, Democrat of New Jersey, led the effort in the Congress to pass the child support bill, which became law in 1984.[14]

Congress also passed a bill, sponsored by Kennelly, Democratic congresswoman Geraldine Ferraro of New York, and Republican senator Robert Dole of Kansas, to reform private pension plans so that widows would be treated more fairly. In 1982 only 10.3 percent of women over age sixty-five received an average pension of at least $2,585, and only about 10 percent of surviving spouses, mainly widows, received pension benefits. The bill lowered the age for vesting, required automatic survivors' benefits in private plans unless both spouses waived them, and liberalized break-in-service rules to take into account women's more frequent departures from the work force. The bill also clarified the authority of state courts to distribute pension benefits in divorce. This was a significant acknowledgement of the work done by homemakers in a marriage. Each of these bills encouraged women to play traditional maternal and housewife roles while making provisions for the sometimes traumatic economic consequences which ensued.[15]

NOW, WLDF, the Women's Equity Action League (WEAL), and other women's groups had little luck with other items on their agenda to help employed women. Congress would not even pass legislation to study the federal work force to determine whether women were being paid less for jobs with skills and responsibilities equal to some men's jobs that received higher pay. The lawmakers did not want to confront the costs or to appear to challenge the idea that women choose jobs with lower pay because of their family priorities. In addition, they had great difficulty addressing *Grove City College* v. *Bell*, a 1984 Supreme Court decision that permitted educational institutions to receive federal higher education student aid funds even if some of the programs in the institution discriminated against women. This decision weakened protection against sex discrimination, which had been enacted into law in Title IX of the Educational Amendments of 1972.[16]

It took four years and acceptance of a limitation on abortion rights, insisted upon by the Catholic Conference of Bishops, before proponents could get a civil rights restoration act passed over the president's veto, in 1988. The conference had lobbied to prevent the act from passing unless a new provision was added forbidding the provision of abortion-related services. Women's groups had great difficulty with being forced to give up a right women already had in order to gain reaffirmation of another right, the right to nondiscrimination in education, that had just been taken away.[17]

In the summer of 1984, Goldsmith and Wilson formed a coalition to advance the idea of a woman candidate for vice president. They believed the battering on women's rights issues and Reagan's overall position on domestic policy made it absolutely essential that he be defeated. Also, a woman on the ticket, they felt, might buttress the chances of Walter Mondale, the Democratic presidential nominee in the 1984 election.[18]

The coalition persuaded Mondale to choose a woman running mate because polling data showed enough of a gender gap to provide the margin of victory. "Gender gap" was a term that had been coined after the 1980 election, when data showed that only 47 percent of women, compared to 55 percent of men, had voted for Reagan. Mondale chose Ferraro as the vice-presidential candidate, but in the wake of disclosures about the financial affairs of Ferraro and her husband, the euphoria over her selection quickly dissipated. The expected Democratic victory did not materialize.

In addition, after Reagan's reelection the polling data showed the gender gap was smaller than it had been in 1980. Pollsters did find increased female interest in politics, but the Republicans had analyzed

women's votes better than the Democrats by dividing women into categories and appealing to them based on whether they were married or
single, working outside the home or not. The election results indicated
fundamentally that women voters in the presidential election did not
vote on the basis of women's rights issues such as reproductive choice,
day care, or job discrimination, and that acceptance of traditional
gender roles was firmly ensconced in the public mind.[19]

Despite the 1984 presidential election results, women's rights leaders and the bipartisan Congressional Caucus on Women's Issues decided to reintroduce the Equal Rights Amendment and to begin a new
push for legislation. They tried to defuse continuing attacks that they
were anti-family by addressing the economic concerns of employed
women. On the first day of the legislative session, in 1985, the ERA
bill was the first measure introduced in the House and Senate even
though proponents did not intend to ask for passage. National Women's
Party spokesperson Elizabeth Chittick announced that the party would
instead focus on "economic issues affecting everyone." California Democratic congresswoman Barbara Boxer agreed that "When we talk about
the need for child care [and] the need for pregnancy leave, these are
not only feminist measures, these are human rights and family issues.
You can't keep the family together if one spouse is underpaid or can't
get child care."[20]

In Reagan's first term, the administration had acknowledged the
increasing concerns of employed mothers and fathers about the care
of children. Women had been nine points less supportive of his election
in the aggregate than men and they were still primarily identified with
the child-care issue. The administration was opposed on fiscal and
ideological grounds, however, to any comprehensive child-care bill.
Child-care programs cost the federal government $2.8 billion in 1980.
The single most expensive item, the child and dependent care tax
credit, accounted for more than one-third of this amount, $956 million.
The other child-care programs, Head Start, Title XX Social Services,
the work incentive program, various child-care food programs, AFDC
child care, and food stamps, were scrutinized by the administration
for "waste" and "fraud." Although the Head Start program escaped
public criticism, it failed to gain significant new funding. The very

costly child-care tax credit also evaded public discussion and, as a middle-class benefit, was one of the few benefits left intact after the 1981 tax bill.[21]

Very little money was left to pay for new legislative proposals after tax cuts, defense budget increases, and the increasing federal deficit. Strategically, the administration reduced federal revenue in order to defeat certain social programs. Federal deficits would allow the cuts in domestic spending without opening an argument over the government's role in providing social services. Responding to constituent views, Congress refused to gut social programs, but Reagan's personal popularity and the prevailing political winds helped Congress to defer the financing question until larger deficits were created.[22]

Like the Eisenhower Republicans, Reagan used the tax code instead of a new social program to address the child-care problem. While insisting he adhered to an ideological pro-family commitment, in 1981 Reagan proposed that employers receive a tax credit for on-site day-care centers, or for paying outside providers to care for their employees' children, or for reimbursing employees for the cost of day care. This employer-sponsored day-care tax provision created another middle-class benefit, even though the child-care tax credit already provided far more for the middle class than the federal government spent for the poor. The economic bias in the provisions caused the National Association for the Advancement of Colored People (NAACP) to ask in 1981—to no avail—that before employers qualified for the credit, they be required to train minorities for jobs in addition to providing day-care centers.[23]

Quality of care became increasingly important as reports of child abuse rose. For example, Eleanor Nathan pleaded not guilty in Martinez, California, to murdering an eleven-month-old infant and torturing twenty other children in an unlicensed day-care center in her home in 1981. On February 10, 1983, she was sentenced to a term of forty-four years and four months to life for first-degree murder. Two children died in a fire at an unlicensed day-care center in southeast Washington, D.C., in 1982, raising questions about day-care licensing in that city.[24]

Heightened interest surrounded the prosecution of charges that first surfaced in March 1984 that Peggy McMartin Buckey, her son Raymond, and other workers had sexually abused eleven children at their McMartin PreSchool in the affluent oceanside city of Manhattan Beach, California, between 1978 and 1983. As the McMartin case went forward, a few of the charges were dropped after two children refused to testify. In early 1990, the jury acquitted both Buckeys on fifty-two counts, but deadlocked on thirteen counts against Raymond after what had become one of the longest, most expensive criminal trials in the United States. The jury that retried Raymond Buckey deadlocked and the prosecutor dropped the charges, bringing an end to the case in 1989.[25]

Discussion of the difficulties of finding good, safe child care continued. The 1982–83 recession threw many communities into double-digit unemployment, making job training, retraining, and child-care services even more pressing issues. In 1983, the House Select Committee on Children, Youth and Families conducted an investigation of poverty and children in female-headed households; the committee chairman, Representative George Miller, Democrat of California, reported that 79 percent of divorced fathers did not pay child support. Moreover, the number of children living with only one parent had increased by 68 percent in twelve years. The parent in such families was usually an employed mother with inadequate child care. These children living in one-parent families were the new generation of latchkey children, just like the uncared-for children of their parents' generation during World War II. Their families either could not find or could not afford child care. While concerns about latchkey children helped to gain passage of the strengthened 1984 child-support enforcement provision, which had been introduced by Barbara Kennelly, they did not fuel demands for more nonparental child care.[26]

The House Select Committee continued to hold hearings on the general topic of improving child-care services. In the Senate, Republican Arlen Specter of Pennsylvania and Democrat Christopher Dodd of Connecticut organized the Children's Caucus in 1983 to consider the same issues. The caucus focused particularly on child abuse and latchkey children, and considered at length the stresses of working mothers and their children. In early 1984, Congressman Miller called for a major national debate on child care, as Congress became more and more active on the issue. Dodd and Specter seconded his call.[27]

Soon there was a virtual cornucopia of nonparental child care strategies proposed in the Congress: vouchers, expanded tax credits, and increased social services, all in time for the 1986 off-year Congressional elections. Since many of their constituents were obviously interested in child care, congressmen felt it was politically risky not to show an interest. Still, there was little, if any, agreement on a specific proposal.[28]

The lack of consensus on the subject of nonparental care surfaced when Edward Zigler, the Yale child-development expert who had briefly served in Nixon's administration, suggested having public schools provide services to meet the needs of employed parents. The public, by a narrow margin, opposed the idea. When asked whether child care should be available as part of public school programs at taxpayer expense, 45 percent of those polled said no and 42 percent favored the proposal; twelve percent expressed no opinion. When the question was phrased to ask whether such programs should be established to take care of the latchkey kids of working parents, the percentage of those in favor dropped by two points. A large percentage of those polled either was reluctant to pay taxes for the purpose, did not care about the children, or thought parents should make arrangements for their own children.[29]

A lack of consensus and the federal deficit delayed serious consideration of day-care legislation, but the momentum kept building. Employers began providing more child-care centers at work sites or paying for services elsewhere in order to maintain employee productivity. American corporations sponsored or paid for only 100 child-care programs in 1978, but by 1985 there were 2,500 of such programs. Developers, prodded by local zoning boards, began to include day-care centers even when not required. Some office parks built child-care facilities to attract tenants. Unions also began to pay greater attention to child-care issues.[30]

As new data and expert opinions were compiled, the battle over child care increased in intensity. The Reagan administration was still ideologically opposed to acknowledging a need for more services. The administration's National Institute of Child Health and Human Development produced a report that tried to minimize the problem. Their survey data showed that the latchkey problem was less widespread than discussion would make it appear. Poor children, they said, were less likely to be at home alone after school than middle-class children.[31]

A 1987 report by the U.S. Census Bureau on the availability of child-care services provided additional ammunition for arguments in favor of a comprehensive day-care program. The report, entitled "Who's Minding the Kids?," showed that in 1986, employed parents spent about $11.1 billion for care of about nine million children but many of them found it almost impossible to find affordable child-center care or home care. In the summer, about 13 percent of school-aged children cared for themselves. This data helped to develop a bipartisan consensus in the Congress that "something" had to be done, even if what was to be done was far from clear.[32]

In the meantime, the Women's Legal Defense Fund (WLDF), the American Association of University Women, the Association of Junior Leagues, the National Federation of Business and Professional Women's Clubs, labor unions, and other organizations as well as the Congressional Caucus on Women's Issues decided to develop parental leave legislation to solve one part of the child-care-services problem. The child-care-services issue was already being managed by a coalition led by child-advocacy groups. There would be no federal appropriations required for parental leave legislation, which would deflect budgetary objections. The leave, as designed by proponents of the bill, would be taken by mothers or fathers to care for children with no presumption in favor of either parent. Because the proposal did not indicate which parent, traditionalists could assume women would take the leave, thus affirming their preference for mother care for children. Feminists felt that a leave policy would help employed parents and their children and clearly erode the identification of child care as a woman's issue —a necessary part of the struggle for women's equity.[33]

Under the Pregnancy Discrimination Act of 1978, as well as several state laws, women were entitled to an unpaid disability or maternal leave with guaranteed job reinstatement upon return to work. The constitutionality of this law was upheld in a 1987 ruling by the U.S. Supreme Court. Lillian Garland had sued her employer, California

Federal Savings and Loan, for refusing to return her to her previous job after pregnancy leave, as required by the state disability law. The bank argued in court that the law discriminated against men by not giving temporarily disabled men the same treatment as women temporarily disabled by pregnancy. On February 9, 1984, a district court agreed with the bank and decided against Garland. Garland appealed and ultimately Justice Thurgood Marshall ruled for the Supreme Court that states may require employers to grant special protection to those who become pregnant. The promotion of equal opportunity must permit "women, as well as men, to have families without losing their jobs," Marshall said. Nonetheless, long before the Supreme Court acted, the negative district court decision in the Garland case had provoked a demand for congressional action.[34]

The district court response had meant that at a time of escalating married women's employment, firing those who became pregnant or assigning them to less visible and less remunerative jobs would continue. Those women who needed to work would have to avoid pregnancy or they might lose their jobs. The court essentially affirmed the mother-care tradition, which assumed that mothers were supported by male breadwinners and should be discouraged from employment that would interfere with their child-raising function.

The California statute under dispute in the Garland case had been written by Congressman Howard Berman, Democrat of California, when he had been a state legislator. Berman now introduced legislation in Congress that would give guaranteed leaves of absence upon the birth or adoption of a child to both parents and additional leave for a woman to cover any disabilities arising from the pregnancy. Women lawyers from WLDF, the Georgetown University Law School, and organizations such as the Association of Junior Leagues, the Pension Rights Center, the American Association of University Women, NOW, and NWPC, refused to support Berman's proposal because they disliked his characterization of pregnancy as a disability. They felt it reinforced the idea of special treatment for women and undermined the case for equality of rights. They persuaded Berman and his colleagues that they could generate broad political support to promote congressional passage of parental leave for mothers *and* fathers.[35]

The resulting comprehensive proposal covered all employers and allowed preexisting health benefits to remain intact, but as the coalition of supporters grew, the proposal was scaled back. In the end, Berman and his colleagues decided not to introduce a universal disability and parental leave bill, believing it too broad and not focused enough on the problem of childbirth-related leave. Although Berman expressed an understanding of the drafters' desire to maintain the principle of equal treatment, politically he thought their bill would fail. There was too much opposition to challenging gender roles.[36]

Nonetheless, Democrat Pat Schroeder of Colorado, the co-chair of the Congressional Caucus on Women's Issues who was also the most senior woman in the House, was happy to push the parental leave bill forward. Schroeder, though not the chair of the most relevant committees, was perhaps the best-known congressional advocate of women's and children's needs. She liked the legislation because it challenged the commitment of conservative family proponents head-on while not doing harm to women's rights. If conservatives were truly interested in helping families, they ought to be willing to let either parent take time off to care for an ill child. If they opposed the bill, their agenda of keeping women subordinated while calling it "maintaining the family" might become clearer. The public might be inclined to reconsider changes in gender roles, in child care at least.[37]

As drafted by the committee, the bill ensured equal, not special, treatment for women. Schroeder, chair of the House Civil Service Subcommittee, also favored the bill's coverage of civil service employees. This ideal feminist bill, H.R. 2020, the Parental and Disability Leave Act, was introduced in the House on April 4, 1985, by Schroeder with a small bipartisan group of twenty cosponsors. Among the organizations endorsing the bill were the American Association of University Women, the American Civil Liberties Union (ACLU), the Association of Junior Leagues, the National Federation of Business and Professional Women's Clubs (BPW), NOW, NWPC, WEAL, WLDF, and labor unions.[38]

Because of the publicity generated by Garland's California case, the media focused attention on H.R. 2020 two weeks after it was introduced. The publicity was good and bad. Organizations that had earlier ignored H.R. 2020 began launching attacks before the bill's proponents were ready to respond. Provoked by the publicity, the U.S. Chamber of Commerce strongly opposed parental leave. The chamber argued that unpaid leave was not free; it would result in an exorbitant increase of business costs. The chamber and other trade groups admitted privately that their main concern was not unpaid parental leave itself, but the strategy for implementing new employee benefits. Congress, employers argued, would open the proverbial flood gates if it required them to provide social programs. Such programs, including child care and elder care, were a worker's responsibility, they said.[39]

Organized labor supported the legislation but successfully demanded that the bill be changed to insure senior employees priority over leave-takers in the event of a layoff. The term "disability leave" was replaced by "medical leave" as suggested by disability rights groups. In response to small-business objections that they could not afford the costs associated with paternity leave, an exemption for businesses with fewer than five employees was added. Eleven months later, a gutted H.R. 4300, the Family and Medical Leave Act, was introduced, followed by S. 2278, introduced by Senators Christopher Dodd and Arlen Specter. The Family and Medical Leave Act became less and less comprehensive as it went through the legislative process. By June 1986, when it was voted out of the necessary House committees, it covered only firms with fifteen or more employees, and capped at thirty-six weeks the maximum amount of leave time in a twelve-month period for each employee. An employee still could take leave for the birth or adoption of a child.[40]

Elder care was added to the bill at the insistence of Republican congresswoman Marge Roukema of New Jersey, who was the ranking Republican on the House Education and Labor-Management Relations Subcommittee. She was willing to support the bill if she could make it more palatable to other Republicans and the White House by making it less feminist and less objectionable to business. She had a two-step strategy in view, which might gain the president's endorsement. There was little objection to this addition from the bill's sponsors because the politically powerful American Association of Retired Persons (AARP) joined the lobbying effort.[41]

Once Roukema got the sponsors to include elder care, however, she used the inclusion to argue that the leave was too costly and must be scaled back even further. Roukema then insisted that they cut the leave to thirteen weeks for medical care and eight weeks for the birth, placement, or adoption of a child. More significantly, she favored raising the employer exemption from fifteen to fifty employees. The bill's sponsors worried that if this kept up, most employed women would be excluded. Schroeder, however, felt she had to go along with the increases in order to get some legislation passed as a beginning. Berman's assessment that a broad bill would elicit negative congressional responses was confirmed. Feminists thought the leave bill was wonderful legislation that would address women's needs and wanted Congress to go on record with a feminist position. Many in Congress, however, saw the need but had no empathy for feminist goals. They acted as though women had an inescapable duty to care for elderly relatives, children, and disabled persons.[42]

To generate new supporters, advocates of the leave proposal decided to emphasize the benefits to men. Edward Zigler set up an advisory panel of social policy experts, including Sheila Kamerman and Alfred Kahn, both of Columbia University, and Dr. T. Berry Brazelton, which recommended a national infant leave policy. Zigler contended that the role of fathers in child care had become more participatory as middle-class mothers entered the work force. He endorsed the legislation as a positive response to these changes. Fathers and mothers needed leave to care for newborn and newly adopted children in the crucial early months, Zigler said. Isabelle Katz Pinzler of the ACLU Women's Rights Project explained that such proposals would help to erase the notion that child care and parental leave are exclusively women's issues. To do otherwise, she said, would reduce the hope of ever having men significantly share the child-rearing burden. The fact that men might well have benefited from the legislation did not ensure its passage.[43]

Searching for consensus in the new Democratically controlled 100th Congress, parental leave sponsors began to appropriate the Reaganite "pro-family" rhetoric by emphasizing that the possibility of leave would benefit both parents and children, not just mothers. Anti-abortion supporters of the legislation began calling it "pro-life," in that it took care of children after birth.[44]

The Supreme Court decision in the Garland case came in the midst of the discussion, in January 1987. NOW and other women's rights organizations that believed equality of rights required that women and men be treated equally feared the high court decision would deal a blow to their efforts. These organizations, like the opponents of protective legislation in the early 1900s, did not want women to be given special treatment that might encourage exclusion and discrimination against women in some jobs. Justice Marshall's opinion protected the feminists' position when he upheld the law because it "allows women, as well as men, to have families without losing their jobs." As amended, however, the congressional bill differed significantly from Berman's California law.[45]

Extensive congressional hearings and the Supreme Court decision failed to persuade enough members to vote for the bill. With continued opposition from business and the White House, Roukema and Republican congressman Jim Jeffords of Vermont refused to mobilize the necessary bipartisan support unless further concessions were made. Once more the bill was watered down as Roukema and Jeffords pressed for changes in the length of leave and employer coverage. Now, for the first three years, the bill would cover companies with fifty or more employees and thereafter those with thirty-five or more employees. The allowable leave was shortened to ten weeks during a two-year period for family reasons and up to fifteen weeks of medical leave in a single year. All leave, of course, was still unpaid. Employers could exempt employees with less than a year of tenure or those who worked less than twenty hours per week. Employers could also deny leave to those earning salaries in the top ten percentile if their absence might prove to be a financial hardship to the employer.[46]

The compromise measure, according to the General Accounting Office, would initially cost employers about $188 million, rising to $212 million, but this was still millions less than what the Chamber of Commerce had insisted parental leave would cost. Despite this good news, only two Republicans on the House Education and Labor Committee, Jeffords and Roukema, voted for the bill. At a standoff, supporters and opponents allowed the medical and parental leave bill to languish until the next session of Congress. The supporters had not allowed for business assertions that the policy would have costs even though the leave was unpaid, and they had not foreseen that business objections, combined with conservatives' insistence on traditional gender roles, would interfere with passage.[47]

While the parental leave bill languished, heightened concern over the plight of employed parents fed a developing public demand that welfare be reformed. Nixon and Carter efforts to reform welfare had foundered on the costs involved. All their calculations had been based on having mothers stay home with young children; they felt that keeping welfare mothers at home, which had been the cornerstone of the welfare policy since the New Deal, should remain a primary goal.

The liberal coalition that wanted child-care services and parental leave was the same liberal coalition that had supported helping welfare mothers in order to support their children. That coalition had evolved and now wanted changes in gender roles and greater opportunities for women.

In the course of the argument for parental leave, women's groups had emphasized how many mothers had jobs and children. Now, in the wake of that debate, it became possible to modify the traditional policy dictating that even welfare mothers should stay home to take care of their children. The old arguments against forcing these mothers to work because juvenile delinquency would increase and children would be ill-cared for lost moral force. While some policymakers entertained alternative notions, such as finding ways for all mothers to stay at home or ways to encourage fathers to stay until children reached school age, these suggestions were not taken seriously. This meant it was possible to reform welfare without making provisions for the mothers to stay at home. As a result, child-care services for welfare mothers became an issue just as they were an issue for other employed mothers.

The politicians' perennial promise to reduce welfare rolls, spurred on by a president whose campaigning and public utterances consistently blasted "welfare cheats," moved the welfare issue to the top of the domestic agenda. There was a public perception that the women and children on welfare, who were actually mostly white, were ghetto blacks lazily living off the public instead of working; this helped to garner public support for the changes. By 1987, Congress, the Reagan administration, and state governors agreed that welfare reforms were achievable. The Omnibus Budget Reconciliation Act of 1981, authored by Republican senators Phil Gramm of Texas and Warren Rudman of New Hampshire, allowed states to redesign Nixon's Work Incentive Program as an employment and training component of Aid to Families with Dependent Children (AFDC).[48]

The success of various new state programs was uneven at best. Most states could only afford job search, job placement assistance, and unpaid community work experience known as "workfare." These programs helped mostly those welfare clients with previous work experience and good educations. Employment rates or earnings did not increase for disadvantaged AFDC recipients, those with no work history, few skills, or bad educations. Such results should not have been surprising. At the beginning of the War on Poverty in 1964, President Lyndon Johnson had acknowledged that these disadvantaged recipients needed comprehensive services, not just short-term training and help in looking for a job.[49]

The increasing cry for welfare reform worried Democratic leaders. If they did not act quickly, Republicans might establish themselves as the serious reformers. Evidence of a hostile Republican takeover was already apparent. President Reagan, in his 1987 State of the Union message, cited Franklin Roosevelt erroneously and out of context in declaring welfare "a narcotic, a destroyer of the human spirit." Democrats seized the reins of the welfare reform bandwagon. Unheeded in the rush, however, were those who cautioned that reform would fail unless jobs above poverty wages were found, and that some people on welfare were unemployable.[50]

The House and Senate proposed bills that required AFDC recipients to find employment. The House bill required all AFDC recipients with children over six to work full-time and those with children under three, part-time. Opponents like Democratic congressman Augustus Hawkins of California, Chairman of the House Education and Labor Committee, made himself unpopular by insisting people would believe the welfare problem solved when it was only covered up. Hawkins, coauthor of the 1978 Humphrey-Hawkins Full Employment and Balanced Growth bill, was a strong advocate of job training and employment for the unskilled. He called the welfare reform bill "slavefare" with recipients working for less money than they had obtained under existing welfare programs and no chance at upward mobility. Hawkins said welfare recipients would be permanently poor and deprived of the needed health care and social services, but his objections were ignored.[51]

Few persons objected to the bill's provisions requiring mothers to work even though the polls showed Americans favored mother care for their own children. Democratic congressman Pat Williams of Montana worried that children would be cared for by people other than their parents. Labor Secretary William Brock responded that some children would be better off in day care under the welfare bill than staying at home with their mothers. Most of the children, Brock said, were from single-parent homes and "if there is a surrogate parent, it's probably a local drug dealer." He continued, "What they get now is an exposure to all that would help to hold them down." He thought that "mothers who received training and better skills would be better parents." "Pro-family" proponents generally believed women should stay at home, but "welfare cheats" were another matter. They usually loved to cite the negative effects of day care on small children but this time they were silent. They were not interested in welfare children. Their arguments were directed at maintaining the white traditional family.[52]

The House of Representatives moved quickly on the legislation, which passed in December 1987 by a vote of 230–194. Almost twenty years after writing the Family Assistance Plan, Daniel Patrick Moynihan, now a Democratic senator from New York, led the cause in the Senate. A less expensive bill, an amended version of the House measure, passed in the Senate in June of 1988 by a vote of 93–3. The House-Senate Conference Committee negotiated a compromise three weeks before the 1988 election and then Reagan quickly signed the Family Support Act of 1988 into law.[53]

The Family Support Act would cost $3.3 billion over a five-year period. The provisions required single parents on welfare with children over the age of three to participate in the new Job Opportunities and Basic Skills (JOBS) program, which offered education, training, and work activities. States had to guarantee child care for parents of children under six and to guarantee that the parents would work no more than twenty hours a week. If parents could not find work, they were required to work sixteen hours a week in a state-organized job. A young parent could substitute working on a high school diploma for a state-sponsored job.[54]

States were ordered to concentrate their efforts on the toughest cases, young persons without high school degrees, long-term recipients, and families with older children close to the limits of eligibility. The states were required to provide recipients with child-care services for twelve months after parents took a job and they could charge parents for child-care services based on a sliding income scale. The act strengthened the 1984 child-support act by requiring the states to implement by 1994 automatic withholding of child-support payments without waiting for the father to become delinquent. Federal money would be paid to the states to develop a computerized tracking system to monitor and improve child-support enforcement. The $3.3 billion price tag for the act would be covered through a variety of tax changes, among them elimination of the dependent care credit for children aged thirteen to fifteen and extension for five years of the Internal Revenue Service's debt collection program. States were ordered to coordinate the services with Head Start and other child-care programs for the poor already in operation.[55]

The work requirements for mothers in the welfare reform bill were no more onerous than most employed women experienced. Many parents worked longer than the twenty hours a week mandated for welfare parents with children under six and the full-time for parents of children above that age. The problem was in matching welfare parents' skills with available jobs that could support them and their children and provide child-care services. Some policy makers suggested that the welfare recipients find employment in day-care centers for their own children or for those of more affluent workers.[56]

Unlike the 1971 Nixon administration Family Assistance Plan that failed in Congress, welfare reform succeeded in 1987 because it promised to save money. Work in exchange for the dole and child-care services only for a limited amount of time, unacceptable in 1971, was applauded in 1988. The presence of so many women in the work force had undermined any incentive to support poor nonemployed mothers on public assistance. Furthermore, the political drumbeat about welfare dependency had eroded any public sympathy for welfare recipients. Congressman Hawkins was correct when he noted that although about half the people on the welfare rolls were not employable under any circumstances, the reforms were not designed to address this problem. Moynihan agreed that there was not enough money in the bill to pay for the various services promised. The federal deficit and the requirement for matching funds from the financially hard-pressed states would make implementation difficult. Before more money could even be approved, however, he thought "the stigma" had to be removed from welfare. Rather than regarding people on welfare as undeserving, "we are finally defining these people as unemployed and that's a breakthrough."[57]

Assuming payment of $32 a week per child for fifty weeks in a year, the $733 million appropriated under the Family Support Act for child-care services for the fiscal year 1992 would pay for less than 500,000 children nationwide. Politicians could now tell their constituents that they had solved the welfare problem, but mothers and children on public assistance soon saw they had been misled by administration and congressional reformers. By 1992, only about 48 percent of the funds appropriated for job training and other services were being used. As Hawkins predicted, the administration and the states wanted to reduce payments or eliminate recipients from the welfare rolls to save money even if they were not being given the required educational services or job training or child care.[58]

Day care for "slum" mothers, abandoned in the 1930s for at-home mother care, came back with a vengeance in the 1988 welfare reform law. The ideal of mother caring for the children at home was only for those who could afford it. If public assistance was required, the ideal was no longer relevant. Accepting the principle of mandatory jobs for welfare mothers did not mean that other employed mothers should have child-care assistance, however. The preference for mother care had been modified when practicality required. Federal child-care support for other employed mothers would require more willingness to abandon the myth of the traditional family and the preference for mother care.

VIII

Toward a National Child-Care Policy, 1988–1990

Women's-rights and child-care groups worked on a child-care bill while the welfare reform proposal was being enacted. They thought the debate over child-care services in the welfare reform legislation would strengthen congressional will to act despite the insistence of the pro-family advocates that the mother-care tradition be maintained.

They believed the 1988 election year would be a good time to enact parental leave legislation and a federal child-care bill. They hoped that the Democratic candidate would support their position and that the Republican candidate would be forced to respond. The child-care problem was getting worse. Over 74 percent of employed women worked full-time and 56.7 percent of married women living with their husbands were in the labor force. Most of these women had children under the age of six.[1]

The issue of women in the work force, or "Who's minding the kids?," was becoming a media growth industry. A Child Care Action Media Campaign gradually gained momentum. This campaign had been launched in 1983 by Elinor Guggenheimer, longtime New York child-care advocate and one of the organizers of the 1960 White House Conference on Child Care, with a board of directors that included the editors of major women's magazines such as *Good Housekeeping, Ladies' Home Journal, Redbook,* and *Working Woman*. By 1988, Guggenheimer's group, which also included child-care experts; the Children's Defense Fund (CDF), the major child advocacy lobby group; and women's rights organizations, had underway a successful media campaign for a national child-care policy. Books and articles, along with television and radio talk shows, frequently debated the subject. Advocates agreed on the need for high-quality, licensed care.[2]

Increasingly, women's organizations became comfortable with a message that downplayed a concern for the rights of women in order to build support for a national child-care policy. Much like the "feminist" social reformers of the 1920s, who disavowed an Equal Rights Amendment to gain support for minimum wages and maximum hours for women to protect motherhood, their message became increasingly "mother and child centered," not woman centered. Some female college students welcomed an expansion of the women's organizations' focus from ERA to other issues. They felt that the movement was broadening its base by taking into account the needs of all women.[3] NOW stood its ground during the developing child-care movement. Beset by financial problems, the ERA fight, the failure of Ferraro's candidacy, and the bloodletting caused by internal leadership fights, the organization refused to make child care its first priority. NOW membership declined during the conservative 1980s. The Ferraro vice-presidential gambit had turned off hardcore activists who wanted the organization to work outside the system and not within it. Molly Yard, president of NOW, noted that child care had always been one of NOW's demands, but chiefly because child care made it possible for mothers to enjoy other rights. NOW was concerned with women's individual rights, whether they had children or not, and would support any child-care proposals that did not violate these principles.[4]

Continuing concern about poor children and welfare women underscored the issue, yet it was the increasing number of divorces, female-headed households, and middle-class wage-earning white women that ignited the child-care movement. Child care became an issue that could generate public support as programs for poor people never could, but a serious move toward legislation required a strong Washington lobby. Some advocates in the labor unions, in the big education unions (the National Education Association and American Federation of Teachers) and other educational associations, and in the human development field such as Edward Zigler had been working to advance child care since the veto of the 1971 legislation.

Although she did not chair the relevant congressional committees and child care was not her only concern, Colorado Democratic congresswoman Schroeder was considered to be an important leader in any legislative effort. Her many media appearances and her exploratory campaign for the Democratic presidential nomination in the summer of 1987 had highlighted the child-care issue, and she was its most visible congressional advocate.[5]

Many issues claimed the attention of women's groups and the Congressional Women's Issues Caucus, including proposed civil rights legislation to overturn the *Grove City* decision and the languishing parental leave bill. The most visible lobby on children's concerns in Congress was still CDF. After Nixon's veto of the 1971 child-care bill, some advocates had feared that the CDF would disintegrate. In fact, it became stronger over the years. With a determined focus on poor children, and using her strong personal contacts in the Democratic establishment, the media, and the civil rights community, Marian Wright Edelman had made CDF a formidable lobby for children.[6]

Edelman's emergence as the principal leader of the children's lobby underscored the view that children were primarily a women's concern. By arguing that children were powerless because they could not vote, by turning out very effective analysis and position papers on every children's issue, CDF had become a widely respected resource for information on children's concerns. Beginning with the labor unions, women's groups, and educational associations that had been part of the earlier coalition, Edelman constructed an Alliance for Better Child Care, made up of 122 religious, educational, child-development, civil rights, and business groups. The alliance wanted to build on the climate generated by the media, increased employment, and stress on mothers to pass legislation that would help the middle class but also benefit poor children.[7]

The interests of the children's lobby and the women's groups coincided in many ways. CDF wanted to make available to poor children what child-development experts had long asserted was best for all children. A lawyer, Edelman had served on the Carnegie Council for Children, worked in the civil rights movement, and was a major proponent of Head Start for poor black children. She had long been disappointed by the federal government's refusal to provide adequate funding for the health, education, and welfare of poor children.[8] Under the proposed bill, all children would be provided with the kind of preschool opportunities available to middle-class children. Those opportunities included quality education and a chance to relate to other children in a setting that promoted learning and development with beneficial experiences. This was not new; child-development experts were promoting the same ideas they had promoted in 1971. Standards about ratios of care-givers to children and the quality of care had always been her concern. Edelman had not changed her positions on these fundamental issues.[9]

Edelman had definite ideas about how the new legislation should differ from the 1971 bill. As a minister's daughter with a strong awareness of the social role of the African-American church, she was willing to support those who wanted to provide funds for church-run day care. Her interest in child development, however, meant that church day-care centers would be held to the same mandatory standards to insure quality on developmental as well as religious grounds. Responding to the shift toward states' rights in the 1980s, Edelman proposed giving the states more control over fund management. The successful Head Start model, which operated outside the public school system, provided a strong case for private-sector services.[10]

The agenda of the women's organizations coincided in many ways with Edelman's. They were all in Elinor Guggenheimer's Child Care Action Campaign together. As middle-class professional women themselves, feminist leaders eagerly endorsed providing all families with the sort of good-quality care they bought for their own children. In addition, they could deflect arguments that the women's movement was a middle-class white women's movement by supporting an issue that would greatly benefit poor and minority-group mothers and children. By always emphasizing that child care was an important concern to fathers and by speaking of parents instead of mothers in their advocacy efforts, women's rights organizations could underscore their desire to weaken gender-specific parenting roles. Supporting child care was seen as another way of supporting equality of options and choices for individual women. They also liked the fact that child care reached beyond their hardcore feminist constituency; the issue helped their organizations remain viable during the backlash against rights in the Reagan years. [11]

But the women's groups were not the leaders in the Alliance for Better Child Care. Edelman and CDF organized and staffed the effort and everyone naturally followed CDF's lead in shaping the debate and strategy. NOW worried that some of the language in the bill seemed to permit sex discrimination against child-care employees. Once congressional staffers, with the help of the CDF-led alliance, had drafted the bill, however, suggestions for modification made little headway. [12]

Under these circumstances, it seemed that Phyllis Schlafly's Eagle Forum, Beverly La Haye's Concerned Women of America, and the other "pro-family groups," flush with their victory over ERA, had been placed on the defensive for once by the women's rights organizations. The women's movement not only cared about children and families, but accepted an emphasis on mothers' child-care responsibilities. Schlafly and the other conservatives appeared to have no choice but to support the "feminist" child-care agenda, but matters were not quite that simple. The pro-family groups had not embraced the feminist agenda. Precisely the opposite had happened.

The feminists made peace with their enemies by reordering their priorities, but Schlafly, for one, did not alter her ideology. She held her "family" policy ground and did not shift position to support any of the women's rights groups' proposals. Instead, she insisted that feminists, insofar as they asserted the importance of "family" concerns, now almost admitted that they had been "anti-family."

But the women's groups' advocacy of parental leave belied any claim that they had abandoned a need to "ungender" child care. As a result, pro-family groups and feminists were both concerned with helping mothers in the workplace. Both said families should be a priority and now they were everybody's major concern, but the "pro-family" groups had no victory to savor. Their major goal of having mothers leave the workplace to stay at home with their children seemed even less likely.[13]

When the child-care alliance's Act for Better Child Care Services (ABC) was introduced into the Congress in November 1987, the perceived threat to the traditional family that had so dominated the 1970s' child-care debates was a less serious barrier. The basic rationale for the bill was that both parents, or the only parent, worked. Unlike 1971, however, now so many families had two wage earners or were single-parent headed and there had been so much media attention to the issue that the rationale was barely controversial.[14]

The legislation declared: "The availability of quality child care is critical to the self-sufficiency and independence of millions of American families, including the growing number of mothers with young children who work out of economic necessity. . . ." A national law was necessary because of an inadequate supply and quality of child care and the "wide differences among the states in child care licensing and enforcement policies." ABC's stated goal was to strengthen the "competitiveness of the United States by providing young children with a sound early childhood development experience."[15]

The bill's sponsors, led by Democratic congressman Dale Kildee of Michigan in the House and Christopher Dodd of Connecticut in the Senate, argued that ABC programs would be cost-effective because they would help reduce "the chances of juvenile delinquency, adolescent pregnancy, and improve the likelihood that children will finish high school and become employed." The program would make it possible for more parents to work or seek education. Making child care more available, according to the sponsors, would have no negative effects and would strengthen the "well-being of families and the national economy."[16]

The bill authorized an appropriation of $2.5 billion to the states to provide a much higher quality program than that mandated for the "unworthy" poor in the welfare reform act. The states would give low-interest loans to nonprofit day-care centers and family-care homes for renovation to meet required building codes. Federal funds would be used to provide night and day care programs and to extend to a full day part-day programs already in existence, such as Head Start. The money could be granted directly to providers or distributed in child-care certificates or vouchers to parents to be used by care-givers who met the requirements of the act.[17]

All funded care-givers would have to have formal training; states would finance the schooling of low-income persons to obtain Child Development Associate credentials. Standards would be developed by a national advisory committee that would include specialists, and be administered by the Department of Health and Human Services. Standards would include staff-child ratios, as well as qualifications, training, and background requirements for personnel. Failure to meet the standards issued by the secretary of health and human services would trigger a funding cutoff. Payments to the state would be based on a sliding fee schedule; parents would make copayments based on the service provided, with family income adjusted for number of children receiving services. The lowest income people would make no payments, but families earning up to 115 percent of the median income in a state would still be eligible.[18]

Republicans, once the bill was introduced, did not want to appear any less responsive than the Democrats to the attractive family issue of child care. However, they countered ABC by introducing their own legislation. Republican senator Orrin Hatch of Utah introduced a bill providing vouchers to working mothers, Title XX Social Services block grants and loans to institutions amounting to about $250 million, and state regulation and licensing of day-care centers. Reflecting the views of the "pro-family groups," other Republicans introduced tax credits to lessen the amount of income taxes paid by a family without regard to whether the mother was in the work force, aiming to reinforce mother care of children. Congress, controlled by the Democrats, went forward early in 1988 with hearings on the ABC bills in the relevant committees.[19]

The principal case for ABC was made in the congressional testimony of Edelman and the witnesses for the 122 organizational members of the Alliance for Better Child Care, as they spoke of the necessity and the benefit to children and the country. In her testimony before the House Human Resources Subcommittee of the Education and Labor

Committee, and before the Senate Subcommittee on Children, Families, Drugs, and Alcoholism of the Labor and Human Resources Committee, Edelman began with a nod toward the pro-family and anti-feminist organizations: "We believe that every mother or primary care-taking parent should have the choice to stay at home with her or his young children. . . ." But she explained that this option was not widely available because

> . . . our society does not currently support parenting at home or help parents when they must go out to work. An essential component of this country's public policies should be adequate income support, children's allowances for families and parental leave policies which allow parents the job security and income support that they need to remain home during the critical early months after childbirth, as well as sound child care policies.[20]

To ward off any strategy of pitting these issues against ABC, she cited injuries experienced by children without proper care: "We cannot wait one minute longer as a nation to put in place policies and resources to protect these children." Then after reciting the data on increases in women's employment and the need for both parents in many two-parent families to work, she noted data on workers' effectiveness when they did not have to worry about their children. Families, she noted, often could not afford to pay for child care at the going rate of $3,000 per year, per child. Children left alone, she explained, "are often consumed by fear that interferes with school work and all areas of their lives." Edelman contended that only a single-minded, comprehensive program would meet the existing needs. The other federal programs, such as Head Start, were so underfinanced, understaffed, and limited that they did not even begin to solve the problem. As for the Child Care Tax Credit for expenses up to a maximum of $2,400 for one dependent and $4,800 for two or more dependents, which had originated in the Eisenhower years, it did nothing to expand the supply of child care or to insure its quality.[21]

Religious groups were divided over funding for church-based day-care programs. The National Council of Churches supported it, but the American Jewish Committee had serious concerns that the separation between church and state might be breached.[22]

State and local officials favored the allocation of funds to the states to design their own programs, but disliked the idea of a national committee setting standards. The high-profile women's rights organizations remained in the background as Sarah Harder, president of the American Association of University Women (AAUW); Beth Wray, president of the National Federation of Business and Professional Women's Clubs (BPW); and Nancy Duff Campbell, managing attorney of the National Women's Law Center, spoke for the feminist constituencies. Quality and affordability were key concerns; these witnesses also emphasized their view that ABC was a complement and not a substitute for the Family and Medical Leave Bill. The AAUW explained that ABC was a way of permitting mothers more independence, which was a main goal of the effort to achieve equality of rights for women.[23]

The Senate hearings were more dramatic. Dodd, chairman of the Children, Families, Drugs, and Alcoholism Subcommittee, opened with a detailed account of his work with Arlen Specter in the Senate Children's Caucus they had established in 1983. Then the committee listened to horror stories from parents and families. Debra and Michael Brooks described the murder of their eleven-month-old son by his unlicensed day-care provider, who struck him while he was trying to crawl away when she was changing his diaper. Tacye and Russ Young described the exorbitant costs of finding a care-giver for their epileptic three-year-old.[24]

The next witness panel consisted of female state and local government officials. Then business representatives came forward to assure everyone of their interest and concern about the issue. They claimed they were doing all they could but competitiveness and better productivity by parents were assured with ABC. This, of course, was the same argument they had used to support corporate tax credits for employee child-care centers.[25]

Opponents of ABC in both the Senate and House committees attacked all of the key points made by the witnesses. Apparently on the advice of Pat Buchanan, their arguments sounded like Nixon's veto message on the 1971 bill: Mother care is optimal and should be promoted above all else. Dr. Karl Zinmeister of the American Enterprise Institute railed against the "mass surrender of child-rearing responsibilities to nonrelatives," calling it "the final triumph of the Industrial Revolution: the industrialization of the family." Schlafly derided ABC as the "federal baby-sitting bill" because it encouraged governmental control of children. She proposed instead a toddler tax credit that would give money directly to families whether the mothers worked or not. Advocates and opponents of the bill assumed incorrectly that mother care had always been traditional. Lieutenant Governor Nick Theodore of South Carolina, for example, noted approvingly that some mothers could continue past practice and ". . . choose to stay at home and can afford to stay home. That's wonderful, and that's a choice which must be preserved." None of the ABC supporters cited the history of father care or the history of care by someone other than parents, which might have helped to illuminate the discussion.[26]

The women's groups and CDF lobbied very hard for ABC. The continued emphasis in women's magazines and other media helped to spread the message that employed mothers needed child-care assistance, as did Schroeder's 1988 Great American Family tour, which consisted of a series of town meetings around the country in which she was joined by Dr. Brazelton and Gary David Goldberg, writer and producer of the TV program "Family Ties." ABC, however, did not pass in 1988.[27]

A Gallup poll taken in May 1988 showed that a plurality of all likely voters in the presidential election would support a candidate who favored more day-care services. In a July 1988 *New York Times* poll, 52 percent of the respondents called for an increase in federal day-care spending. But the poll reported "broad disagreement" about the role government should have in financing church-sponsored day care and in providing subsidies to mothers who stay home. This broad disagreement slowed ABC's momentum but it, in itself, did not cause the effort to fail. The Catholic Conference of Bishops objected to prohibitions against using funds for sectarian activities, and prohibitions against religious discrimination by providers.[28]

Edelman agreed to remove these clauses, but the ACLU, the National Education Association, the Parent-Teacher Association, and other organizations in the ABC alliance objected to her acquiescence, which they insisted would permit the use of funds for religious purposes and what they regarded as religious discrimination. They believed the Catholic conference wanted to establish a precedent to demand federal funds for church schools in competition with the public schools. Edelman brushed off their complaints. Church-state concerns, she asserted, could be pursued in the courts *after* the bill was enacted. Her response was not appreciated by the affected organizations.[29]

Edelman's agreement also deeply irritated some members of Congress. Significantly, Democratic congressman Augustus Hawkins of California, chair of the House Education and Labor Committee overseeing all education and labor issues, and a firm supporter of women's rights and help for poor children, moved to block the bill. Edelman faced the prospect of losing legislation she regarded as critical and having CDF responsible for the defeat.[30]

Instead of renegotiating, Edelman mounted a full-court offensive to subdue critics and to discourage congressional doubters. Time was running out and she did not believe compromise was possible between members of her coalition. She engaged heavy hitters like Coretta Scott King and Jesse Jackson to press the Congress for immediate passage. Over Hawkins's objections, the bill was voted out of committee.[31]

By this time, however, the presidential election was at hand. Republican candidate George Bush used a very effective strategy to avoid supporting the bill and to keep the vote of his partisans who were interested in child-care services.

He unveiled his backing for a national child-care policy consisting of tax credits in a speech before a National Federation of Business and Professional Women's Clubs (BPW) national meeting two weeks before the Republican convention. At the convention, Bush said that women had helped to bring about America's prosperity and cited the BPW as one of a "thousand points of light." A Gallup poll in October 1988 asked whether day care for working parents should be a priority for the next president. Thirty-nine percent of those polled thought it should be a top priority; 42 percent, a medium priority; 17 percent, a low priority; and 2 percent thought it should have no priority. Bush repeated his support for some form of federal help for child care and jumped behind Schlafly's Toddler Tax Credit, which would provide a $1000 tax credit for up to two children per family under age five. The Democratic candidate, Michael Dukakis, was mostly silent on the subject but said he supported ABC despite worries about the costs.[32]

ABC did not get to the floor of Congress. The House spent the last days of the session on another hot political issue, how to combat illegal drug use and the drug trade. Voter opinion two days after the election showed that 28 percent of Bush voters and 55 percent of Dukakis voters wanted more child care. The candidates' staffs were obviously reading the polls all along.[33]

Edelman pushed the Senate for quick passage of ABC in order to have something to show for the 1988 session, but the Senate took up the bill along with the other child-care proposal, Family and Medical Leave. Because they were both regarded as women's issues by the politicians, the legislative fate of ABC became tied to the parental leave bill on which Schroeder and the women's rights organizations, not Edelman, had played the leading role.[34]

In September, candidate Bush said he favored parental leave, encouraging Senate Republican support. Then he equivocated, making clear that he wanted business to voluntarily institute such policies. West Virginia Democratic senator Robert Byrd, the Senate majority leader, equivocated as well. He thought the Democrats would be helped politically with women's votes by passing child-care legislation but he was not sure whether to push for one of these bills or both. Byrd, whose support of women's issues in the past had been lukewarm at best, actually met with women's rights organization leaders to discuss strategy.[35]

In the end, Byrd, who wanted to challenge the Republicans, decided to put both bills on the floor. The U.S. Chamber of Commerce and the National Federation of Independent Businessmen stepped up their lobbying campaigns against the leave bill, which they characterized as the first of a series of expensive "congressionally ordered benefits like child care and universal health insurance." To defuse the lobbyists' claims, Nine to Five, the national association of working women, released a study that showed there would be no additional financial burden on small businesses from a leave bill. In fact, as Nine to Five executive director Karen Nussbaum explained, a leave policy "appears to be good for small business job growth." Using government data, the study found that employment among small businesses with parental leave policies grew at a 21 percent faster rate than in businesses without such policies.[36]

Both bills moved toward the floor for a vote in October. NOW strongly supported the parental leave bill, but on ABC, Molly Yard was very concerned about Edelman's changes and the bill's heavy emphasis on mothering. Although bothered by the discrimination issues as well as the weak targeting on poor children, African-American child-care advocates and civil rights groups such as the National Institute for Black Child Development and the NAACP did not want to publicly oppose Edelman. Her sincerity and commitment over the years and their joint efforts to secure full funding for Head Start made criticism difficult.[37]

Thus opponents within the Alliance for Better Child Care either kept silent publicly or steered discussion toward the act's voucher provisions that made it harder to trace discrimination on the basis of race, sex, or religion with the use of federal funds. Vouchers would be given to parents to buy care instead of having the funding paid to the provider by the government agency. Authorizing vouchers might also open the door to long-standing demands for education vouchers for use in private and religious schools. Once combined, the parental leave and the child-care legislation was stalled. Then, Byrd tacked on a bill outlawing child pornography, which some Republicans wanted very much. But most Republicans cared more about obstructing parental leave and the child-care bill.[38]

Joined by Senate Democrats Alan Dixon of Illinois, David Boren of Oklahoma, James Exon of Nebraska, Howell Heflin of Alabama, Daniel Melcher of Montana, and Sam Nunn of Georgia, Republicans supported a parliamentary maneuver to continue the debate until the end of the session unless the child pornography bill was withdrawn. Drug policy and other urgent matters awaited Senate action. The rhetoric was strident. Dodd accused the Republicans of a "filibuster by silence." In desperation, the Bush-Schlafly toddler tax credit was added at the last minute, but even that failed.[39]

The necessity for federal child-care regulations, the insistence by sponsors on making leave parental instead of maternal, and the possible financial drain on small business from mandated leave drew the loudest objections. The bill was not brought to a vote and Democrats did not have a likely Republican veto of child-care proposals to use as a last-minute campaign issue.[40]

In the aftermath of the legislative debacle, a *New York Times* editorial came back to the essential point, that ". . . the subject of poor children risks being swallowed up in the larger subject of day care." The *Times* believed that day care was "being swallowed up in a golden glow of generalized virtue about children" . . . Letting "the two subjects blur" would be detrimental to poor children. The *Times* proposed a program for thirteen million poor children, with special assistance to young mothers during pregnancy, and child care to permit them to stay in school, as well as advice and help with caring for their babies. It acknowledged that if full Head Start funding were achieved for all eligible three- to five-year-old children, that would be the most important day-care initiative.[41]

ABC failed to pass because polls showed deep division among the American people over endorsing federal financing of nonparental child care. If polls had shown strong support, candidates Bush and Dukakis would have moved the issue front and center and both parties in Congress would have worked out a bill. Likewise, strong support for parental leave during a political campaign would have stimulated passage even if the Chamber of Commerce did not like it. Bush managed to have it both ways. He mollified anyone who cared about child care by supporting it in theory even though he waffled. Dukakis believed that nonparental child care would not win over any new liberal supporters.

When all was said and done, most of the public still believed mothers were responsible for child care. Balancing jobs and children was difficult but did not require changing the natural order of things.

The 1988 debate and the election of Bush made clear that the only way a child-care bill would become law would be if it included Bush's proposals. The defection of some Democrats had made it unlikely that a measure could be passed by veto-proof margins. The debate also made clear that proposals made by Hawkins and other influential committee chairmen, as well as the White House, would have to be added to ABC to make it palatable.

Many Republicans and some Democrats remained convinced that no new child-care program was needed. They thought the problem was not regulation or supply of child care per se, but that working families needed more income, which they could spend for child care—or however else they chose to spend it. To accomplish this end, House and Senate Republicans introduced President Bush's (and Schlafly's) toddler tax proposal again along with ABC when Congress reconvened in 1989. The refined proposal gave direct payments to those too poor to pay taxes. Poor families with enough income could choose either the Bush $1000 credit or the refundable version of the existing credit, but not both. Bush reiterated the claim that his plan would avoid bureaucracy and expand maximum "parental choice" of child care by a relative, or neighbor, or in private or church centers.[42]

Senator Orrin Hatch remained convinced that some attention to supply was necessary. He reintroduced his proposal for a child-care block grant administered by the states at $250 million a year over the next three years as well as a tax credit. He also supported the ABC plan and wanted a measure passed that would combine the proposals.[43]

Former Reagan White House official Gary Bauer, now with the Family Research Council, encouraged adoption of Bush's plan as "philosophically sound" but wanted, in addition, a plan that explicitly provided funds for mothers who stayed at home. He recognized that Bush's pledge of "no new taxes" meant there was little money available.[44]

The Alliance for Better Child Care attacked both Hatch's and Bush's proposals. Edelman denounced Hatch's plan as "a politically cosmetic bill that talks about the private sector and has no minimum standards." She thought Bush's proposal was insincere since the amount of the credit was insufficient to pay for child care and wrongheaded because it did nothing about the supply and quality problems. Edelman had the votes: the ABC bill passed 11–5 in the Senate committee and was ready for floor action in April. Hatch and fellow Republican senator James Jeffords of Vermont joined the Democrats in favor of the bill.[45]

On the other side of the Capitol, House members weighed in with their own tax credit proposal to help employed mothers. In addition, Representative Hawkins came up with his own child-care plan, which his staff had begun working on after his 1988 dispute with Edelman over religious discrimination and vouchers. Hawkins believed in federal funding of social programs and wanted to address the supply and quality issues as well as the affordability problem. He proposed fully funding Head Start and creating licensed centers for pre–Head Start children, under the original ABC plan. He avoided the religious discrimination issue altogether by simply ignoring it. To insure the support of the teachers' unions, Hawkins proposed to include the public schools as service providers for after-school care. The committee prohibited any sectarian activity, including worship and instruction, in any of the authorized programs. Hawkins's bill was favorably reported out of the full committee on June 27, 1989, by a 23–11 vote.[46]

Child-care legislation in both houses moved forward, while the weakened Family and Medical Leave bill, in which feminists had a clear stake, was also reintroduced in early 1989. The legislation cleared the Senate and House committees by the end of April and differences were relatively minor. Representative Roukema assured her colleagues that opposition to the leave bill would end once the Democrats assured business that the bill would not open the door to other mandated benefits, like child care and health insurance, as they feared. Democrats, however, led by Senator Edward Kennedy of Massachusetts, chairman of the Labor and Human Resources Committee, saw nothing wrong with mandating benefits for needed employee services. They thought such a strategy was entirely proper, in view of the Reagan-Bush policies of low taxes, high corporate profits, and federal budget deficit accumulations.[47]

President Bush, attempting to blunt the issue, still opposed any mandated leave legislation, and repeated his desire that more companies voluntarily adopt leave policies. The U.S. Chamber of Commerce still argued that mandated benefits would cause productivity to suffer and that costs would be passed on to consumers in higher prices. Schroeder and other feminists acknowledged privately that the watered-down version of the Family and Medical Leave bill was hardly worth passing, but they had to back it in public because it contained the principle of shared responsibility for children. Republican senator David Durenberger of Minnesota and other Republicans offered their support of the leave bill if shared responsibility were discarded. They suggested they might end their opposition and vote for it if the provisions were made to apply only to mothers and not fathers.[48]

While floor action on the leave bill was delayed, Senate advocates of the child-care legislation decided to get a bill through by adding something for everyone. Changes in the ABC structure, including tax credits, relaxed quality standards, and less money was the price of passage. In the new reality of lowered voices, combat fatigue from the Reagan years, and the evidence of disagreements on substance, this strategy succeeded. Just before the Senate floor vote, succumbing to reality, Edelman in an op-ed piece in the *Washington Post* characterized the changes and concessions as positive developments. She embraced the compromises that brought the bill to the floor, asking for quick passage, but she refused to address the church-state issue that had bothered the ACLU and other groups in her coalition. They did not interfere with passage.[49]

The modified Act for Better Child Care Services passed in the Senate in June 1989, after seven days of floor debate. Hatch explained his support of the bill because it "does not make the federal government a child care provider; it does not give the government a monopoly on child care; it does not prohibit participation by religious institution[s]; and, it does not require the licensing of close relatives who provide care." In a self-congratulatory back-slapping exercise, Dodd credited Hatch and Maryland's Democratic senator Barbara Mikulski for working out the agreements that made it possible to bring the bill to the floor. Hatch, Dodd pointed out, "has not lost his conservative credentials. I have not lost my progressive ones . . . we decided to drop our ideology . . . to see if we could work out a legislative product that reflected our respective points of view."[50]

Hatch's usual supporters, including Schlafly's Eagle Forum, attacked him for backing ABC, with its provision for child-care centers. Angered, he responded that their criticisms were unfounded: the bill did not create a large bureaucracy and was not "biased" toward institutional care, as they claimed. Schlafly could not defeat child care in the Senate, but in the end she got some of the tax credit help for families with stay-at-home mothers that she wanted.[51]

Considerable speculation about Hatch's support of the child-care provision and willingness to attack the pro-family conservatives swirled around the Capitol. Some speculated that his youth in a poor family and his experience as chairman of the Senate Committee on Labor and Human Resources when the Republicans had controlled the Senate between 1980 and 1986 made him sympathetic to the problems of the poor. Schlafly opined, "He has a feminist staff, so that's all he hears."

Paul Weyrich and others on the right had answers that were less generous and more politically charged. They thought Hatch wanted to be appointed to the Supreme Court; he would need Democratic allies for confirmation and child care might gain him some friends on that side of the aisle.[52]

Hatch's support did not completely convince some of his Republican colleagues, including one of only two women senators and the only female Republican, Nancy Kassebaum. She criticized the bill because there were already numerous programs as well as the existing dependent child-care tax credit. The legislation would also, Kassebaum said, be falsely institutionalizing the expectation that government could solve the problem. A maximum of one million child-care slots might be funded through ABC, but the latest data showed a need for at least eighteen million places. Bush's income supplement tax credit might be enough to "help many low-income women stay at home with their children," Kassebaum said, but "the government cannot protect its citizens from hard choices that are very difficult to make. The decision to work or not to work cannot be made revenue neutral." In the end, however, despite her complaints about the deficiencies of the legislation, even Kassebaum voted for it. She was persuaded that some services would be better than nothing.[53]

ABC, as passed by a vote of 63–37, contained enough of the original ABC bill to permit Edelman and the child-care alliance, including the feminist organizations, to claim victory. It authorized $1.75 billion in new child-care services, $2 billion in income tax credits, and $400 million for a block grant to the states to improve existing child-care services. As in the 1988 welfare reform bill, states, not the federal

government, would set health and safety standards. The states, however, received extra financial incentives if they followed national
guidance.[54]

To defer the church-state problem, parental vouchers could be used
for sectarian programs so long as constitutional requirements were met.
This meant, in effect, leaving the policy to be litigated in the courts.
There were three tax credits included: the existing Dependent Care
Tax Credit (DCTC) was expanded to cover parents too poor to pay
taxes, thereby making them eligible for payments which could offset
child-care expenses; a supplement to the current earned-income tax
credit was established to provide up to $750 a year to low-income
families with children under age four; and credit was granted for services to the estimated thirteen million children without health care.
The bill provided a phased-in expansion of the Dependent Care Tax
Credit to include a credit for family health insurance expenses. This
would provide low- and moderate-income families with a refundable
credit amounting to as much as $500 a year to offset eligible out-of-
pocket expenses.[55]

To pay for the tax credits, the federal excise tax on telephone service,
implemented to raise money for the Vietnam War, would be retained.
The new Senate majority leader, George Mitchell, succeeded in gaining
a floor vote, breaking opponents' delaying tactics by threatening to
hold the Senate in session when they were scheduled to adjourn for
the two-week July fourth recess. The bill passed, but the real consensus
was a commitment to avoiding a threat to vacation plans.[56]

After the vote, critics within the original child-care alliance and
opponents of institutional child-care services complained about the
bill. On the right, some thought the bill was still "blatant discrimination
against the mother who takes care of her own children." According to
William Safire, conservative syndicated columnist, Hatch, the "darling
of the New Right on school prayer and abortion," deserved credit for
using the bill to get vouchers and tuition tax credits for religious and
private centers, but the bill preserved the ABC institutional care structure and warranted a Bush veto.[57]

On the other side, the NEA and the American Jewish Committee
(AJC), both members of the ABC alliance, quickly voiced their own

objections. Edelman had continued to ignore their disapproval of using vouchers to fund care in religious child-care centers, which they saw as a breach of the wall between church and state. The NEA predictably attacked Hatch's voucher system as "a real precedent for vouchers for elementary and secondary public assistance for private and parochial education." The AJC predictably characterized the aid to religiously operated centers as "the opening round in the tuition tax credit battle . . ."[58]

The Senate had acted but in the House of Representatives, the Hawkins Education and Labor Committee held out. It passed a Hawkins bill which included many of the ABC features before the Fourth of July recess, but refused to endorse the Senate position which permitted vouchers for sectarian centers run by religious groups. The House Ways and Means Committee passed Democratic representative Thomas Downey's income tax credit proposal for the working poor in late July 1989; it was much like the Bush-Schlafly toddler tax credit. Hawkins did not oppose the credit but the Ways and Means Committee also expanded block grant funding to the states, which could be used for child-care services. This expanded funding could be substituted for a child-care bill.[59]

With little hope for a truce between the differing approaches of two House committees, national child-care legislation was held at a standoff after the Ways and Means Committee action. Congress managed, however, to express deep concern about child care without actually passing or spending anything. The difference between the House and Senate versions of child-care legislation were vast. Even if a congressional compromise was achieved, Bush had so many reservations about child care that he was likely to veto anything more than the most weak-kneed approach to the problem. Bush responded to women voters' concerns by appointing more women to administrative posts than any president before, but he remained committed to his version of child care; tax credits, not ABC. No one discussed how to implement any of the proposals under discussion or how they meshed with the child-care provisions of the welfare reform bill passed in 1988. The running battle over the child-care bill continued through the summer of 1989 as Edelman and the child-care coalition refused to give up and the relevant House committees disagreed, with each insisting on its own bill on the subject.[60]

Negotiations between Ways and Means and Education and Labor were fruitless. Downey, head of the Ways and Means subcommittee responsible for the bill, and George Miller, chairman of the Select Committee on Children, Youth, and Families and a member of Hawkins's Education and Labor Committee, informed Edelman that they were going to insist on their own proposals. None of this jockeying for position in the Congress provided help for those who needed child-care services, but the issues were serious and reflected turf fights as well as politicians' understanding of what their constituents wanted. The controversy became more heated as the House and Senate bills had to be reconciled in conference between managers of the bill from both bodies.[61]

Hawkins's bill prohibited the use of federal funds to support religious activities and religious discrimination, and the Senate bill permitted both under certain circumstances. Some people trivialized this as a concern with whether children sang "Jesus Loves Me" as part of the routine in a day-care center, but the ACLU thought it mattered very much to parents who might not want their children influenced toward any particular religion and that a law allowing such activities would violate the First Amendment. But without the church-state provision, there were not enough votes to pass a child-care bill.[62]

The drama played itself out as Downey and Miller decided to join forces with the Republicans to bypass the necessity of dealing with ABC, as well as the ban on church-run centers and the standards in the Hawkins bill. Hawkins angrily told the press that it was "unconscionable that Downey is insisting on substituting his proposals. All he has to do is to agree to both." In a last-ditch effort, Edelman brought children to the Hill to lobby House Speaker Thomas Foley, who was not there to see them. They met instead with Senate majority leader George Mitchell, who expressed support of their cause. Edelman accused Miller and Downey of "bad motives" and, in turn, Downey called her "immature" and Miller called her "hysterical."[63]

Amid the contention, the real issue was whether the Democrats would join with the Republicans in having a child-care program with fewer standards and less money while telling the public that they were doing something about child care. The likelihood that a child-care bill would be passed in the next session of Congress was enhanced by the public controversy between Edelman, Downey, and Miller. Downey and Miller would need to protect their reputations as child-care advocates. Furthermore, the Senate bill was ready for conference, awaiting House action.[64]

The entire Congress and the administration were prepared to pass a bill because it addressed everyone's concerns in some fashion. The tax credit at least acknowledged the needs of stay-at-home moms and the child-care services provisions were too stingy to motivate anyone to abandon the mother-care tradition. Increasing objections to the emphasis on child-care centers for children of employed middle-class mothers in two-parent households encouraged the tax credit Bush favored.

Magazine editors on the board of the Child Care Action Media Campaign reported receiving increasing negative mail from individuals who described themselves as mothers at home. The writers complained about articles encouraging child-care centers. The campaign's board of directors discussed the issue but could not agree on exactly how to deal with the complaints. According to Irene Natividad, chairwoman of the National Women's Political Caucus, they acknowledged, however, the need to consider publishing more about families in which the husband supported the family and the mother cared for the children.[65]

President Bush, in his 1990 State of the Union message, indicated he understood the child-care problems of women "working outside the home." He wanted government to "expand child-care alternatives for parents," but without specifications. He knew some form of a child-care bill would be passed by the Congress and was projecting his understanding that ignoring the needs of working mothers was no longer politically palatable.[66]

At the end of March 1990, the House passed its child-care bill, which essentially consisted of Downey's Ways and Means Committee's grants to the states, which could be used for child-care services, and Hawkins's provisions expanding Head Start to a full school day in places where it was part-day and giving some after-school care and classes for latchkey children at school, plus $100 million in incentive grants to businesses to set up day care and to states to upgrade quality of care. Vouchers and the earned-income tax credit were also included. This hodgepodge went to the House-Senate conference in April, where it awaited inclusion with other legislation and was passed before the end of the congressional session in the Omnibus Budget Reconciliation Act of 1990 in October.[67]

In the meantime, the House passed the Family and Medical Leave bill in May 1990. The bill, much weakened since Schroeder had first introduced it, covered businesses with fifty or more employees, granting twelve weeks of unpaid leave but with health benefits intact. The bill, as watered down, affected only 5 percent of employers and 44 percent of employees. The National Federation of Independent Business said the bill backed by "organized labor and the more radical feminist groups . . . is just the first step toward 100 percent coverage and paid leave." The favorable 237–187 vote was larger than expected, but still well short of the two-thirds majority needed to override a threatened presidential veto. After the leave bill passed in the Senate by voice vote on June 14, 1990, Bush vetoed it, as promised. The House tried and failed to override his veto on July 25, 1990.[68]

President Bush signed the child-care bill, including the block grants, tax credits, and Hawkins's before- and after-school proposals, on November 5, 1990. After all of the discussion and controversy, the child-care bill promised only the most minimal help for parents trying to balance jobs and children. In addition, the administration kept delaying implementation, projecting a start date of no earlier than sometime after September 1, 1991.[69]

As of January 1992 the federal budget included $825 million under the new child-care provision, called the Child Care and Development Block Grant, compared to the $2.5 billion appropriation requested when ABC was first introduced almost five years before. After subtracting a required 25 percent for before- and after-school developmental programs and 20 percent for administrative costs, about $494 million for child-care services would be available. At an average cost of $45 per child for fifty weeks a year, only about 220,000 additional children could be served nationwide. Recognizing the inadequacy of the funding and in order to preserve state discretion, the bill permits the states to set eligibility levels and to target certain areas or specific income groups. As of January 1, 1992, the states planned to limit eligibility to those who make less than 75 percent of the state median income, which is on the average no more than $30,000 for a family of four.[70]

According to the Department of Health and Human Services, when the program is implemented, states must establish voucher programs under which eligible parents can receive certificates to pay to the child-care provider of their choice. The church-state problem was handled in the regulations by prohibiting state grants to church-run centers that engage in religious activities. However, the state must give vouchers to parents to pay for services from the provider of their choice, which may include church centers ineligible for grants from the state. The state can impose no requirements on the religious centers except health and safety rules.

The department recommends that parents inquire at their county social services agency to see if they are eligible for the child-care programs established. The states will be required to inform the public of the eligibility rules and the availability of the funds. Child-care centers receiving funding must be licensed and non-center providers must register with the state. The only requirements that may be imposed on child-care providers are those designed to insure health and safety and the prevention and control of infectious diseases, including immunization.

The legislation acknowledged the poor salaries and wages of the mostly-female work force employed in the child-care field. States may, but are not required to, use some of the funds to improve the quality of child-care services including improving care-takers' wages, salaries, and other compensation. Each year the states must submit a report to the Department of Health and Human Services on their efforts. The department is expected to monitor the state programs.[71]

Not much new money or quality assurance was achieved for child-care services but at least a start was made. The debate over the child-care bill and parental leave, however, had a larger meaning for those who were concerned about women's rights. In the polls and in the political debate, not enough people were willing to engage in new thinking on the care-giver role.

The small amounts of money and grudging acceptance of some child-care subsidy for other than welfare mothers occurred not just because of budgets, but because of ideological concerns over gender roles and what was good for children. In addition, the Family and Medical Leave bill failed, in part, because maternity leave could gain acceptance but not leave for mothers *and* fathers. It was not only a question of business costs but the idea of men actually taking child-care leave that was hard for the public to comprehend.

Everyone agreed that mothers who had jobs needed time off to take care of children, but endorsing a change in gender roles by encouraging fathers to take equal responsibility will take more time. The deflection of the 1971-style motherhood arguments in the debate on the child-care bill and the large number of votes for parental leave showed progress, but the president and other opposing politicians will only change their thinking concerning responsibility for children when enough of their constituents do.

IX

The Next Agenda

The enactment of federal child-care legislation in 1990 and the growing number of states with parental leave laws were positive developments on the child-care front. The debate in Congress over child care and the national Family and Medical Leave legislation showed the mother-care tradition had eroded somewhat. The discussions also underscored how much work still needed to be done to create a new pattern of fathers and mothers taking equal responsibility for the care of their offspring.

While women's employment increased and the new feminine mystique grew in the 1980s, mothers who already had employer-sponsored leave and day care were increasingly discontented. The problem was discussed wherever employed mothers gathered. For example, the American Bar Association Commission on Women in the Profession reported in 1988 that 25 percent of law firm associates, the entry level job for lawyers, were women but only 6 percent of law firm partners were women. Female lawyers complained that sex discrimination was the cause of this disparity; the ABA passed additional resolutions condemning discriminatory practices. The commission detailed several reasons for the "glass ceiling": female lawyers lacked mentors; they were not given important case assignments; senior attorneys sometimes acquiesced to clients' requests not to have a woman lawyer; women were excluded from clubs and other social environments where business contacts are made; they were told they could not become partners because they were not "rainmakers," lawyers who bring in significant business. The commission complained that female lawyers were also forced to sacrifice career advancement to have children, while men did not suffer professionally from having children. [1]

Women lawyers provided graphic testimony about the "child-care problem," and the "mommy track." A growing number of firms provided all that feminist and child-care advocates had been asking for: flexible working hours, child care, and lenient parental leave. Yet women who took advantage of these "mommy" provisions often found themselves left behind when it came to partnerships, choice assignments, and stature. Nowhere in their protests, however, did they suggest that "daddy" ought to work flexible hours or share the burden of rearing their children. "In our society and in the legal world, to take parental leave is wimp-like," noted Alice E. Richmond, a partner in a major firm. "The kind of toughness that is needed to be perceived as a go-getter lawyer is more harmed if a man takes parental leave than if a woman does."[2]

These views did not exist exclusively among lawyers or among professional women. In fact, expressions of this sort could be heard whenever working women and the subject of child care were discussed. A group of young women planning a national conference on "I'm Not a Feminist But" talked of scheduling their professional work and child care and reentering and entering the work force as issues. During the extended discussion, no one even mentioned the possibility that the fathers of the children might have to juggle the same issues.[3]

The controversy that ensued, in 1989, when Felice Schwartz, the founder and president of Catalyst, a nonprofit research and advisory organization that worked with corporations to foster the career and leadership development of women, proposed a "mommy track" for employed mothers, offered hope that women might be concluding that emphasizing their responsibility for mothering was a very bad idea. In the prestigious *Harvard Business Review*, Schwartz agreed with corporate leaders who believed "the cost of employing women in management is greater than the cost of employing men." She thought that as the socialization of boys and girls and their expectations grew more alike, workplace behavior would become the same.[4]

For the immediate future, however, management needed to recognize "career primary" and "career family women." Career family women needed leave to take care of elderly parents, flexible hours, and child care. Career primary women should be treated like "everyone else," i.e., like men. In view of demographics showing an increasingly female work force and labor pool, management should know that "part-time employment is the single greatest inducement to getting women back on the job expeditiously and the provision women themselves most desire." Moreover, business should value women, who because of child-rearing stay on a plateau in the same job for years, instead of devaluing them. Schwartz insisted that studies showed the rate of turnover in management positions was two and one-half times higher for women than men. She said that one-half of all women in an anonymous consumer goods company returned to their jobs late or not at all. Schwartz concluded that women "have a greater tendency to plateau or to interrupt their careers in ways that limit their growth and development."[5]

While many employed women complained about the "career family" or "mommy track," Schwartz accepted the idea. Her position made clear that while feminists might argue for flextime, parental leave, and child care by emphasizing the need for both mothers and fathers to have these options, employers view them as help solely for employed mothers. Schwartz essentially acknowledged that "motherhood supports" did not radically transform gender roles, and could retard the more modest goal of women's upward mobility on the job.[6]

Pat Schroeder, Eleanor Smeal, Irene Natividad, and other female political leaders recognized immediately that Schwartz's prior feminist record made her argument useful for those who thought women should be defined mainly as mothers and should accept constraints on their opportunities gladly. Schroeder responded in a *New York Times* Op-Ed piece: "Of course, the business people love it because it's what they don't feel free to say, and here's a woman saying it for them." She insisted that Schwartz's article represented "casual scholarship," based on "unidentified studies at unnamed corporations about undefined turnover rates."[7]

Even if actual and correct, Schwartz did not consider or describe attributing factors such as "rigid relocation demands, better job opportunities at other corporations, or downturns in the company's fortunes," Schroeder said. She went on to note Bureau of Labor Statistics reports on high turnover rates in all types of jobs for women and men. Finally, Schroeder pointed out that numerous employers had instituted employment practices to make it possible to combine productivity and family obligations. "Employers are finding that meeting employees' needs makes companies more productive and more competitive," she said. Paraphrasing a popular saying of the women's movement, Schroeder said, "If men gave birth, paid parental leave would have been written into the Constitution by the Founding Fathers."[8]

Eleanor Smeal, president of the Fund for a Feminist Majority, told me she was outraged that the *Harvard Review* would publish an article like the Schwartz piece, making it appear that women wanted a "mommy track," without any real data. Molly Yard, president of NOW, and Irene Natividad, of the National Women's Political Caucus, each voiced similar complaints about the article and attacked the views expressed. Yard thought effort ought to be devoted to giving men the same flexibility. "It's not something that should be thought of only in terms of women." Natividad, the mother of a four-year-old boy, said her husband had been "fuming about the recent 'mommy track' discourse, which seemed to leave men like him out of the parenting picture." He took care of their son and they both thought change in the work environment that would benefit everyone was the answer.[9]

Faith Wohl, head of DuPont's Work Force Partnering Division, cited data that undermined Schwartz's views, even though DuPont's chief executive officer, Richard Heckert, was also chairman of the board of Catalyst. Their company's three-year study showed that both men and women were becoming more concerned about relocation, child care, synchronizing vacations, and other family issues. Wohl decried the notion that women, unlike men, should not have children to get ahead. "That's a choice some women may want to make, but it's not a price they should have to pay for a promotion."[10]

Sylvia Hewlett, whose 1986 book criticized the feminist movement for failing to give enough attention to reconciling the demands of the family and the workplace, distanced herself from Schwartz's views:

> There's no way we can afford a second track for anyone, given the changing demographics of who is entering the work force. I've un-covered over the last five years a lot of bottom-line reasons why we have to be supportive of parents across the board, but I resent terribly the notion that children are a women's issue.

Hewlett, just two years earlier, had demanded government-sponsored child care to substitute for mother care, without explaining the negative effects on women's employment mobility.[11]

Schwartz's defenders, however, accepted the idea of women having constrained choices. Betty Jane Frye, director of Options, a firm that helps relocating spouses find jobs, asked, "Why can't we have both kinds of people and say up front they will cost more for a while? Women haven't been willing to admit that before." Jerome M. Rosow, president of the Work in America Institute research group, insisted that Schwartz was only talking about "the reality of what's happening. It is not a question of being derailed from a career, but rather going at a slower pace. What we are seeing is an elaboration of choice." Richard Lewis, chief executive officer of Corporate Annual Reports, thought the idea could help the fast-track woman. "Of course," he joked, "there might be men who want to be on a 'daddy track,' but there is a real world to consider here. Men accept the idea that a woman might take time off to take care of a baby. At the same time, men would not understand why another man would take time off, and men know that."[12]

Schwartz tried to calm her critics, claiming she had only been discussing "a whole variety of options." Women might be put on a fast track after pregnancy, she said. Her response accentuated the nar-rowness of her analysis. As Schroeder angrily pointed out, Schwartz assumed women had certain kinds of jobs, predominantly professional and independent. She also presumed each family had a male bread-winner or that women were independently wealthy.[13]

Several of the letters to the *Harvard Business Review* in response to the Schwartz article made these same assumptions. Many focused on the increasing role of fathers in sharing parenting as a solution. In a joint letter, the ACLU, Women's Rights Project, NOW, NWPC, and other feminist organizations questioned the assumption that child care should be "primarily the province and responsibility of women." The writers also suggested "reallocating some sex-role expectations and tasks more evenly between women and men."[14]

Rosabeth Moss Kanter, a tenured professor in the Harvard Business School, who criticized Schwartz's article for its lack of "data backing up broad assertions," was named editor of the *Harvard Business Review*. Critics of the Schwartz article felt that their protests had led to Kanter's appointment, but the "mommy track" flap had a deeper significance. Smeal and WLDF president Judith Lichtman, at least, agreed that it signaled the dangers to women's employment opportunities of losing sight of the goal of individual rights in pursuit of "family policy."[15]

The Supreme Court soon reinforced the message that the work of protecting women's rights needed at least as much attention as child care. The Court, in scheduling oral argument in a Missouri abortion case on April 26, 1989, conveyed one reminder; it was clear that the right of a woman and her physician to choose abortion was in serious jeopardy, given the political composition of the Court. Reagan-appointed Justices Anthony M. Kennedy, Sandra Day O'Connor, and Antonin Scalia, along with Chief Justice William H. Rehnquist and a holdover from the Kennedy years, Byron R. White, were known generally to be anti-choice on the abortion issue.

The threat to *Roe* v. *Wade* immediately became a burning issue for the leaders of the women's rights organizations. The pro-choice cause became a coalition effort as NOW, the WLDF, the NWPC, and the National Women's Law Center dedicated time and resources to full-scale mobilization. Spearheaded by NOW, in league with Planned Parenthood, the National Abortion Rights Action League (NARAL), the Fund for a Feminist Majority, and other groups, they first organized a march to urge the Supreme Court not to overturn *Roe* v. *Wade*, which brought at least 250,000 marchers to Washington on April 9, 1989. Crowd counts varied from NOW's estimate of 600,000 to media figures of 250,000. Everyone agreed it was the largest protest march in Washington since the August 1963 march on Washington for civil rights. On April 5, 1992, another "march for women's lives" organized by NOW and other groups brought as many or more people to the capital.[16]

The 1992 march showed that the mobilization achieved in the 1989 march could be sustained during a presidential election year. The 1989 march, however, was a watershed. It included people of all ages, men (some 40 percent of the marchers) and women, movie stars such as Jane Fonda, Glenn Close and Cybill Shepherd. More significantly, however, it brought a new constituency to the cause, which appeared to grow by the 1992 march. Many participants said they had never marched for anything before. Some carried coat hangers to evoke the days of illegal abortions. Banners urged the United States Supreme Court to keep abortion "safe and legal." Placards ranged from "Nostalgic for Choice" to "Hoyas for Choice." In remembrance of the women's suffrage movement, some women wore white.

Conspicuously absent were African-American or other racial minority women and men. Leaders of the women's rights march blamed economics and pointed out that anti-abortion marches were also mostly white. Religion certainly played a role. As Donna Brazile, a board member of Voters for Choice, said: "There's a lot of anti-abortion fervor in the black community because of the ministers. If the minister says, 'This is genocide, this is sterilization,' you're not going to get the choir girls out of the loft." Fundamentally, however, despite the presence of Faye Wattleton as head of Planned Parenthood, the women's rights organizations and the anti-abortion groups had few African-American, Latino, or Asian-American members. The organizations had been started by middle-class white women and men and mostly stayed that way.[17]

The most vocal movement leaders understood the mobilization effect of the 1989 march. Some saw choice as a way of reenergizing younger women who had benefited from the struggle for women's rights, but had not been actively supporting the cause. Many young women at the march agreed with Natividad, the first woman of color to head the NWPC, who thought this could be "the catalytic, politicizing issue for the 'Me Generation.' " One young student marcher, an anti-apartheid activist, said she had never been much interested in feminism before, but "now I understand the connection between assaulting women's individual rights and other human-rights concerns." While Natividad found it "frustrating" to be still working on the abortion issue, if it brought younger women aboard the women's movement, "I would say that's a bigger plus, frankly." Gloria Steinem partly disagreed. Not only was working on abortion after fifteen years not an "invigorating" experience, the movement, she contended, had always drawn its power from older women. Younger women had to experience life's unequal choices and "women have always been the only group that grows more radical with age."[18]

Even before deciding the abortion case, the Supreme Court delivered a major assault on rights in mid-June 1989 in interpreting Title VII of the Civil Rights Act of 1964, which prohibits sex and race discrimination in employment. Justices Kennedy, O'Connor, Scalia, Rehnquist, and White gutted remedies for discrimination against women on the job. The Court effectively reversed eighteen years of case law by holding that an employer never has the burden of proving the necessity of a practice in the workplace that excludes and discriminates against minorities or on the basis of sex.[19]

The Court, in another 5–4 decision, permitted white male Birmingham firefighters to challenge promotions of qualified blacks that were made as a result of a consent decree designed to end litigation over the effects of race discrimination in that city. The city had used an affirmative action plan to hire and later to promote blacks to remedy longtime prohibitions against blacks applying for jobs in the fire department. The white firefighters did not file a motion to intervene until after the consent decree was entered, ending the original lawsuit, and the promotions and hirings had already been made. The Court decision meant that the blacks who had acquired jobs would be demoted or fired.[20]

Any suggestion of fairness on the part of the Court was controverted by a decision the same day which threw out a sex discrimination complaint on the grounds that it was filed too late. Three women employees at AT&T Technologies challenged a seniority system in which the rules were changed to protect incumbent males in a job category when the women became eligible for the positions. In an opinion written by Justice Scalia, the Court said Title VII requirements that a complaint was lost unless filed within three hundred days meant they should have sued within three hundred days of the rule change and not within three hundred days of the time it affected them.[21]

In another Title VII case, the Court upheld the right of a woman to be promoted to partner at the accounting firm of Price Waterhouse. The woman, a senior manager at the firm, was not promoted to partner in 1983 even though she brought in more business than any of the other partnership candidates. Her peer review evaluations contained mixed reviews. Some praised her for "outstanding performance" while others criticized her "macho" and "abrasive" manner. Justices White and O'Connor concurred with Blackmun, Marshall, and Stevens in the personal victory for the plaintiff. The announced rule, however, would permit discrimination to be a motivating factor if the employer could prove by a preponderance of the evidence that it would have made the same decision absent the discrimination. Price Waterhouse lost because they could not prove they would have made the same decision if there had been no discriminatory motive.[22]

Finally, the Court rejected an African-American woman's complaint of harassment in the terms and conditions of her employment at a credit union. She was the target of racial epithets and given unusual cleaning duties which no white employee was required to perform. The Court rejected her complaint because the harassment occurred while she was on the job and not while she was making a contract to be hired. The 1866 Civil Rights Act under which she sued permitted the recovery of money damages for illegal discrimination in the making of contracts including employment contracts. Her problems, according to the Court, fell under private contract law in each state and Title VII of the Civil Rights Act of 1964. The Court announced this even though Title VII does not cover employers with less than fifteen employees and such employers hire nearly 50 percent of the nation's work force, including large percentages of women.[23]

Justice Thurgood Marshall summed up the Court's rulings as difficult to characterize "as a product of anything other than a retrenching of the civil rights agenda." Marshall said the civil rights movement should work to strengthen state laws. In his opinion he wrote:

> Most importantly, there is the Congress. With the mere passage of corrective legislation, Congress can in an instant regain the ground which was lost last term in the realm of statutory civil rights. And by prevailing upon Congress to do so, we can send a message to the Court that the hyper-technical language games played by the Court . . . in its interpretations of civil rights enactments are simply not accurate ways to read Congress's broad intent in the civil rights area.[24]

Immediately after the employment discrimination decisions, the Leadership Conference on Civil Rights, a coordinating lobby representing civil rights groups, organized a series of meetings for the civil rights and liberties groups to decide on new congressional legislative proposals. Women's groups, WLDF, NOW, and the National Women's Law Center, as well as the women's rights project of the ACLU participated along with the NAACP Legal Defense Fund, the NAACP, and the Lawyer's Committee on Civil Rights. Everyone knew the task would be difficult despite the fact that key members of Congress, including Senators Howard Metzenbaum, Democrat of Ohio, Edward Kennedy, and Congressman Hawkins quickly announced their desire to introduce remedial legislation. The problem was how to draft legislation that would remedy the whole array of problems in the decisions and that would forestall as many problems as possible in the future.[25]

If there were any doubters left in the leadership of the women's organizations about the need for pouring their resources into the individual rights cause, the Supreme Court's July 3, 1989, abortion decision was convincing. The Court, on the last day of the term, issued a 5–4 decision in *Webster* v. *Reproductive Health Services* that narrowed sharply *Roe* v. *Wade*. In a Rehnquist opinion joined by Justices Kennedy, O'Connor, Scalia, and White, the Court approved a state's right to impose sharp new distinctions on the right to choose abortion and denied abortion choice the status of a fundamental constitutional right.[26]

The Court upheld three provisions in a Missouri law which barred public employees from performing or assisting in abortions not necessary to save a pregnant woman's life; the use of public hospitals, clinics, and any other public building from being used to perform abortions, even if no public funds were involved; and required doctors who believed a woman requesting an abortion might be at least twenty weeks pregnant to perform tests to determine whether the fetus was viable. Truman Medical Center in Kansas City performed nearly all the hospital abortions conducted in Missouri. It was a private hospital, but because it was built on land leased from the state, it fell within the statute's definition of a "public facility." Essentially abortion was still legal, but states were given a green light to confine and restrict it without fearing court reversals.[27]

The Court majority did not expressly overrule *Roe* v. *Wade*, only because O'Connor and Rehnquist insisted that the Court could take an anti-abortion stance without doing so. Rehnquist, who wrote the majority opinion, and White had both dissented in *Roe* v. *Wade*, which had been decided by a 7–2 vote. O'Connor and Rehnquist simply thought the Missouri case could be decided without overruling *Roe* v. *Wade*. Rehnquist said he did not see why "the states' interest in protecting potential human life should come into existence only at the point of viability," as *Roe* v. *Wade* announced, but *Missouri* did not seek to limit abortions before viability, so the case did not need to go that far. O'Connor continued to view *Roe* v. *Wade's* approach as "problematic" but she too thought this case did not require an overruling and that there would be "time enough to re-examine *Roe* and to do so carefully."[28]

Scalia, who like Kennedy was exercising his first vote on abortion, was irritated because O'Connor and Rehnquist would not overrule in this case. He wanted the Court to "go beyond the most stingy possible holding today." Otherwise, he thought, they who were appointed and given life tenure to insulate them from the popular will would be subjected to more mail and demonstrators on the issue outside the Court building. Scalia's views assumed that the public did not realize that court decisions are political as well as a matter of interpreting law.[29]

Predictably, women's rights advocates expressed deep disappointment as the anti-abortion leaders expressed joy at the decision. President Bush made no public comment, but his chief of staff, John Sununu, read a statement welcoming the decision and asking that *Roe v. Wade* be completely reversed. Accepting the Court's opening for state restrictions, Randall Terry, head of Operation Rescue, an anti-abortion group, predicted "an avalanche of new legislation." Kate Michaelman of NARAL thought the decision would heighten fear among pro-choice advocates and cause them to become better organized since they could not rely on the courts. Both sides prepared to do battle in the states.[30]

Essentially, those who favored the cause of elevating the legal, social, and economic status of women faced on July 5, 1989, a three-front war. The anti-abortion activists only had to fight for their issue. The anti-child-care and parental-leave forces had "family" to defend; the child-care lobbyists led by CDF had their goal well targeted and civil rights groups could focus on the discrimination cases. The women's rights advocates, however, had to organize state-by-state pro-choice campaigns and also had to fight for congressional legislation to reverse the Supreme Court's employment discrimination decisions *and* for parental-leave and child-care legislation.

One effect of *Webster*, which could benefit the movement in the long run, was that the Court decision required the kind of grassroots organizing that was not done well enough in the ERA fight. There was some time. NOW, NWPC, Planned Parenthood, and NARAL quickly organized for the state-by-state campaigns that would be necessary. In much of the country, the legislative battles would not begin until January 1990, because most state legislatures had already adjourned. Eleven state legislatures were still in session, but several were restricted to budget-related issues. In January, forty-four legislatures would convene for regular sessions; the other six met biennially and would not meet again until 1991. Of all the state legislatures still in session or about to be called for special sessions, only Florida's indicated an intention of dealing with the subject.[31]

A nationwide Gallup poll, reported on July 11, 1989, found that 55 percent of people nationwide opposed the *Webster* decision. In the polls, men and women generally expressed similar views but, significantly, a larger proportion of women than men indicated that their voting decisions in the future would be more influenced by a candidate's position on abortion.[32]

Pro-choice voters played a major role in victories by Douglas Wilder in the Virginia gubernatorial race, James Florio in the New Jersey gubernatorial race, and in David Dinkins's victory in the New York City mayoral race. The same results were reported in any number of local races, including that of a San Diego councilwoman who was denied the sacrament of Communion by her bishop for her pro-choice position. Governor Bob Martinez of Florida confidently called a special session of the Florida legislature right after the *Webster* decision for the express purpose of adding more restrictions to what was already one of the most restrictive state abortion laws. He was roundly defeated in the legislature, as local NARAL and NOW supporters organized the opposition.[33]

In Michigan a tough anti-abortion parental consent statute passed in both houses but not by enough votes to override a veto by pro-choice Governor James Blanchard. But anti-choice forces in Pennsylvania achieved a major victory. A strong restrictive law was passed that even required a married woman to obtain written consent from her husband before she could have an abortion. Although spousal consent was later overturned by an appeals court, Governor Bob Casey of Pennsylvania, a Democrat, was anti-choice and supported the legislation. Observing the strength of the pro-choice coalitions in other elections, however, state Republicans decided to run a pro-choice woman, state Auditor General Barbara Hafer, against Casey in the 1990 governor's race, but she lost.[34]

A bipartisan group of House and Senate members introduced a freedom of choice act to codify *Roe* v. *Wade;* in the House it was Congresswoman Schroeder, Republican William Green of New York, California Democrats Don Edwards and Barbara Boxer, Oregon Democrat Les AuCoin, and, in the Senate, Mikulski, Metzenbaum, California Democrat Alan Cranston, and Oregon Republican Robert

Packwood. They quickly gathered at least one hundred House and twenty-two Senate cosponsors. In addition to the legislation, the women's groups organized successful nationwide rallies on November 12, beginning at dawn in Kennebunkport, Maine, and ending at nightfall in San Francisco.[35]

Many women seemed not to connect the Supreme Court employment discrimination and abortion decisions to their disinterest in promoting women's rights. In December 1989, *Time* magazine published a cover story summarizing the angst of women who had nothing favorable to say about feminists but who wanted the fruits of the feminist movement. Only 33 percent of the women it polled wanted to be called feminists, but 62 percent thought feminists had been helpful to women and only 18 percent thought they had been harmful.[36]

Some polls, however, indicated that an overwhelming percentage of women thought there was still a need for a strong women's movement. Gloria Steinem's view that women became more radical as they got older was confirmed in a *New York Times* poll that showed most women believed "despite their gains, it is still a man's world," with sharp age and race differences in patterns of response. Women ages eighteen to twenty-nine, "those least likely to have faced all the concerns of marriage, child care and the work force," had the fewest complaints. Those aged thirty to forty-four, an age that included marriage, work, and children, and who were the first generation raised to expect to balance these concerns, were the most "confused and frustrated." Only 43 percent of black women felt any improvement in men's attitudes, compared with 61 percent of white women, and nearly 25 percent of black women felt men's attitudes had actually gotten worse, compared with only 15 percent of white women who felt that way.[37]

By the next year, the situation was not as clear as it had seemed in 1989. In the 1990 elections, abortion seemed overshadowed by the federal budget crisis and the move toward war in the Persian Gulf. In the governors' races, pro-choicers lost key elections. Robert Casey defeated Barbara Hafer in Pennsylvania, James Blanchard of Michigan lost, and George Voinovich, former mayor of Cleveland, won in Ohio. However, there were major pro-choice victories. Lawton Chiles defeated Bob Martinez in Florida and Ann Richards won in Texas. Idaho governor Cecil Andrus, who vetoed a restrictive abortion bill in 1989, easily won reelection, and a number of anti-abortion state legislative candidates were defeated. In the Congress, abortion rights supporters gained eight seats in the House and two in the Senate. New fights over abortion legislation would certainly ensue in state legislatures and more court challenges were expected.[38]

Pro-choice activists at the grassroots level still seemed not to understand that the threat to abortion rights was connected to the erosion of other rights and to the debate in Congress over parental leave and child care. They did not understand the negative effects of the family and mothering emphasis, which resulted in a watered-down child-care bill with minimal funding for nonparental child-care services and in the vetos of the parental leave legislation and the omnibus civil rights bill to overturn the destructive employment discrimination decisions by the Supreme Court. In both cases, Congress failed to override the president's veto. *The New York Times* did not get the point, either. The newspaper of record missed the feminist goal of making the leave bill parental so that either men or women might take it. They thought President Bush's view that leave ought to be negotiated between workers and employers, was "a good point" because the "percentage of women receiving maternity leave" had increased enormously.[39]

The protest of about 150 Wellesley students in April 1990 at the announcement that Barbara Bush would speak at their commencement showed their understanding of the assault on women's opportunities. They thought that she too faithfully represented traditional gender roles and that her husband had a poor record in support of women's rights, parental leave, child care, and other concerns. The reaction to their protest was disappointing. Instead of discussing the reality of transformations underway and encouraging them, a concerted defense of traditional roles ensued. First, the school announced that Raisa Gorbachev, an educated woman in her own right, would come. This made the protesters somewhat happier, but the news media discussions mainly focused on motherhood and the validity of a life-style for mothers that put family first. They entirely missed the point the protesting students had made connecting the emphasis on mothering with the erosion of women's rights. As one of the students said on "The MacNeil/

Lehrer NewsHour" public television show on the subject, it showed what hard times the women's movement had fallen on that people could discuss women's rights issues only tangentially while discussing Barbara Bush. She noted the absence of television talk shows highlighting the connections between the Supreme Court decisions and the employment and child-care burdens women faced and the perpetuation of gender roles.[40]

By the end of 1991, there was still no national parental leave bill. The Congress passed the legislation again in November. President Bush vetoed it again and there were still not enough votes to override his veto. In the meantime, a few more states enacted laws requiring businesses to grant unpaid leave. By the end of 1991, eleven states had such laws.[41]

The legislation to overturn the Supreme Court's 1989 employment discrimination reversals had been vetoed and was back in the Congress, where it faced an erosion of support because of race baiting and opposition to paying damages to women who suffered sexual harassment on the job.

The angry reaction of many women to the treatment of Professor Anita Hill when she testified that Supreme Court nominee Clarence Thomas sexually harassed her when she worked for him at the Equal Employment Opportunity Commission inspired action on the stalled civil rights employment discrimination legislation before the Congress. Opposition to former Klansman David Duke's campaign for governor of Louisiana generated additional support for the legislation. Congress accepted the business community's insistence on a cap on the amount that could be recovered in sex discrimination cases. President Bush stopped calling the proposal a quota bill and it was passed by overwhelming Congressional majorities and signed into law on November 21, 1991.[42]

The 1992 March For Women's Lives was designed to advance a strong pro-choice position in the November elections. NOW, the Fund for a Feminist Majority, NARAL, and other organizations hoped to elect pro-choice candidates in state and local races as well as to the Congress; the announcement that the Supreme Court would decide the constitutionality of Pennsylvania's restrictive abortion law fueled their concern. They also hoped to defeat President Bush, who, in a three-man race with Arkansas Governor Bill Clinton and wealthy business-man H. Ross Perot, was the only anti-abortion candidate. Bush's anti-choice position, his opposition to parental leave and the civil rights legislation they supported, as well as his Supreme Court nomination of Clarence Thomas, made him anathema to women's rights proponents.[43]

The Pennsylvania abortion law in question required notification of the husband before an abortion could be performed, parental consent for minors, a twenty-four-hour waiting period, and an explanation by the doctor of alternatives to abortion. The American Civil Liberties Union and Planned Parenthood challenged the state law. They also joined the state in asking for a fast review in the case. Both sides hoped to use a decision in a presidential election year to garner support on one side of the issue or the other. Bush appointees Justices David H. Souter and Clarence Thomas were expected to be deciding votes. Justices Harry Blackmun and John Paul Stevens remained as the justices who publicly favored upholding *Roe* v. *Wade*.[44]

Dianne Feinstein, who along with Barbara Boxer won the Democratic primary in the California U.S. Senate elections, told the 1992 marchers: "I hope today begins a series of marches . . . throughout the United States to support abortion-rights candidates." NOW president Patricia Ireland pointed out that the organization for the march provided the group "with the mechanisms in place to get out the vote." She wanted more women to run for office in the confidence that committed women would work for them, and hoped for women candidates "who we can believe in with all of our hearts." She got her wish. An unprecedented number of women ran for office, including senatorial primary winners Carol Moseley Braun in Illinois and Lynn Yeakel in Pennsylvania.[45]

The struggle to maintain abortion rights became even more complex after the Supreme Court announced the decision in the Pennsylvania case on June 29, 1992, the next to last day of the term. Kennedy retreated from his 1989 position in *Webster* that he would overrule *Roe* v. *Wade* but not in order to take a pro-choice position. O'Connor forged a new majority based on a joint opinion with Kennedy and Souter, which deftly upheld the Pennsylvania restrictions, except for the requirement to notify the husband before an abortion could be performed.[46]

The O'Connor joint opinion affirmed *Roe* v. *Wade* while overruling its central premise that a woman and her physician alone could make the abortion decision in the first trimester. The decision permitted state regulation even in the earliest months of pregnancy, so long as any regulation was not an unspecified "undue burden." Blackmun and Stevens complained about the abandonment of the trimester principle, which had preserved the woman's unfettered right to choose along with her physician in the first three months of pregnancy. Having no other alternative, however, they concurred in O'Connor's joint opinion to constitute a five-person majority. Thomas, in his first abortion decision, joined in the vitriolic anti-choice position of dissenters Rehnquist, Scalia, and White.[47]

The Court decision underscored the importance of the presidential contest between Bush and Clinton to the future of the abortion issue. Blackmun noted, "I am 83 years old, I cannot remain on this court forever, and when I do step down, the confirmation process for my successor well may focus on the issue before us today."[48]

Kate Michaelman, head of NARAL, denounced "George Bush's court" for leaving "*Roe* v. *Wade* an empty shell that is one Justice Thomas away from being destroyed." The anti-choice groups had won a victory, which they chose to characterize as a defeat, for mobilization purposes. Wanda Franz, president of the National Right to Life Committee, took advantage of the fact that O'Connor's opinion produced press headlines that *Roe* v. *Wade* was affirmed. Describing the decision as a loss for her side, she insisted: "The fact that abortion advocates are not satisfied even with a reaffirmation of *Roe* shows their extremism."[49]

The battle would continue in the states over the imposition of regulations, in cases attacking specific state regulations as an undue burden, and in continuing efforts to gain congressional approval of the Freedom of Choice legislation, which would codify *Roe* v. *Wade*. But the announcement that the court had affirmed abortion rights would make passing the legislation harder. In addition, even if legislation were passed, a hostile Supreme Court could declare it an unconstitutional invasion of a state's right to regulate.[50]

In practical terms, as before *Roe* v. *Wade*, affluent women could obtain an abortion in their home state or by traveling out of state. The fate of poor women would depend on where they lived, whether they could find someone who would perform an abortion, and whether they could afford the operation in states where it was permitted but more closely regulated and therefore more expensive. Many women who sought an abortion would be assailed with counseling designed to persuade them to abandon their choice, with printed materials describing the "unborn child." The Court's decision represented the latest line in a series of assaults on the concept of women's rights. Women's sex discrimination claims had long been given weak legal protection in the courts. A cap on damages for sex discrimination in employment had to be accepted in order to obtain passage of the 1991 Civil Rights Act. What had been a fundamental right to choose abortion in the first trimester, only to be restricted for the most compelling reasons, had disappeared.[51]

The majority justices in the Pennsylvania case noted that the "ability of women to participate equally in the economic and social life of the nation" has been facilitated "by their ability to control their reproductive lives." Only two justices, Blackmun and Stevens, however, rejected the notion that the state's interest in potential life means that a woman's right to choose must be constrained at every stage of pregnancy. The O'Connor joint opinion concluded that a state may "enact persuasive measures which favor childbirth over abortion, even if those measures did not further a health interest." A majority of the justices seemed to perceive women largely as mothers or potential mothers.[52]

This view of women had broad acceptance. Although only about 20 percent of mothers were full-time homemakers in 1992, the emphasis on family and women as mothers remained as firmly ensconced as ever even among women who were busy balancing jobs and children. It permeated not only the Supreme Court opinion but the presidential political campaigns. Republicans spoke of preserving family values and Democrats agreed. They disagreed, however, about how to achieve the goal.[53]

The Democrats promised to "make it easier for parents to build strong families" by enacting pay equity and passing the Family and Medical Leave legislation and "ensuring quality and affordable child care opportunities for working parents . . ." The Republicans worried that "the traditional family is under assault," claimed credit for the watered-down child-care bill, and endorsed "pro-family policies: job-sharing, telecommuting, compressed work weeks, parental leave negotiated between employer and employee and flextime." The platforms represented a bipartisan consensus that some help with child care is necessary. There was no consensus, however, in favor of a redefinition of gender roles to make child care more than a mother's responsibility.[54]

Pat Schroeder told pro-choice marchers at the abortion rights rally on April 9, 1989: "You know what happened in the eighties? Ronald Reagan got elected and said 'Put down your picket signs and put on your little dress-for-success suits.' Well, a lot of people put down their picket signs and lost their rights."[55]

Among too many women society's emphasis on family and mothering and their own experience of trying to balance jobs and children seems to reinforce traditional attitudes instead of giving them greater understanding of the link between women's rights and their responsibilities. This is so, even while women complain about job stress and too many demands on their time and energy.

Middle-class women responded to the old feminine mystique discussed in Friedan's book by getting a job. Some sought personal development and the opportunity to change their lives. Among all of their difficulties, the decline in availability of servants by the 1960s made life even more depressing at home. Even the television sit-com mothers of the 1960s baked the pies and cleaned and took care of the children, more often than not without household help.

Today, some white middle-class mothers who have husbands to support them are leaving the work force because of the stress, the costs of child care, and the desire to take care of their homes and families. The polls show little interest among women in insisting that their husbands share the housework and child-care burden, or in asking their husbands to become stay-at-home dads. In other words, feminist consciousness seems to be the last thing on their minds.[56]

During the first half of 1990, participation of women aged twenty to forty-four in the labor force declined slightly from 74.5 percent to 74 percent, for the first time since 1948. Between 1990 and 1991, the numbers of employed women declined. There were 53,130,000 women employed in November 1990 and 53,049,000 in November 1991. There was also a 10 percent increase in birthrates between 1985 and 1990. Furthermore, large numbers of wives in 1991 *Washington Post* and *USA Today* polls said they would quit work if they did not need the money; husbands were not asked. They also believed that having a mother work caused a preschool child to suffer. Some young women say that they spend a great deal of time contemplating the comfort of a "motherhood and apple pie fantasy life."[57]

Awareness of high though stabilizing divorce rates and the necessity for work and the interest in careers displayed by some younger women means that the retreat is mostly just that—a fantasy.

If the exit of middle-class women from the work force is more than an artifact of the 1990s recession, remedying the child-care and job discrimination problems for employed women who do not have that choice will become a low-priority public concern. Poor, divorced women, most African-American women, and large numbers of women from other racial minority groups have always had to balance jobs and children. The passage of a child-care bill with even minimal services came about because of white middle-class women and not because of poor women's needs.

The parents introduced in the beginning of this book have a large stake in the resolution of child-care issues. Law firm attorneys Connie and David Chandler, and Vernon Johnson and Penny Davis who work at the state transportation department are also affected differentially by the passage of the child-care bill, the failure of parental leave, and public opinion concering child care and women's rights.[58]

Connie and David remain eligible for the long-standing child-care income tax credit but are not likely to benefit from the 1990 child-care legislation. Their employer might establish a day-care center under the tax credit provisions and charge less than the for-profit center Connie already uses. The states might choose to raise standards, which would insure better quality care by requiring more care-givers per child, but this is up to the states and there are no federal standards.

Connie and David's income either singly or together is too high for any assistance or for the new tax credits. Penny and Vernon have low enough incomes to probably be eligible for all of the new tax credits, which, taken together, would within five years be worth about $3,000 additional income each year. Vernon could ask for child-care assistance in the form of a voucher in order to help with payment to his neighbor. Penny could ask for a voucher or direct payments to the child-care center at work. The amounts they would receive, however, would depend on how much the state allocated for this purpose from the limited amounts available.

One way to look at solutions is to say that what Penny needs besides more income is to have her children's father help with their care. Upon divorce a court decree should require not just child-support payments, but burden sharing or shifting to take care of the children in order to impress upon the parties the seriousness of their obligations. Neither fathers nor mothers should be able to simply walk away without some pressure being brought to bear. They could either have shared custody or the parent who does not have custody could pay an additional amount for nonparental care. The parent without custody should also be required to help with other chores that drain custodial parents of time and energy, such as baby-sitting, transportation to doctors' appointments and other child-care services or to school. These arrangements will be difficult to implement but they are important ways of beginning to change the thinking of parents. Monetary responsibilities could be enforced in the same way as other child-support orders, by garnishment if necessary.

When parents have never been married to each other, custodial fathers or mothers should be able to have the same sort of legally sanctioned burden-sharing arrangements. Fathers or mothers who do not possess financial resources may have time that can be used to help in caring for their offspring.

Connie's and David's income and status should make them good candidates for deciding to shift work and child-care responsibilities, if they can agree that David should adjust his aspirations. They could take turns caring for the children and being employed full-time or could each become part-timers. That way they would both share equally the opportunity for upward mobility on the job, any negative fallout, and the responsibility for their two children.

If they do not adjust their roles, then, under the circumstances, Connie is a prime candidate to become a stay-at-home mom. If she stays married and returns to the work force after the children are older, she will be far down the professional ladder. If she and David divorce after she has left the work force, the economic effects on their family could be devastating.

More public financing and better standards for child care and paid parental leaves would help Vernon and Penny and people like them. One could ask, however, why taxpayers should pay for parents to have time off unless those who are not parents are also given the same benefit. Most public policy decisions in the domestic arena are made because there is a large constituency for them. There is not yet a strong enough constituency for these policies because there is deep ambivalence and well-entrenched attitudes about gender roles and the care of children.

If we were not ambivalent about paying for nonparental child-care services, we would find the money in the budget to pay for the costs just as we pay for military hardware and other items essential for defense or for the general welfare or for protecting the environment.

If we wanted to abandon the idea of mothers at home responsible for children and fathers away at work, we would faster change the workplace environment and the way we manage tasks. We would also pay child-care workers more, and elevate the occupational status so that men and women would be equally likely to take the jobs.

Therefore, changes in attitudes toward gender roles and the responsibility for child care are preconditions for the kind of change that should occur. We could begin with parenting and child-care courses in middle school. Both boys and girls need to learn how to care effectively for children and that child care is mother's and father's responsibility. Boys especially need to learn that caring for a baby does not undermine masculinity.

Women in the pro-family coalition like Beverly La Haye and Phyllis Schlafly resist change. They seem to like the celebration of motherhood and the belief that husbands and children love mothers for their sacrifices.

Much of the public still thinks of women who work out of necessity as unfortunate and women at home as the paradigm. Tax policy and other policies generally reflect this rule because the pro-family coalition promotes these illusions and many other people feel insecure about changing gender roles. A majority of the Democrats in Congress are willing to pass child-care and parental leave legislation although they are careful not to alienate those who endorse the traditional family illusion. Republican presidents respond by insisting on weakening the legislation or vetoing it because they are responding to their important constituency, the pro-family groups.

Men and women need to take to heart the evidence from child-development experts, the lessons of history, and their own common sense. Children can be and have been taken care of successfully by fathers, mothers, and others throughout history. Using nonrelative care-givers who have been screened carefully to make sure they are responsible is no reason to feel guilty. Acculturation and myth interfere with absorbing this fact.

We need to insist on fathers and mothers sharing the care of their offspring as well as the opportunity to enjoy the fulfillment of individual rights. Whatever else we do, we must understand that advocating women's rights and greater opportunity for women in the workplace and in every avenue of public life is inconsistent with an insistence on mother taking care of children and housework. To demand mother care and women's employment while professing a dedication to equality of rights for women is not only illogical but wishful thinking. Without such understanding, the conflicts that arise from the belief that women must handle both job and child care effectively to be considered successful will continue. Defining child care primarily as women's sphere reinforces the devaluing of women and prevents their equal access to power. Until these concepts are generally accepted, those who seek to advance the cause of women's rights will remain embattled.

Notes

INTRODUCTION

The Problem

1. Alan Flippen, "3 States Proceed with Measures on Family Leave," *Washington Post*, December 31, 1991, p. A4; California, Oregon and Hawaii laws became effective on January 1, 1992; Cathy Trost, "Survey Fortifies Parental Leave Backers," *Wall Street Journal*, August 9, 1990, p. B1.
2. Mary Beth Norton et al., *A People and a Nation: A History of the United States* (Boston: Houghton Mifflin, 1990), p. 987.
3. Phyllis Schlafly, *The Power of the Positive Woman* (New Rochelle, N.Y.: Arlington House Publishers, 1977), pp. 139–40; Barbara Ehrenreich, *The Hearts of Men: American Dreams and the Flight from Commitment* (Garden City, N.Y.: Anchor Press/Doubleday, 1983), pp. 50–51, 120.
4. Norton et al., *A People and a Nation*, p. 990.
5. Betty Friedan, *The Feminine Mystique* (New York: W. W. Norton, 1963).
6. U.S. Department of Labor, *Working Women: A Chartbook*, August 1991, Bulletin 2385; telephone conversation with Tom Nardone, Labor Force Statistics staff—Bureau of Labor Statistics, Department of Labor, December 31, 1991.
7. U.S. Department of Labor, *Working Women: A Chartbook*, August 1991, Bulletin 2385.

8. Labor force participation data from Tom Nardone, Labor Force Statistics—Bureau of Labor Statistics, Department of Labor: December 31, 1991.

9. Bureau of Labor Statistics, Department of Labor: December 31, 1991; Deborah Fallows, *A Mother's Work* (Boston: Houghton Mifflin, 1985); also note the story of Carol Bauer, wife of Reagan's Family Policy assistant in Susan Faludi, *Backlash: The Undeclared War Against American Women* (New York: Crown Publishers, 1991), pp. 263–67.

10. U.S. Census Bureau, "Who's Minding the Kids"; Brooke A. Masters, "U.S. Finds Child-Care Bills Hit Poor Women Hardest," *Washington Post*, July 27, 1989, p. A1, report issued July 26, 1989. Since there were 52 million children, this meant that about 22 million children had stay-at-home mothers, nine million under the age of five and the remainder between the ages of five and fourteen. When working and nonworking mothers were considered, less than one child in five was in custodial care. The Census Bureau surveyed 1650 working mothers nationwide between September and November 1986. The next day the *Post* published a correction saying they should have made clear that child care is a family expense, not just a woman's expense, July 28, 1989, p. A3; the latest published data is from the 1986 survey. The 1988 survey was still in data tapes January 1992. The 1988 survey showed only a slight increase over the numbers and percentages reported in 1989 from the 1986 data. Conversation with Martin O'Connell, Population Fertility Branch, U.S. Census Bureau, December 31, 1991.

11. U.S. Census Bureau, "Who's Minding the Kids"; conversation with Martin O'Connell, Population Fertility Branch, U.S. Census Bureau, December 31, 1991.

12. National Commission on Working Women, Women and Work Fact Sheet, Bureau of Labor Statistics; Kevin D. Thompson, "The Executive Parent Survival Guide," *Black Enterprise*, May 1991, pp. 41–50, 44.

13. Deborah Rankin, "The Tough New Cutbacks in Child Care," *New York Times*, December 18, 1988, p. F9; Tamar Lewin, "Tax Law Shift May Affect How the Baby Sitter Is Paid," *New York Times*, October 11, 1989, p. A14.

14. Lewin, "Tax Law Shift May Affect How the Baby Sitter Is Paid," p. A14.

15. Sara Rimer, "Child Care at Home: Two Women, Complex Roles," *New York Times*, December 26, 1988, p. A1; N. R. Kleinfield, "Inviting Danger In," *New York Times*, December 9, 1991, p. B1.

16. Rimer, "Child Care at Home," p. A1.

17. Ibid.

18. Ibid.

19. Ibid.; Kleinfield, "Inviting Danger In," p. B1; Barbara Katz Rothman, *Recreating Motherhood Ideology and Technology in a Patriarchal Society* (New

York: W. W. Norton, 1989), pp. 198–208, proposes that care-givers should have some rights to visit or continue to be connected to children they nurture. The assumption is that these nannies regard their function as more than a job.

20. Tamar Lewin, "Small Tots Big Biz," *New York Times Magazine*, January 29, 1989, pp. 30–31, 89–92; Customer Service, Kinder Care by Phone, January 9, 1991.

21. Kirsten O. Lundberg, "What's New in Day Care: A Tool to Keep Women in the Work Force," *New York Times*, February 26, 1989, p. A13.

22. Hal Morgan and Kerry Tucker, *Companies That Care: The Most Family Friendly Companies in America—What They Offer and How They Got That Way* (New York: Simon and Schuster/Fireside, 1991); most of the companies have well over 500 employees, pp. 336–38.

23. Conversation with Arlene Johnson, Work and Family Information Center Conference Board, April 1991.

24. Lundberg, "What's New in Day Care," p. A13; Janet Guyon, "Inequality in Granting Child-Care Benefits Makes Workers Seethe," *Wall Street Journal*, October 23, 1991, p. A1.

25. Conversation with Arlene Johnson.

26. Frank Swoboda, "IBM's Bold New Leave Policy Has Its Benefits," Washington Business, *Washington Post*, December 19, 1988, p. A1; Frank Swoboda, "IBM Sets Flexible Work Rules to Ease Home, Office Strains," *Washington Post*, October 19, 1988, p. A1.

27. Ibid.

28. Ibid.

29. Ibid.

30. Conversation with Joan Wallach, Link Resources Corporation, April 1991, and fax; a 1985 federal government study based on a survey of 55,800 households estimated one million people worked at home on their main job eight hours a week, more than three-fourths were farmers; the Link Resources surveys were done in 1988 and 1990.

31. Liz Spayd, "Increasingly in Area, Home Is Where the Workplace Is," *Washington Post*, April 22, 1991, p. A1.

32. Terri Shaw, "Ending the Commute; Transforming Today's Home Offices" and "Home Is Where the Office Is," *Washington Post*, July 6, 1989, p. A16; Kathleen Christensen, *Women and Home-Based Work: The Unspoken Contract* (New York: Holt, 1988); Spayd, "Increasingly in Area, Home Is Where the Workplace Is," p. A1. The women homework survey was done in 1985.

33. Lundberg, "What's New in Day Care," p. A13; Policy Analysis for California

Education, *Conditions of Children in California* (School of Education, University of California, Berkeley, California, 1989), pp. 92–94.

34. Phillip Gold, "Bringing Child Care to Work Breaks Home-Office Barriers," *Insight*, March 13, 1989, pp. 40–41.

35. Ibid.; conversation with Ali, February 1992.

36. See note 35 above.

37. Lena Williams, "Child Care at Job Site Easing Fears," *New York Times*, March 16, 1989, p. C1. Report on a two-day visit to the center.

38. Ibid.

39. Ibid.

40. Stride Rite, Information Office, April 18, 1991; Tamar Lewin, "Aging Parents: Women's Burden Grows," *New York Times*, November 14, 1989, p. A1; Cindy Skrzycki, "Family Concerns Spark Changes at Work," *Washington Post*, September 3, 1989, p. B4; Cindy Skrzycki, "Family Blessings, Burdens," *Washington Post*, December 24, 1989, p. H1.

41. Peter T. Kilborn, "When Work Means Bring the Kids," *New York Times*, October 5, 1989, p. A22; Harriet Presser, "Shift Work and Child Care Among Young Dual Earner American Parents," *Journal of Marriage and the Family* 50 (1988), pp. 133–48.

42. Barbara Marsh, "Business Offers Parents Help Caring for Kids," *Wall Street Journal*, September 5, 1991, p. B1.

43. Morgan and Tucker, *Companies That Care*, p. 24; child-care workers at about $183 a week make less money than parking lot attendants ($240), bartenders ($239), hairdressers ($230), gas station attendants ($225), cashiers ($202), Bureau of Labor Statistics, 1990.

44. Sue Shellenbarger, "Companies Team Up to Improve Quality of Their Employees' Child Care Choices," *Wall Street Journal*, October 17, 1991, p. B1; Vance Stanton, "A Celebration of Child Care: Stride Rite Center Marks 20th Year," *Boston Globe*, June 30, 1991, p. 26.

45. Shellenbarger, "Companies Team Up."

46. Elizabeth Pleck, *Domestic Tyranny: The Making of Social Policy Against Family Violence from Colonial Times to the Present* (New York: Oxford University Press, 1987), pp. 175–81; 196–200.

47. Kleinfield, "Inviting Danger In," p. B1; Lisa W. Foderaro, "Nanny Pleads Not Guilty in Death of Baby," *New York Times*, January 17, 1992, p. B5; William Glaberson, "Swiss Au Pair Found Not Guilty of Fire That Killed Baby," *New York Times*, July 8, 1992, p. A1.

48. Bernard Weintraub, "Say Hello to the Nanny From Hell," *New York Times*, January 5, 1992, p. H13; Rita Kempley, " 'Cradle': and Down Will Come Baby," *Washington Post*, January 10, 1992, p. D1.

49. Walter Goodman, "Cameras at Day-Care Centers," *New York Times*, June 20, 1991, p. C18.
50. Karen S. Peterson, "Stay Calm: Most Day Care Is No Nightmare," *USA Today*, June 21, 1991, p. 1D.
51. Ibid.
52. David Mills, "Oprah: Children's Crusader," *Washington Post*, November 13, 1991, p. B1.
53. Letter to editor from Barbara Shroyer Roman of Fairhope, Ala., *New York Times Magazine*, February 19, 1989, p. 12; Paul Gaston, *Women of Fair Hope* (Athens: University of Georgia Press, 1984), pp. 54–55; 77–85; Sandra Evans, "Mothers Making Themselves More at Home: Many Women Forgo Return to Working World Despite Pressures," *Washington Post*, October 2, 1989, p. A1; Mothers First, a Washington, D.C., group, joined Formerly Employed Mothers at Loose Ends of Chicago and Mothers at Home of Arlington, Virginia, as organized voices of those who traded work for child care in this period.
54. Barbara Bush on National Public Radio, Weekend Edition, Saturday, September 30, 1989, reported in Donnie Radcliffe, "Barbara Bush's Old-fashioned Views," *Washington Post*, October 3, 1989, p. D2; at about the same time Bobbie Kilberg, deputy assistant to the president for public liaison, was considering a proposal to set up a day-care center on site for the 1,700 employees of the White House, Sandra Evans, "Patter of Little Feet May Resound in White House Offices," *Washington Post*, December 7, 1989, p. B1.
55. Americans' Use of Time Project, University of Maryland, *Ms.*, September 1989, p. 86; not much change had taken place by 1991; the Conference Board reported that two out of five husbands almost never cooked, cleaned the house, or shopped for food, whether or not a woman had a job; women also paid bills and made arrangements for car repairs and other traditionally "male" tasks, Alan Otten, "People Patterns," *Wall Street Journal*, February 22, 1991, p. B1.
56. Arlie Hochschild with Anne Machung, *The Second Shift: Working Parents and the Revolution at Home* (New York: Viking, 1989), pp. 43–56.
57. Use of Time Project, University of Maryland, *Ms.*, September 1989, p. 86; Hochschild, *The Second Shift*, pp. 89–90.
58. *Playboy* Roper Poll, reported in *Washington Post*, April 7, 1991, Sunday Business section, p. H2; Barbara Vobejda, "Children Help Less at Home: Dads Do More," *Washington Post*, November 22, 1991, p. 1; as mother's education level rises the less housework she has children do and the more

husbands do; poor, black families share work with children more than non-black families.

59. "Odd Jobs," *Washington Post*, April 7, 1991, p. D2, Gallup survey of 503 women and *Playboy* Roper Poll.

60. Ellen Goodman, "Sharing Housework: An Uneasy Truce," *Washington Post*, August 1, 1989, p. A21; Robert Kuttner, "She Minds the Children, He Minds the Dog," *New York Times Book Review*, June 25, 1989, p. 3; most of the complaining parties in divorce proceedings are wives, but that does not mean husbands do not want divorces.

61. Letter to the editor from Amy Ellen Schwartz of Medford, Mass., *New York Times*, July 9, 1989, p. E26, complaining about Carol Lawson, "Girls Still Apply Makeup, Boys Fight Wars," June 15, 1989, p. C1.

62. Letter to the editor from James Snow of Baltimore, *New York Times Book Review*, July 23, 1989, p. 4, complaining about Arlie Hochschild's *The Second Shift*; Saraj Parasuraman et al., "Work and Family Variables as Mediators of the Relationship Between Wife's Employment and Husband's Well-Being," *Academy of Management Journal* 32 (1989), pp. 185–201: a sample of accountants and wives showed that husbands of employed women had lower levels of job satisfaction, marital adjustment, and quality of life than those whose wives did not have paid jobs. If they had good child care, the dissatisfaction levels were lower.

63. Skrzycki, "Family Concerns Spark Changes at Work," p. B4. Carol Hymowitz, "Stepping Off the Fast Track," *Wall Street Journal*, June 13, 1989, p. B1; Morgan and Tucker, *Companies That Care*, p. 27; Richard Berke, "Study Sees Shift in Plans for Birth," *New York Times*, June 22, 1989, p. A16; *Playboy Magazine*, Roper Poll.

64. Skrzycki, "Family Concerns Spark Chages at Work," p. B4.

65. Julia Lawlor, "Suit Puts Spotlight on Daddy Stress," *USA Today*, June 21, 1991, p. B1.

66. Lisa Belkin, "Bars to Equality of Sexes Seen Eroding, Slowly"; *New York Times*, August 20, 1989, pp. A1, A25; Lynn Norment, "The Trials and Triumphs of Working Mothers," *Ebony*, September 1989, p. 38.

67. Dalton Narine, "New Rules for Today's Black Couples," *Ebony*, September 1989, pp. 46, 48, 50.

68. Laura Randolph, "Secrets About Black Men That Every Black Woman Should Know," *Ebony*, May 1991, pp. 38–44, 42, highlighting Washington, D.C., psychiatrist Dr. Harry Edwards who said, "even in the liberated 90s those old-fashioned feelings have not gone away."

69. Lenore Weitzman, *The Divorce Revolution* (New York: The Free Press, 1985), pp. 323–56.

70. Cathy Trost, "To Cut Costs and Keep the Best People, More Concerns Offer Flexible Work Plans," *Wall Street Journal*, February 18, 1992, p. B1.

71. Elizabeth M. Fowler, "More Stress Found in the Workplace," *New York Times*, September 12, 1989, p. D12; Alison Leigh Cowan, "Women's Gains on the Job: Not Without a Heavy Toll," *New York Times*, August 21, 1989, pp. A1, A14.

72. Claudia Deutsch, "The Fast Track's Diminished Lure," *New York Times*, October 6, 1991, p. C25.

73. Betty Friedan, *The Second Stage* (New York: Simon and Schuster, 1981), p. 121; Janet Elder, "Working Overtime a Bind for Parents," *New York Times*, February 9, 1989, p. C1; Sherry Suib Cohen, "Beyond Macho: The Power of Womanly Management," *Working Woman*, February 1989, p. 77; Susan McHenry and Linda Lee Small, "Does Part-time Pay Off," *Ms.*, March 1989, p. 88; Cynthia Marano, executive director, Wider Opportunities for Women, "No Way Out: Working Poor Women in the U.S.," 1988; Stanley D. Nollen, "The Work-Family Dilemma: How HR Managers Can Help," *Personnel*, May 1989, pp. 25–30; Carol Lawon, "With Job Sharing, Time for the Family," *New York Times*, June 1, 1989, p. C1; Amanda Bennett, "Managing, Fathers Make More Use of On-Site Day Care," *Wall Street Journal*, September 1, 1991, p. B1; Barbara Vobejda, "As Single Fathers Head More Families," *Washington Post*, May 13, 1992, p. A21.

CHAPTER I

Searching for Solutions

1. Phyllis Palmer, *Domesticity and Dirt: Housewives and Domestic Servants in the United States, 1920–1945* (Philadelphia: Temple University Press, 1989), pp. xii–xiii.

2. Deborah Fallows, *A Mother's Work* (Boston: Houghton Mifflin, 1985).

3. Gilbert Steiner, with Pauline H. Milius, *The Children's Cause* (Washington, D.C.: Brookings Institution, 1976); Gilbert Steiner, *The Futility of Family Policy* (Washington: Brookings Institution, 1981); Edward Zigler and Edmund Gordon, eds., *Day Care: Scientific and Social Policy Issues* (Boston: Auburn House Publishing Co., 1982); Sylvia Hewlett, *A Lesser Life: The Myth of Women's Liberation in America* (New York: William Morrow & Co., 1986); Sheila Kamerman and Alfred Kahn, *Maternity Policy and Working Women* (Columbia University Press, 1983); Arlie Hochschild with Anne Machung, *The Second Shift: Working Parents and the Revolution at Home* (New York: Viking, 1989): she includes black, Asian, and Hispanic couples

among the fifty she interviewed; Ruth Sidel, *Women and Children Last: The Plight of Poor Women in Affluent America* (New York: Viking, 1981).

4. Delores Hayden, *Redesigning the American Dream: The Future of Housing, Work and Family* (New York: W. W. Norton, 1984).

5. Nathan Cobb, "The Baby Gurus," *The Boston Globe Magazine*, June 17, 1990, pp. 14–16, 27–35.

6. Susan Faludi, *Backlash: The Undeclared War Against American Women* (New York: Crown Publishers, 1991).

7. Hewlett, *A Lesser Life*.

8. Conversation with Eleanor Smeal, March 1989.

9. See, for example, Mary Ruggie, *The State and Working Women: A Comparative Study of Britain and Sweden* (Princeton: Princeton University Press, 1984), pp. 38, 161; Robert J. Samuelson, "The Daddy Track," *Washington Post*, March 29, 1989, p. A25; references in the Women's Research Institute study.

10. Hochschild, *The Second Shift*.

11. "Modern Maturity," Public Broadcasting System, March 3, 1988.

12. Brazelton, T. Berry, *Working and Caring* (Reading, Mass: Addison-Wesley Publishing Co., 1985); Burton White, *A Parent's Guide to the First Three Years* (Englewood Cliffs, N.J.: Prentice Hall, 1981); Sandra Scarr, *Mother Care/Other Care* (New York: Basic Books, 1984); Judy Mann, "Myths About Day Care," *Washington Post*, September 6, 1985, p. C3; Trish Hall, "Child Care as Seen by Children," *New York Times*, January 26, 1989, p. C1.

13. Brazelton, *Working and Caring*; White, *A Parent's Guide*; Scarr, *Mother Care/Other Care*; *Washington Post*, September 6, 1985, p. C3; Hall, "Child Care as Seen by Children," p. C1.

14. Brigitte and Peter Berger, *The War Over the Family: Capturing the Middle Ground* (Garden City, N.Y.: Anchor Press/Doubleday, 1983); George Gilder, *Wealth and Poverty* (New York: Basic Books, 1981), pp. 70–72, 88; Susan Cohen and Mary Fainsod Katzenstein, "The War Over the Family Is Not Over the Family," in Sanford Dornbusch and Myra H. Strober, *Feminism, Children and the New Families* (New York: The Guilford Press, 1988), pp. 25–45.

15. Genesis 2:23–25, 2:16–17, 3:7, 3:15, 3:22; Gerda Lerner, *The Creation of Patriarchy* (New York: Oxford University Press, 1986), ch. 9; Jerry Falwell, *Listen America* (New York: Doubleday, 1980), p. 150; Cohen and Katzenstein, "The War Over the Family," pp. 25–45; Muslims have similar beliefs.

16. Lionel Tiger and Robin Fox, *The Imperial Animal* (New York: Holt, Rinehart and Winston, 1971), pp. 56–75, 142–46, 179.

17. Phyllis Schlafly, *The Power of the Positive Woman* (New Rochelle, N.Y.: Arlington House, Publishers, 1977); Jerry Falwell, *Listen America*, p. 150; Cohen and Katzenstein, "The War Over the Family," pp. 25–45.

18. Nancy Makepeace Tanner, *On Becoming Human* (Cambridge, England: Cambridge University Press, 1981), pp. 156–58; Lerner, *The Creation of Patriarchy*, pp. 39–43; Clifford Geertz, *The Interpretation of Cultures* (New York: Basic Books, 1973), pp. 33–54.

19. Ruth Bleier, *Science and Gender: A Critique of Biology and Its Theories on Women* (New York: Pergamon Press, 1984), pp. 121–23, 131–37; Tanner, *On Becoming Human*, pp. 156–58.

20. Bleier, *Science and Gender*, pp. 121–23, 131–37; Tanner, *On Becoming Human*, pp. 156–58. Alice Rossi, "A Bisocial Perspective on Parenting," *Daedalus* 106 (1977), pp. 1–22, believes that biology shapes what is learned but mother care is not genetically determined. Gender roles, including mother's responsibility for child care, can be unlearned, but they work and do not need changing. Also, the experience of pregnancy would probably make mothers bond with children more than fathers; Robert Karen, "Becoming Attached," *Atlantic Monthly* 265 (1990), pp. 35–50, 63–70, notes: "Throughout this article, for simplicity's sake, I'll refer to the primary caregiver as the mother—though fathers and non-related adults can also be primary caregivers—and I'll use the male pronoun for the infant." (p. 38); Helen H. Lambert, "Biology and Equality: A Perspective on Sex Differences," *Signs* 4 (1978), pp. 97–117.

21. Nancy Chodorow, *The Reproduction of Mothering: Psychoanalysis and the Sociology of Gender* (Berkeley and Los Angeles: University of California Press, 1978).

22. Ibid.

23. Carroll Smith-Rosenberg, "Female World of Love and Ritual," *Signs* 1 (1975), pp. 1–26.

24. Carol Gilligan, *In a Different Voice: Psychological Theory and Women's Development* (Cambridge: Harvard University Press, 1982), pp. 25–40, 128–50; Carol Gilligan, Janie Victoria Ward, and Jill McLean Taylor, with Betty Bardige, ed., *Mapping the Moral Domain: A Contribution of Women's Thinking to Psychological Theory and Education* (Cambridge: Harvard University Press, 1989): they believe that as girls become involved in the institutional roles of the world of men the more they advance in school, or in the professions, their "voices" change, although the concern with care and personal involvement is not totally expunged. This theory may account for women's behavior but it may also account for the fact that women have

been dominated by men; see Joan C. Williams, "Domesticity as the Dangerous Supplement of Liberalism," *Journal of Women's History* 2 (1991), pp. 69–88.

25. Gilligan, *In a Different Voice*, pp. 25–40.
26. Ibid., pp. 128–50; Francesca M. Cancian, "The Feminization of Love," *Signs* 11 (1986), pp. 692–709.
27. *EEOC* v. *Sears, Roebuck & Co.*, 39 *FEP Cases* 1672 (N.D. Ill. 1986): "Women's History Goes to Trial: *EEOC* v. *Sears, Roebuck and Company*," *Signs* 11 (1986), pp. 751–79; preface by Jacqueline Dowd Hall, introduction to documents by Sandi Cooper, and testimony of Rosalind Rosenberg and Alice Kessler-Harris; Stephanie Riger, "Comment on 'Women's History Goes to Trial,' " *Signs* 13 (1988), pp. 897–903.
28. Riger, "Comment on 'Women's History Goes to Trial,';" supporters of fairer employment practices should not be unduly concerned, however; if difference theory did not exist, opponents would find another rationale to justify their rejection.
29. Joan Scott, *Gender and the Politics of History* (New York: Columbia University Press, 1988).
30. Ibid.
31. Mary Joe Frug, "Securing Job Equality for Women: Labor Market Hostility to Working Mothers," *Boston University Law Review* 59 (1979), pp. 55–103; Joan C. Williams, "Deconstructing Gender," *Michigan Law Review* 87 (1989), pp. 797–845 (see especially notes 100–103); Tamar Lewin, "Feminist Scholars Spur Rethinking of Law," *New York Times*, September 30, 1988, p. B9.
32. Frug, "Securing Job Equality for Women," pp. 55–103; Williams, "Deconstructing Gender," pp. 797–845.
33. See note 32 above.

CHAPTER II

Father Care, Other Care

1. Phyllis Palmer, *Domesticity and Dirt: Housewives and Domestic Servants in the United States, 1920–1945* (Philadelphia: Temple University Press, 1989), p. xiii.
2. Theresa LaFromboise and Anneliese M. Heyle, "Changing and Diverse Roles of Women in American Indian Culture," *Sex Roles* 2 (1990), pp. 455–76.
3. LaFromboise and Heyle, "Changing and Diverse Roles"; Nancy Shoemaker, "The Rise or Fall of Iroquois Women," *Journal of Women's History* 2 (1991),

pp. 39–57; Sara Evans, *Born for Liberty: A History of Women in America* (New York: The Free Press, 1986), pp. 7–19.

4. Steven Mintz and Susan Kellogg, *Domestic Revolutions: A Social History of American Family Life* (New York: The Free Press, 1988), pp. 2, 12–13, 36–41; Laurel Ulrich, "Housewife and Gadder: Themes of Self-Sufficiency and Community in Eighteenth-Century New England" in Carol Groneman and Mary Beth Norton, eds., *To Toil the Livelong Day* (Ithaca: Cornell University Press, 1987), pp. 14–50.

5. Lois Greene Carr and Lorena Walsh, "A Planter's Wife: The Experience of White Women in Seventeenth Century Maryland," in Nancy F. Cott and Elizabeth H. Pleck, eds., *A Heritage of Her Own* (New York, Simon & Schuster, 1979), pp. 29–30; Evans, *Born for Liberty*, pp. 7–19, 26–27.

6. Mintz and Kellogg, *Domestic Revolutions*, pp. 12–13; Laurel Thatcher Ulrich, *Good Wives: Images and Reality in the Lives of Women in Northern New England* (New York: Random House, 1982), pp. 9–15, 23–28, 50–51, 70–71.

7. John W. Blassingame, *The Slave Community* (New York: Oxford University Press, 1979), pp. 13–16.

8. Ibid.,; Deborah Gray White, *Ain't I a Woman: Female Slaves in the Plantation South* (New York: W. W. Norton, 1985), pp. 142–60.

9. White, *Ain't I a Woman*, pp. 142–60.

10. Mintz and Kellogg, *Domestic Revolutions*, pp. 22–23.

11. Ibid., pp. 40–41; Daniel Blake Smith, *Inside the Great Houses: Planter Family Life in Eighteenth-Century Chesapeake Society* (Ithaca: Cornell University Press, 1980), pp. 175–230.

12. Mintz and Kellogg, *Domestic Revolutions*, pp. 34–35.

13. Alan McFarlane, ed., *The Diary of Ralph Josselin, 1616–1683* (London: Oxford University Press, 1976), pp. 1–195, gives ample evidence of Josselin's total involvement with his children; Robert H. Bremner et al., *Children and Youth in America: A Documentary History*, 3 vols. (Cambridge: Harvard University Press, 1970), vol. 2, 1600–1865, p. 27; Mintz and Kellogg, *Domestic Revolutions*, pp. 1–24.

14. John Demos, *A Little Commonwealth: Family Life in Plymouth Colony*, chs. 6, 7 (New York: Oxford University Press, 1970); John Demos, *Past, Present and Personal: The Life Course in American History* (New York: Oxford University Press, 1986), pp. 41–67; Carol Karlsen, *The Devil in the Shape of a Woman: Witchcraft in Colonial New England* (New York: W. W. Norton, 1987), pp. 154–81; John Demos, *Entertaining Satan: Witchcraft and the Culture of Early New England* (New York: Oxford University Press, 1982), pp. 60–64, 197–209, 394–95.

15. Laurel Thatcher Ulrich, *Good Wives*, pp. 9–20, 50–51, 70–71; Lyle Koehler, *A Search for Power: The Weaker Sex in Seventeenth Century New England* (Urbana: University of Illinois Press, 1980), ch. 3; Marylynn Salmon, *Women and the Law of Property in Early America* (Chapel Hill: University of North Carolina Press, 1986), pp. 185–93.

16. Bremner et al., *Children and Youth in America*, vol. 3, 109–10; Demos, *A Little Commonwealth*, chs. 6, 7; Catherine M. Scholten, *Childbearing in American Society, 1650–1850* (New York: New York University Press, 1985), pp. 50–55.

17. David Levin, *Cotton Mather: The Young Life of the Lord's Remembrancer, 1633–1703* (Cambridge: Harvard University Press, 1978), pp. 10–13, 16, 94–95.

18. Page Smith, *John Adams*, vol. 1, 1735–1784 (Garden City, N.Y.: Doubleday and Co., Inc., 1962), pp. 8, 11–13; Dumas Malone, *Jefferson and His Time: Jefferson the Virginian*, vol. 1 (Boston: Little, Brown and Co., 1948), pp. 4, 20, 27, 37, 42–43; the teachers were male.

19. Irving Brant, *James Madison: The Virginia Revolutionist, 1751–1789* (Indianapolis: Bobbs-Merrill Co., 1941), pp. 49–50.

20. Elizabeth P. McCaughey, *From Loyalist to Founding Father: The Political Odyssey of William Samuel Johnson* (New York: Columbia University Press, 1980), pp. 12–13, 17. Recollections of other significant Revolutionary-generation leaders reflect the central role fathers played and the practice of sending children away from home: see, for example, Noel B. Gerson, *Light Horse Harry: A Biography of Washington's Great Cavalryman General Henry Lee* (Garden City, N.Y.: Doubleday and Co., Inc., 1966), p. 3.

21. Marvin Zahnhiser, *Charles Cotesworth Pinckney* (Chapel Hill: University of North Carolina Press, 1967), pp. 10–11.

22. Nancy F. Cott, "Eighteenth-Century Family and Social Life, Revealed in Massachusetts Divorce Records," in Cott and Pleck, eds., *A Heritage of Her Own*, p. 107.

23. Edmund Morgan, *The Puritan Family: Essays on Religion and Domestic Relations in Seventeenth-Century New England* (1944; reprint ed., New York: Harper & Row, 1966), pp. 75–81, 106–8; Linda Kerber, *Women of the Republic: Intellect and Ideology in Revolutionary America* (Chapel Hill: University of North Carolina Press, 1980), pp. 181–83; Ross W. Beales, Jr., "In Search of the Historical Child: Miniature Adulthood and Youth in Colonial New England," in N. Ray Hiner and Joseph M. Hawes, *Growing Up in America: Children in Historical Perspective* (Urbana: University of Illinois Press, 1985), pp. 7–24.

24. Ethel Armes, ed., *Nancy Shippen: Her Journal Book* (Philadelphia: J. B.

Lippincott Co., 1935), pp. 291–92; Margo Culley, ed., *A Day at a Time: The Diary Literature of American Women from 1764 to the Present* (Old Westbury, N.Y.: Feminist Press, 1985).

25. Kerber, *Women of the Republic*, pp. 8–12.
26. Ibid., pp. 7–12, 35.
27. Evans, *Born for Liberty* p. 56; Alice Rossi, ed., *The Feminist Papers from Adams to De Beauvoir* (New York: Columbia University Press, 1973), pp. 10–11, 13.
28. Kerber, *Women of the Republic*, pp. 24–26.
29. Ibid.
30. Virginia Moore, *The Madisons* (New York: McGraw-Hill, 1979), pp. 1–47, 172.
31. Carl Kaestle, *The Evolution of an Urban School System, New York City, 1750–1850* (Cambridge: Harvard University Press, 1973), pp. 58–59; Mark Van Doren, ed., *The Correspondence of Aaron Burr and His Daughter Theodosia* (New York: Covici, Friede, 1929), pp. 12–13, 24–25.
32. Kathryn Kish Sklar, *Catharine Beecher: A Study in American Domesticity* (New York: W. W. Norton, 1976), pp. 3, 7, 9–10. Edward James et al., *Notable American Women*, vol. 2, p. 393.
33. See discussion of Schlafly, Falwell, and difference theory in Chapter One.
34. Nancy Cott, *The Bonds of Womanhood: Woman's Sphere in New England, 1780–1835* (New Haven: Yale University Press, 1977), ch. 2; Gerda Lerner, "The Lady and the Mill Girl: Changes in the Status of Women in the Age of Jackson, 1800–1840," in Cott and Pleck, eds., *A Heritage of Her Own*, pp. 189–93; Kerber, *Women of the Republic*, pp. 284–88; Barbara Welter, "The Cult of True Womanhood, 1820–1860," *American Quarterly* 18 (1966), pp. 131–75; Mary P. Ryan, *Cradle of the Middle Class: The Family in Oneida County, New York, 1790–1865* (Cambridge: Harvard University Press, 1981), pp. 40–41, 71–72, 85–86.
35. See note 34 above.
36. See note 34 above.
37. Mintz and Kellogg, *Domestic Revolutions*, pp. 49–51; Mary E. Ryan, *Cradle of the Middle Class*, pp. 230–35; Susan Strasser, *Never Done: A History of American Housework* (New York: Pantheon Books, 1982), pp. 18–25.
38. Nancy Cott, *The Bonds of Womanhood*, pp. 28–31, 55–57; Alice Kessler-Harris, *Out to Work: A History of Wage-Earning Women in the United States* (New York: Oxford University Press, 1982), ch. 2; Gerda Lerner, "The Lady and the Mill Girl," pp. 189–93; Thomas Dublin, *Women at Work: The Transformation of Work and Community in Lowell, Massachusetts, 1826–1860* (New York, Columbia University Press, 1979), pp. 23–57.

39. Lerner, "The Lady and the Mill Girl," pp. 189–93.

40. Ibid.

41. Ibid.

42. Hasia Diner, *Erin's Daughters in America: Irish Immigrant Women in the Nineteenth Century* (Baltimore: Johns Hopkins University Press, 1983), pp. 8–19. Beginning in the early nineteenth century, 52.9 percent of Irish immigrants were female. Among Germans, women were 41 percent; among Jewish immigrants, males and females were almost equally divided.

43. Ibid.

44. Christine Stansell, *City of Women: Sex and Class in New York, 1789–1860* (Urbana: University of Illinois Press, 1986), pp. 52–54; Cott, *Bonds of Womanhood*, pp. 43–62; Kessler-Harris, *Out to Work*, pp. 58–60.

45. Alexis de Tocqueville, "On American Women and American Wives," quoted in Nancy Cott, ed., *Root of Bitterness: Documents of the Social History of American Women* (Boston: Northeastern University Press, 1986), pp. 117–26.

46. Mrs. A. J. Graves, *Woman in America: Being an Examination into the Moral and Intellectual Condition of American Female Society* (New York: Harper and Bros., 1841), pp. 143–49, 152–64, in Cott, ed., *Root of Bitterness*, pp. 141–47.

47. Catharine E. Beecher, *Treatise on Domestic Economy*, rev. 3rd ed. (New York: Harper and Row, 1847), pp. 25–27, 33–34, 36–43, in Cott, ed., *Root of Bitterness*, p. 174; Sklar, *Catharine Beecher*, pp. 151–67.

48. Anne L. Kuhn, *The Mother's Role in Childhood Education: New England Concepts, 1830–1860* (New Haven: Yale University Press, 1947), pp. 4–5, 8–9, 73; Faye Dudden, *Serving Women: Household Service in Nineteenth-Century America* (Middletown, Conn.: Wesleyan University Press, 1983), ch. 4; Glenna Matthews, *Just a Housewife: The Rise and Fall of Domesticity in America* (New York: Oxford University Press, 1987), pp. 95–97; Strasser, *Never Done*, pp. 164–66.

49. Mintz and Kellogg, *Domestic Revolutions*, pp. 46–49; Daniel Blake Smith, *Inside the Great Houses*, pp. 25–54. The transformation occurred earlier in wealthy planter families. Ryan, *Cradle of the Middle Class*, pp. 71–72, 85–86.

50. Anne L. Kuhn, *The Mother's Role in Childhood Education*. "The Mother sways the dominion of the heart, the father that of the Intellect," pp. 150–72.

51. John Boswell, *The Kindness of Strangers: The Abandonment of Children in Western Europe from Late Antiquity to the Renaissance* (New York: Pantheon

Books, 1988); Stephen Brobeck, "Images of the Family: Portrait Paintings as Indices of American Family Culture, Structure and Behavior, 1730–1860," *The Journal of Psychohistory* 5 (1977), pp. 81–106; Mintz and Kellogg, *Domestic Revolutions*, pp. 46–49; Jay Fliegelman, *Prodigals and Pilgrims: The American Revolution Against Patriarchal Authority, 1750–1800* (Cambridge, England: Cambridge University Press, 1982), pp. 36–66; Ryan, *Cradle of the Middle Class*, pp. 97–98; Demos, *Past, Present and Personal*, pp. 41–67.

52. Ryan, *Cradle of the Middle Class*, pp. 158–63; Carl Degler, *At Odds: Women and the Family in America from the Revolution to the Present* (New York: Oxford University Press, 1980), pp. 45–51; Stansell, *City of Women*, 158–62.

53. See note 52 above.

54. John Mack Faragher, *Women and Men on the Overland Trail* (New Haven: Yale University Press, 1979), pp. 168–87; Harriet Noble's story of "Emigration from New York to Michigan" in Elizabeth Ellet, *Pioneer Women of the West* (New York: Charles Scribner's Sons, 1856), pp. 388–95.

55. Elizabeth Geer Diary and Letter 1847 from 35 *Transactions* of the Oregon Pioneer Association (1907), pp. 153, 171–78 in Cott, ed., *Root of Bitterness*, 1973, pp. 227–28, 255; John Mack Faragher and Christine Stansell, "Women and Their Families on the Overland Trail to California and Oregon, 1842–1867," in Cott and Pleck, *A Heritage of Her Own*, pp. 247–67; Glenda Riley, *The Female Frontier: A Comparative View of Women on the Prairie and the Plains* (Lawrence: University Press of Kansas, 1988), pp. 1–13; Julie Roy Jeffrey, *Frontier Women: The Trans-Mississippi West, 1840–1880* (New York: Hill and Wang, 1979), pp. 68–78, explains these women wanted fathers to take charge of male children as soon as they were old enough to do manual labor.

56. Evans, *Born for Liberty*, pp. 101–7.

57. Anthony to Stanton (1856) in *Elizabeth Cady Stanton/Susan B. Anthony: Correspondence, Writing, Speeches*, ed., Ellen Carol DuBois (New York: Schocken Books, 1981), p. 61; Stanton to Anthony (1857) in Eleanor Flexner, *Century of Struggle: The Woman's Rights Movement in the United States* (Cambridge: Harvard University Press, 1972), p. 90; Evans, *Born for Liberty*, p. 103.

58. Address of Elizabeth Cady Stanton on the divorce bill. Before the Judiciary Committee of the New York Senate, in the Assembly Chamber, February 8, 1861, in Jamil Zainaldin, *Law in Antebellum Society* (New York: Alfred A. Knopf, 1983), p. 216.

59. Bremner et al., *Children and Youth in America*, vol. 2, 1600–1865, p. 364; U.S. Bureau of Education Circular of Information No. 3, *Legal Rights of Children*, 1880.

60. *Mercein* v. *People ex. rel. Barry* 25 *Wend.* 641 (1840).

61. Michael Grossberg, *Governing the Hearth: Law and Family in Nineteenth-Century America* (Chapel Hill: University of North Carolina Press, 1985), pp. 234–47; Ryan, *Cradle of the Middle Class*, pp. 71–74, 99–100; Kuhn, *The Mother's Role*, pp. 38–67.

62. Degler, *At Odds*, pp. 165–69; about 60 percent of divorces in the late nineteenth century did not involve children; Grossberg, *Governing the Hearth*, p. 253; William L. O'Neill, *Divorce in the Progressive Era* (New Haven: Yale University Press, 1967), pp. 198–230; Nelson Manfred Blake, *The Road to Reno: A History of Divorce in the United States* (New York: Macmillan, 1962), pp. 130–51. With the abolition of the maternal custody presumption in the twentieth century after the 1960s women's rights movement, some fathers claimed custody even when they did not want it to reduce a wife's financial claims in a divorce; Nancy D. Polikoff, "Why Mothers Are Losing: A Brief Analysis of Criteria Used in Child Custody Determinations," *Women's Rights Law Reporter* 7 (1982), pp. 235–43.

63. Jacqueline Jones, *Labor of Love, Labor of Sorrow: Black Women's Work and the Family from Slavery to the Present* (New York: Basic Books, 1985), pp. 1–5.

64. John Hope Franklin and Alfred Moss, Jr., *From Slavery to Freedom: A History of Negro Americans* (New York: Alfred A. Knopf, 1988), pp. 97, 104–5.

65. Ibid., pp. 104–8.

66. Catherine Clinton, *The Plantation Mistress: Woman's World in the Old South* (New York: Pantheon Books, 1982), pp. 87–90.

67. Jones, *Labor of Love*, pp. 22–24; Clinton, *The Plantation Mistress*, pp. 16–22.

68. Jones, *Labor of Love*, pp. 23–24; Clinton, *The Plantation Mistress*, pp. 16–28.

69. Jones, *Labor of Love*, p. 27.

70. John W. Blassingame, *Slave Testimony: Two Centuries of Letters, Speeches, Interviews and Autobiographies* (Baton Rouge, Louisiana State University Press, 1977), p. 133.

71. Mary Frances Berry and John Blassingame, *Long Memory: The Black Experience in America* (New York: Oxford University Press, 1982), p. 75.

72. Blassingame, *Slave Testimony*, p. 133.

73. Berry and Blassingame, *Long Memory*, p. 75.

74. Herbert Gutman, *The Black Family in Slavery and Freedom 1750–1925* (New York: Vintage Books, 1977), pp. 76–78; Dorothy Sterling, ed., *We Are Your Sisters* (New York: W. W. Norton, 1984), p. 41; Theodore Rosengartner, *Tombee: Portrait of a Cotton Plantation* (New York: McGraw-Hill, 1987), p. 153; White, *Ain't I a Woman*, pp. 126–28.

75. Michael P. Johnson and James L. Roark, *Black Masters: A Free Family of Color in the Old South* (New York: W. W. Norton, 1984), pp. 66–67; Suzanne Lebsock, *The Free Women of Petersburg* (New York: W. W. Norton, 1984), pp. 87–111; Franklin and Moss, *From Slavery to Freedom*, pp. 138–57; Larry Koger, *Black Slaveowners: Free Black Slave Masters in South Carolina, 1790–1860* (Jefferson, N.C.: McFarland & Co., 1985), pp. 80–101.

76. Lebsock, *The Free Women of Petersburg*, pp. 87–111; Franklin and Moss, *From Slavery to Freedom*, p. 141.

77. Franklin and Moss, *From Slavery to Freedom*, pp. 142–45; Sharon Harley, "Northern Black Female Workers: Jacksonian Era," in Sharon Harley and Rosalyn Terborg-Penn, eds., *The Afro-American Woman: Struggles and Images* (Port Washington, N.Y.: Kennikat Press, 1978), p. 8; Paula Giddings, *When and Where I Enter: The Impact of Black Women on Race and Sex in America* (New York: William Morrow & Co., 1984), pp. 47–9.

78. Sarah and Angelina Grimké, born into a wealthy slaveholding family in South Carolina, left the South and became Quakers in Philadelphia. Angelina Grimké, *An Appeal to the Women of the Nominally Free States*, 2d ed. (Boston: Isaac Knapp, 1838), pp. 13–16, 19–23, 49–53, 60–61. Southern women "hold their own sisters and brothers in bondage. Southern families often present the most disgusting scenes of dissension, in which the mistress acts a part derogatory to her own character as a woman . . ." excerpted in Cott, *Root of Bitterness*, pp. 194–99; Franklin and Moss, *From Slavery to Freedom*, pp. 152–54.

79. Theda Perdue, "Cherokee Women and the Trail of Tears," *Journal of Women's History* 1 (1989), pp. 14–30.

CHAPTER III

Mother Care, Other Care

1. Dudley Cornish, *The Sable Arm: Negro Troops in the Union Army, 1864–1865* (New York: Longman Green, 1956), pp. 287–88; Cindy Aron, "To Barter Their Souls for Gold: Female Federal Clerical Workers in

Nineteenth-Century America," Ph.D. diss., University of Maryland, 1981, pp. 6, 10, 38.

2. Alice Kessler-Harris, *Out to Work: A History of Wage-Earning Women in the United States* (New York: Oxford University Press, 1982), pp. 75–78.

3. James W. Geary, *We Need Men: The Union Draft in the Civil War* (DeKalb: Northern Illinois University Press, 1991), pp. 105–6; James McPherson, *Battle Cry of Freedom: The Civil War Era* (New York: Oxford University Press, 1988), pp. 476–84.

4. Aron, "To Barter Their Souls for Gold," pp. 75–79.

5. Leon Litwack, *Been in the Storm So Long: The Aftermath of Slavery* (New York: Alfred A. Knopf, 1979), p. 114, 125–43.

6. Jacqueline Jones, *Labor of Love, Labor of Sorrow: Black Women's Work and the Family from Slavery to the Present* (New York: Basic Books, 1985), pp. 66–67; Litwack, *Been in the Storm*, p. 547.

7. *Proceedings: Constitutional Convention of South Carolina*, pp. 836, 838 (Charleston: printed by Denny & Perry, 1868; reprinted Arno Press and *New York Times*, 1968).

8. Ellen Carol DuBois, *Feminism and Suffrage: The Emergence of an Independent Women's Movement in America* (Ithaca, N.Y.: Cornell University Press, 1978).

9. Eleanor Flexner, *Century of Struggle: The Woman's Rights Movement in the United States* (Cambridge, Mass.: Harvard University Press, 1959, 1972), pp. 162–63; Sara Evans, *Born for Liberty: A History of Women in America* (New York: The Free Press, 1989), pp. 125–30.

10. Flexner, *Century of Struggle*, pp. 181–85; Evans, *Born for Liberty*, pp. 125–30.

11. Ibid., pp. 119–30.

12. Litwack, *Been in the Storm*, pp. 357–58.

13. Ibid.

14. Herbert Gutman, *The Black Family in Slavery and Freedom, 1750–1925* (New York: Vintage Press, 1977), pp. 207–8; Rebecca Scott, "The Battle over the Child: Child Apprenticeship and the Freedmen's Bureau in North Carolina," in N. Rasy Hibner and Joseph M. Hawes, eds., *Growing Up in America: Children in Historical Perspective* (Urbana: University of Illinois Press, 1985), pp. 193–207.

15. Litwack, *Been in the Storm So Long*, p. 229.

16. Ibid.

17. Ibid., pp. 244–247.

18. Eric Foner, *Reconstruction: America's Unfinished Revolution, 1863–1877* (New York: Harper & Row, 1988), pp. 170–75.

19. Pete Daniel, *The Shadow of Slavery, 1901–1969* (Urbana: University of Illinois, 1972); Foner, *Reconstruction*, pp. 170–75.
20. Jones, *Labor of Love*, pp. 58–68, 79–95; Claudia Goldin, "Female Labor Participation: The Origin of Black-White Differences," *Journal of Economic History* 37 (March 1977), pp. 87–108, and critique of Goldin by Harold Woodman, pp. 109–12.
21. Burton Hendrick, *The Life of Andrew Carnegie*, 2 vols. (Garden City, N.Y.: Doubleday Doran and Co., 1932), vol. 2, p. 275.
22. Mary Beth Norton et al., *A People and a Nation: A History of the United States* (Boston: Houghton Mifflin, 1990), pp. 529–34.
23. Ibid., pp. 536–43.
24. Ibid.; Kessler-Harris, *Out to Work*, pp. 139–40.
25. John Hope Franklin and Alfred Moss, Jr., *From Slavery to Freedom: A History of Negro Americans* (New York: Alfred A. Knopf, 1988), pp. 227–83.
26. Kessler-Harris, *Out to Work*, pp. 119–38; Aron, "To Barter Their Souls for Gold," pp. 12–52.
27. Elizabeth Pleck, "A Mother's Wages: Income Earning Among Married Italian and Black Women" in Nancy F. Cott and Elizabeth H. Pleck, eds., *A Heritage of Her Own* (New York: Simon and Schuster, 1979), pp. 367–92.
28. Margaret O'Brien Steinfels, *Who's Minding the Children? The History and Politics of Day Care in America* (New York: Simon and Schuster, 1973), pp. 38–39; Carl Degler, *At Odds: Women and the Family in America from the Revolution to the Present* (New York: Oxford University Press, 1980), pp. 139–42; David Musto, *The American Disease: Origins of Narcotic Control* (New Haven: Yale University Press, 1973; Oxford University Press expanded edition, 1987), pp. 1–10, 94.
29. Rose Schneiderman, "A Cap Maker's Story," in Gerda Lerner, *The Female Experience: An American Documentary* (New York: Macmillan, 1985), pp. 38–40.
30. Ibid.
31. Kessler-Harris, *Out to Work*, pp. 139–418; Pleck, "A Mother's Wages," pp. 367–92; Jones, *Labor of Love*, pp. 110–51.
32. Pleck, "A Mother's Wages," pp. 367–92.
33. Linda Gordon, *Woman's Body, Woman's Right: Birth Control in America* (New York: Penguin Books, 1977, reprint ed. 1983), pp. 48, 130–31; Nancy Cott, *The Grounding of Modern Feminism* (New Haven: Yale University Press, 1987), pp. 165–67; on housework changes see generally Susan Strasser, *Never Done: A History of American Housework* (New York: Pantheon Books, 1982).

34. Kessler-Harris, *Out to Work*, pp. 108–17.

35. Ibid.

36. Steinfels, *Who's Minding the Children?*, pp. 37–38.

37. Ibid.

38. Lawrence Friedman, *The History of American Law* (New York: Simon and Schuster, 1985), p. 494; Christine Stansell, *City of Women: Sex and Class in New York, 1789–1860* (Urbana: University of Illinois, 1987), pp. 209–14.

39. Michael Steven Shapiro, *Child's Garden: The Kindergarten Movement from Froebel to Dewey* (University Park and London: Pennsylvania State University Press, 1983), pp. 91–92 and notes there cited; Charles Loring Brace, *The Dangerous Classes of New York and Twenty Years of Work Among Them* (New York: Wynkoop and Hallenbeck, 1872); Anna Hallowell, "The Care and Saving of Neglected Children," *Journal of Social Science*, September 1880, p. 122; John N. Foster, "Ten Years of Child Saving Work in Michigan," National Conference of Charities and Corrections (NCCC), *Proceedings* (1884), pp. 132–42.

40. Robert H. Bremner et al., *Children and Youth in America: A Documentary History*, 3 vols. (Cambridge: Harvard University Press, 1970), vol. 2, pts. 7–8, pp. 1452–60; Mary Elizabeth Pidgeon, *Employed Mothers and Child Care*, Women's Bureau Bulletin No. 246 (Washington, D.C.: Government Printing Office, 1953), pp. 11–15; Steinfels, *Who's Minding the Children?*, pp. 34–37; Shapiro, *Child's Garden*, pp. 1–19.

41. Bremner et al., *Children and Youth in America*, vol. 2, pts. 7–8, pp. 1452–60; Steinfels, *Who's Minding the Children?*, pp. 34–37; Shapiro, *Child's Garden*, pp. 1–19.

42. Bremner et al., *Children and Youth in America*, vol. 2, pts. 7–8, pp. 1452–60; Steinfels, *Who's Minding the Children?*, pp. 34–37.

43. Shapiro, *Child's Garden*, pp. 1–19.

44. Ibid, pp. 19–28.

45. Ibid.

46. Ibid., pp. 65–85.

47. Ibid., pp. 85–105, 131–50.

48. Ibid.

49. Steinfels, *Who's Minding the Children?*, pp. 38–50; Barbara M. Brenzel, *Daughters of the State: A Social Portrait of the First Reform School for Girls in North America, 1856–1905* (Cambridge, Mass.: MIT Press, 1983), pp. 115–35; Shapiro, *Child's Garden*, p. 185; Jane Addams, *Twenty Years at Hull House* (New York: Macmillan, 1910), pp. 167–74. They had a kin-

dergarten and a day nursery for sixteen years; Addams used the terms interchangeably. She complained that "The long hours of factory labor necessary for earning the support of a child leave no time for the tender care and caressing which may enrich the life of the most piteous baby."

50. Steinfels, *Who's Minding the Children?*, pp. 44–48.
51. Ibid.
52. Alfreda Duster, ed., *Crusade for Justice: The Autobiography of Ida B. Wells* (Chicago: University of Chicago Press, 1971), pp. 249–50.
53. Ibid.
54. Paula Giddings, *When and Where I Enter: The Impact of Black Women on Race and Sex in America* (New York: William Morrow & Co., 1984), p. 100; W. E. B. Du Bois, ed., *Efforts for Social Betterment Among Negro Americans* (Atlanta: Atlanta University Press, 1909); W. E. B. Du Bois, ed., *Some Efforts of Negroes for Social Betterment* (Atlanta: Atlanta University Press, 1898); Fannie Barrier Williams, "The Need of Social Settlement Work for the City Negro," *Southern Workman*, September 1904, pp. 501–6; Jacqueline Rouse, "The Legacy of Community Organizing: Lugenia Burns Hope and the Neighborhood Union," *Journal of Negro History* 69 (1984), p. 114; see also Jacqueline Rouse, *Lugenia Burns Hope: A Black Southern Reformer* (Athens: University of Georgia Press, 1989), pp. 57–90; Ralph E. Luker, "Missions, Institutional Churches, and Settlement Houses: The Black Experience, 1885–1910." *Journal of Negro History* 69 (1984), pp. 101–13.
55. Steinfels, *Who's Minding the Children?*, pp. 62–66.
56. Ibid.
57. Valerie Sher Mathes, "Nineteenth-Century Women and Reform: The Women's National Indian Association," *American Indian Quarterly* 14 (1990), pp. 1–18.
58. Ibid.
59. D. S. Otis, *The Dawes Act and the Allotment of Indian Lands*, ed. Francis Prucha (1934; reprint, Norman: University of Oklahoma Press, 1973), pp. 64–81, 82–97.
60. Ibid.
61. Lynn Y. Weiner, *From Working Girl to Working Mother: The Female Labor Force in the United States, 1820–1980* (Chapel Hill: University of North Carolina Press, 1985), pp. 3–9.
62. Ibid., pp. 47–58.
63. Ibid., pp. 31–46.
64. Kessler-Harris, *Out to Work*, pp. 93–94; Weiner, *From Working Girl to Working Mother*, pp. 51, 61–62; Grace Dodge, ed., *Thoughts of Busy Girls,*

Who Have Little Time for Study, Yet Find Much Time for Thinking in Phillip Foner, *Women and the American Labor Movement* (New York: Macmillan, 1979), p. 103.

65. Kessler-Harris, *Out to Work*, pp. 93–94; Weiner, *From Working Girl to Working Mother*, pp. 52–66.

66. Barbara Allen Babcock, Ann E. Freedman, Eleanor Holmes Norton, and Susan C. Ross, *Sex Discrimination and the Law, Causes and Remedies* (Boston: Little, Brown & Co., 1975), p. 29.

67. Gordon, *Woman's Body, Woman's Right*, p. 138 and nn. 4, 5.

68. Viviana A. Zelizer, *Pricing the Priceless Child: The Changing Social Value of Children* (New York: Basic Books, 1985), pp. 208–21.

69. Barbara Ehrenreich and Deirdre English, *For Her Own Good: 150 Years of the Experts' Advice to Women* (New York: Doubleday, 1978), pp. 173–83 and notes there cited; Charlotte Perkins Gilman, "On Women's Evolution from Economic Dependence," *Women and Economics* (5th ed., Boston: Small, Maynard and Co., 1913, originally published 1898), in Cott, *Root of Bitterness*, pp. 369–70.

70. Duster, ed., *Crusade for Justice*, pp. 242–45, 250–55; most black women leaders of the period had no children.

71. Ibid.

CHAPTER IV

Reinforcing the Mother-Care Tradition, 1900–1930

1. Linda Gordon, *Woman's Body, Woman's Right: Birth Control in America* (New York: Penguin Books, 1977, reprint ed. 1983), pp. 48, 130–31; Nancy Cott, *The Grounding of Modern Feminism* (New Haven: Yale University Press, 1987), pp. 165–67; Ben J. Wattenberg, *The Birth Dearth* (New York: Pharos Books, 1987).

2. Gordon, *Woman's Body, Woman's Right*, pp. 48, 130–31; Cott, *Grounding of Modern Feminism*, pp. 165–67; on housework changes see generally Susan Strasser, *Never Done: A History of American Housework* (New York: Pantheon Books, 1982).

3. Steven Mintz and Susan Kellogg, *Domestic Revolutions: A Social History of American Family Life* (New York: The Free Press, 1988), pp. 109–18.

4. Alice Kessler-Harris, *Out to Work: A History of Wage-Earning Women in the United States* (New York: Oxford University Press, 1982), pp. 112–17.

5. Cott, *Grounding of Modern Feminism*, pp. 215–19.

6. Ibid., pp. 218–20; Dorothy Brown, *American Women in the 1920's Setting a Course* (Boston: Twayne Publishers, 1987), pp. 43–45.
7. Cott, *Grounding of Modern Feminism*, pp. 187–94.
8. Ibid.
9. Mintz and Kellogg, *Domestic Revolutions*, pp. 102–29.
10. Ibid., pp. 123–25.
11. Kessler-Harris, *Out to Work*, pp. 172–79.
12. Cott, *Grounding of Modern Feminism*, pp. 187–88; Blanche Crozier, "Marital Support," *Boston University Law Review* 15 (1935), pp. 28–58.
13. Kessler-Harris, *Out to Work*, pp. 169–74.
14. Dorothy Ross, *G. Stanley Hall: The Psychologist as Prophet* (Chicago: University of Chicago Press, 1972), pp. 280–308; Barbara Ehrenreich and Deirdre English, *For Her Own Good: 150 Years of the Experts' Advice to Women* (New York: Doubleday, 1978), pp. 177–82, 194; Mintz and Kellogg, *Domestic Revolutions*, pp. 119–25.
15. Ehrenreich and English, *For Her Own Good*, pp. 183–86.
16. Ibid.
17. Ibid., pp. 186–89
18. Ibid.
19. Cott, *Grounding of Modern Feminism*, pp. 182–83.
20. Ibid., p. 183; the titles of the articles resonate in current "mommy track" discussions.
21. Cott, *Grounding of Modern Feminism*, pp. 182–84; Lynn Weiner, *From Working Girl to Working Mother* (Chapel Hill: University of North Carolina Press, 1985), pp. 83–91; Lois Scharf, *To Work and to Wed: Female Employment, Feminism, and the Great Depression* (Westport, Conn.: Greenwood Press, 1980), p. 85.
22. See note 21 above.
23. Evelyn Nakano Glenn, *Issei, Nisei, War Bride: Three Generations of Japanese-American Women in Domestic Service* (Philadelphia: Temple University Press, 1986), pp. 67–78, 206–10; Bonnie Thornton Dill, "Our Mothers' Grief: Racial Ethnic Women and the Maintenance of Families," Center for Research on Women, Memphis State University, Research Paper no. 4, May 1986; Vicki Ruiz, *Cannery Women Cannery Lives: Mexican Women, Unionization, and the California Food Processing Industry, 1930–1950* (Albuquerque: University of New Mexico Press, 1987), pp. 10–17.
24. Leslie Woodcock Tentler, *Wage-Earning Women: Industrial Work and Family Life in the United States, 1900–1930* (New York: Oxford University Press, 1979), pp. 137–39.
25. *Muller* v. *Oregon* 208 *U.S.* 412 (1908), pp. 421–22; Joan Hoff, *Law, Gender*

and Injustice (New York: New York University Press, 1991), pp. 196–205; Kessler-Harris, *Out to Work*, ch. 7.

26. *United Auto Workers* v. *Johnson Controls, Inc.*, 59 *United States Law Week*, March 20, 1991, pp. 4209–19.

27. Ibid.

28. Kessler-Harris, *Out to Work*, pp. 187–88.

29. Ibid., pp. 219–24; Maurine Greenwald, *Women, War, and Work* (Ithaca: Cornell University Press, 1990), pp. 13–32.

30. Kessler-Harris, *Out to Work*, pp. 219–24.

31. Ibid., p. 98.

32. Margaret O'Brien Steinfels, *Who's Minding the Children? The History and Politics of Day Care in America* (New York: Simon and Schuster, 1973), pp. 54–57.

33. Ibid.

34. Weiner, *From Working Girl to Working Mother*, pp. 126–27.

35. Ibid.; Robert H. Bremner et al., *Children and Youth in America: A Documentary History, Volume 2, 1866–1932* (Cambridge: Harvard University Press, 1971), p. 365; see also Ehrenreich and English, *For Her Own Good*, p. 131.

36. Helen Russell Wright, *Children of Wage-Earning Mothers: A Study of a Selected Group in Chicago*, U.S. Labor Department, Children's Bureau publication no. 102 (Washington, D.C.: Government Printing Office, 1922), p. 43, in Tentler, *Wage-Earning Women*, p. 150.

37. Tentler, *Wage-Earning Women*, p. 155.

38. Ibid., pp. 158–61.

39. Ibid.

40. Weiner, *From Working Girl to Working Mother*, pp. 128–30; Steinfels, *Who's Minding the Children?*, pp. 60–68.

41. Weiner, *From Working Girl to Working Mother*, p. 131.

42. Ibid.; Steinfels, *Who's Minding the Children?*, pp. 60–68.

43. Steinfels, *Who's Minding the Children?*, pp. 57–61.

44. U.S. Department of Health, Education and Welfare, Children's Bureau, *Five Decades of Action for Children: A History of the Children's Bureau*, Dorothy E. Bradbury, director of Children's Bureau, Reports, 1962, pp. 15–16; Kessler-Harris, *Out to Work*, pp. 320–21; Brown, *Setting a Course*, pp. 33–35, 61–63.

45. Martha May, "Bread Before Roses: The American Workingmen, Labor Unions and the Family Wage," in Ruth Milkman, ed., *Women, Work and Protest: A Century of U.S. Labor History* (Boston: Routledge, Kegan and Paul, 1985), pp. 1–21.

46. Mary Frances Berry, *Why ERA Failed: Politics, Women's Rights, and the Amending Process of the Constitution* (Bloomington: Indiana University Press, 1986), p. 43.
47. J. Stanley Lemons, *Woman Citizen: Social Feminism in the 1920's* (Urbana: University of Illinois Press, 1973), pp. 16–17, 32, ch. 6; Susan Becker, *The Origins of the Equal Rights Amendment: American Feminism Between the Wars* (Westport, Conn.: Greenwood Press, 1981), pp. 128–30.
48. Susan Ware, *Holding Their Own: American Women in the 1930's* (Boston: Twayne Publishers, 1982), pp. 89–94; William Chafe, *The American Woman: Her Changing Social, Economic, and Political Roles, 1920–1970* (New York: Oxford University Press, 1972), pp. 42, 112–13, 127–28.
49. Berry, *Why ERA Failed*, p. 57.
50. See note 48 above.
51. Kessler-Harris, *Out to Work*, p. 152.
52. Ibid., pp. 204–14; Cott, *Grounding of Modern Feminism*, pp. 117–30.
53. See note 52 above.
54. Cott, *Grounding of Modern Feminism*, pp. 134–35.

CHAPTER V

Extending the Mother-Care Tradition, 1930–1960

1. Steven Mintz and Susan Kellogg, *Domestic Revolutions: A Social History of the American Family* (New York: The Free Press, 1988), pp. 151–60; 177–82.
2. Lynn Weiner, *From Working Girl to Working Mother* (Chapel Hill: University of North Carolina Press), pp. 109–10; Lois Scharf, *To Work and to Wed: Female Employment, Feminism, and the Great Depression* (Westport, Conn.: Greenwood Press, 1980), p. 85, 43–55.
3. Scharf, *To Work and to Wed*, pp. 55–65.
4. Ibid., pp. 106–8.
5. Weiner, *From Working Girl to Working Mother*, pp. 84–88; Scharf, *To Work and to Wed*, pp. 45–55; 106–8; Alice Kessler-Harris, *Out to Work: A History of Wage-Earning Women in the United States* (New York: Oxford University Press, 1982), pp. 250–60.
6. Scharf, *To Work and to Wed*, pp. 107–8.
7. Kessler-Harris, *Out to Work*, pp. 264–65; Scharf, *To Work and to Wed*, pp. 114–17.
8. Linda Gordon, "Social Insurance and Public Assistance: The Influence of

Gender in Welfare Thought in the United States, 1890–1935," *American Historical Review* 97 (1980), pp. 19–54.

9. Ira De Reid, "The Negro in the United States," in the *Report of the Committee on Socially Handicapped—Dependency and Neglect*, White House Conference on Child Health and Protection, 1930, 32 vols., pp. 279–312.

10. Margaret O'Brien Steinfels, *Who's Minding the Children? The History and Politics of Day Care in America* (New York: Simon and Schuster, 1973), pp. 65–67.

11. Sonya Michel, "American Women and the Discourse of the Democratic Family in World War II" in Margaret Randolph Higonnet, et al., eds., *Behind the Lines: Gender and the Two World Wars* (New Haven: Yale University Press, 1987), p. 156.

12. Kessler-Harris, *Out to Work*, pp. 274–287.

13. Michel, "American Women and the Discourse of the Democratic Family," p. 159.

14. Ibid., p. 165.

15. Catherine Mackenzie, "Would Continue Day Care Centers," *New York Times*, September 20, 1945, p. 26.

16. Jacqueline Jones, *Labor of Love, Labor of Sorrow* (New York: Basic Books, 1985), pp. 254–55.

17. Steinfels, *Who's Minding the Children?*, pp. 67–72.

18. Maureen Honey, *Creating Rosie the Riveter: Class, Gender, and Propaganda* (Amherst: University of Massachusetts Press, 1984), pp. 36–37, 50, 81.

19. Ibid.

20. Carl Degler, *At Odds: Women and the Family in America from the Revolution to the Present* (New York: Oxford University Press, 1980), p. 420; "16 Babies Burned in Maine Nursery," *New York Times*, February 1, 1945, p. 25.

21. "16 Babies Burned in Maine Nursery," *New York Times*, February 1, 1945, p. 25; "Better Child Care Urged after Fire," *New York Times*, February 2, 1945, p. 22.

22. See note 21 above.

23. Ibid.

24. Ibid.; Eugenia Kaledin, *Mothers and More: American Women in the 1950s* (Boston: Twanye Publishers, 1984), pp. 32, 203.

25. Catherine Mackenzie, "Parent and Child," *New York Times*, August 19, 1945, sec. 6, p. 27, discusses Abigail F. Brownell, "Child Care Facilities for Dependent and Neglected Negro Children in Three Cities, New York, Philadelphia and Cleveland."

26. Weiner, *From Working Girl to Working Mother*, p. 136.

27. Ruth Milkman, *Gender at Work: The Dynamics of Job Segregation by Sex*

During World War II (Urbana: University of Illinois Press, 1987), pp. 100–101.

28. Barbara Ehrenreich and Deirdre English, *For Her Own Good: 150 Years of the Experts' Advice to Women* (Garden City, N.Y.: Anchor Press/Doubleday, 1978), pp. 191–207.

29. Evelyn Nakano Glenn, *Issei, Nisei, War Bride: Three Generations of Japanese-American Women in Domestic Service* (Philadelphia: Temple University Press, 1986), pp. 67–78; 206–10; Bonnie Thornton Dill, "Our Mothers' Grief: Racial Ethnic Women and the Maintenance of Families," Center for Research on Women, Memphis State University, May 4, 1986.

30. Vicki Ruiz, *Cannery Women Cannery Lives: Mexican Women, Unionization, and the California Food Processing Industry, 1930–1950* (Albuquerque: University of New Mexico Press, 1987), pp. 10–17.

31. Ibid.

32. Elsie George, "The Women Appointees of the Roosevelt and Truman Administrations: A Study of Their Impact and Effectiveness" (Ph.D. diss., American University, 1972); Nancy F. Cott, "Feminist Politics in the 1920s: The National Woman's Party," *Journal of American History* 71 (1984), pp. 43–68, 59.

33. Kessler-Harris, *Out to Work*, pp. 262–72.

34. Ibid., p. 135.

35. Scharf, *To Work and to Wed*, pp. 133–38.

36. Ehrenreich and English, *For Her Own Good*, pp. 192–203; Mintz and Kellogg, *Domestic Revolutions*, pp. 121–37.

37. Ibid.

38. Ibid.

39. Ehrenreich and English, *For Her Own Good*, pp. 203–13; Mintz and Kellogg, *Domestic Revolutions*, pp. 121–23.

40. Scharf, *To Work and to Wed*, pp. 153–55; Virginia Byerly, *Hard Times Cotton Mill Girls: Personal Histories of Womanhood and Poverty in the South* (Ithaca, N.Y.: ILR Press, 1986); Judith E. Smith, "Our Own Kind: Family and Community Networks in Providence" in Cott and Pleck, eds., *A Heritage of Her Own*, pp. 393–411; Phyllis Palmer, *Domesticity and Dirt: Housewives and Domestic Servants in the United States, 1920–1945* (Philadelphia: Temple University Press, 1989), p. 4.

41. Byerly, *Hard Times Cotton Mill Girls*, pp. 34–39; 125–27.

42. Smith, "Our Own Kind: Family and Community Networks in Providence," in Cott and Pleck, eds., *A Heritage of Her Own*, pp. 393–411; Kessler-Harris, *Out to Work*, pp. 269–71.

43. See note 42 above.

44. Elaine Tyler May, *Homeward Bound: American Families in the Cold War Era* (New York: Basic Books, 1988), pp. 1–15, 76, 89–91.
45. Mintz and Kellogg, *Domestic Revolutions*, pp. 179–82.
46. George Gallup, *The Gallup Poll Public Opinion 1935–1971* (New York: Random House, 1972), pp. 598–99, Gallup Poll, interviewing date, 8-16 to 8-21, publication date September 14, 1946. Question: "England allows $1 per week for each child under 16; should we have this?" Yes—30 percent; No—61 percent; No opinion—9 percent. When the question was changed to whether respondents approved of a family allowance to support children: 36 percent said yes and 46 percent of those with children under 16 said yes.
47. Frank Stricker, "Cookbooks and Lawbooks: The Hidden History of Career Women in Twentieth-Century America" in Cott and Pleck, eds., *A Heritage of Her Own*, pp. 476–98; Cott, *The Grounding of Modern Feminism*, pp. 209–45; Betty Friedan, *The Feminine Mystique* (New York: W.W. Norton, 1963; Dell paperback, 1963), pp. 50–52.
48. Mintz and Kellogg, *Domestic Revolutions*, pp. 123, 187–88.
49. Ibid., pp. 190–94.
50. Ibid., pp. 123, 187–88; Michael Zuckerman, "Dr. Spock, The Confidence Man," in Charles Rosenberg, ed., *The Family in History* (Philadelphia: University of Pennsylvania Press, 1975), pp. 179–207.
51. Ehrenreich and English, *For Her Own Good*, pp. 206–8.
52. "The New American Domesticated Male," *Life* 36 (1954), pp. 42–45; Nancy Cleaver, "Are You a Dud as a Dad?," *American Home*, August 1950, p. 21; May, *Homeward Bound: American Families in the Cold War Era*, pp. 140–49, 208–19.
53. See note 52 above.
54. Ibid.
55. Friedan, *Feminine Mystique*, p. 225; Barbara Ehrenreich, *The Hearts of Men* (Garden City, N.Y.: Anchor Press/Doubleday, 1983), pp. 88–97.
56. See note 55 above.
57. See note 55 above.
58. Kaledin, *Mothers and More*, pp. 93–94.
59. Weiner *From Working Girl to Working Mother*, pp. 89–96.
60. Ibid., pp. 89–96.
61. Kaledin, *Mothers and More*, ch. 2.
62. Ibid.
63. Mary Frances Berry, *Why ERA Failed: Politics, Women's Rights, and the Amending Process of the Constitution* (Bloomington: Indiana University Press, 1986), pp. 59–60; see generally, Leila J. Rupp and Verta Taylor, *Survival*

in the Doldrums: The American Women's Rights Movement, 1945 to the 1960s (New York: Oxford University Press, 1987); 96 *Congressional Record*, 81st Congress, 2d sess., 1950, pp. 861–73; 99 *Congressional Record*, 83rd Congress, 1st sess., 1953, pp. 8951–74.

64. William Chafe, *The American Woman: Her Changing Social, Economic and Political Roles, 1920–1970* (New York: Oxford University Press, 1972), pp. 160–72; Valerie Oppenheimer, *The Female Labor Force in the United States: Its Growth and Changing Composition* (Berkeley: University of California Press, 1967), pp. 138–39; U.S. Department of Labor, Women's Bureau, Employed Mothers and Child Care, Bulletin no. 246, 1953.

65. Steinfels, *Who's Minding the Children?*, p. 72.

66. Internal Revenue Code, 1954, ch. 736, section 214, 68A Stat. 70, repealed by Tax Reform Act of 1976, Public Law No. 94–455, section 504 (b) (1), 90 Stat. 1520, 1565.

67. *Smith* v. *Commissioner of Internal Revenue*, 40 U.S. Tax Appeals Reports 1038 (1939); the amount of the deduction was decreased by the amount by which the combined adjusted gross income of husband and wife exceeded $4,500; Stephen Ambrose, *Eisenhower*, 2 vols. (New York: Simon and Schuster, 1984), II, p. 58, the 1954 tax bill did not lower rates but did increase deductions thereby providing a tax cut of 7.4 million for 1954. Thanks to reductions in defense Eisenhower was able to balance the budget despite the tax cut.

68. 100 *Congressional Record*, 83rd Congress, 2d sess., March 18, 1954, debate on the Internal Revenue Code of 1954 pp. 3516–3561; Kelley, p. 3539; McCormack, p. 3550.

69. Internal Revenue Code, 1954, ch. 736, section 214, 68A Stat. 70, repealed by Tax Reform Act of 1976, Public Law No. 94–455, section 504 (b) (1), 90 Stat. 1520, 1565.

70. House Committee on Ways and Means, *Hearings*, 83d Congress, 1st sess., House No. 102, June and July 1953, pp. 69–71.

71. Ibid.

72. House Committee on Ways and Means, *Hearings*, 83d Congress, 1st sess., House No. 102, June and July 1953, pp. 31–33, 46–52.

73. *Public Papers of the Presidents*: Dwight Eisenhower, 1954, p. 716, No. 199, August 16, 1954; also budget message, second part, January 21, 1954. The change from a deduction to a credit took place in the Tax Reform Act of 1976. The allowable credit was 20 percent of expenses up to $4,000 amounting to $400 for one child and up to $800 for two children.

CHAPTER VI

Challenging the Mother-Care Tradition, 1960–1980

1. Lois Scharf, "ER and Feminism" in Joan Hoff-Wilson and Marjorie Lightman, eds., *Without Precedent: The Life and Career of Eleanor Roosevelt* (Bloomington: Indiana University Press, 1984), p. 247.
2. Scharf, "ER and Feminism," pp. 248–49.
3. Ibid.; Margaret Mead and Frances Bagley Kaplan, eds., *American Women: The Report of the President's Commission on the Status of Women and other Publications of the Commission* (New York: Charles Scribner's Sons, 1965), pp. 30 and 32; as usual with study commissions, the Women's Bureau and commission staff actually did the work from the beginning. They also kept in touch with the White House in shaping the study. Cynthia Harrison, *On Account of Sex, The Politics of Women's Issues* (Berkeley: University of California Press, 1988), pp. 136–39.
4. Harrison, *On Account of Sex*, pp. 89–105, 140; Barbara Ehrenreich and Deirdre English, *For Her Own Good: 150 Years of the Experts' Advice to Women* (New York: Doubleday, 1978), pp. 258–60.
5. Pauli Murray, *Song in a Weary Throat: An American Pilgrimage* (New York: Harper and Row, 1987), pp. 347–55; Harrison, *On Account of Sex*, pp. 89–105, 140; Ehrenreich and English, *For Her Own Good*, pp. 258–60.
6. Betty Friedan, *The Feminine Mystique* (New York: W.W. Norton, 1963), pp. 11–27.
7. Ibid.
8. Ibid.
9. Rochelle Gatlin, *American Women Since 1945* (Jackson: University Press of Mississippi, 1987), pp. 115–16.
10. Alice Echols, *Daring to Be Bad: Radical Feminism in America 1967–1975* (Minneapolis: University of Minnesota Press, 1989), pp. 387–89.
11. Harrison, *On Account of Sex*, pp. 192–95; Jo Freeman, "The Women's Liberation Movement: Its Origins, Organizations, Activities and Ideas" in Jo Freeman, ed., *Women: A Feminist Perspective* (Palo Alto, Calif.: Mayfield Publishing Co., 1975, 1979), pp. 557–73.
12. Gatlin, *American Women Since 1945*, pp. 77–96; Sara Evans, *Personal Politics: The Roots of Women's Liberation in the Civil Rights Movement and the New Left* (New York: Knopf, 1979), pp. 204–21.
13. Judith Hole and Ellen Levine, *Rebirth of Feminism* (New York: Quadrangle

Books, 1971), p. 85; Gatlin, *American Women Since 1945*, pp. 115–18; A. M. Jaggar and Paula S. Rothenberg, *Feminist Frameworks: Alternative Theoretical Accounts of the Relations Between Women and Men* (2d ed., New York: McGraw-Hill, 1979, 1984), p. 120; Alice Echols, *Daring to Be Bad*, pp. 3–4.

14. Daniel P. Moynihan, *The Negro Family: The Case for National Action* (Washington, D.C.: Government Printing Office, 1965); Andrew Billingsley, *Black Families in White America* (Englewood Cliffs, N.J.: Prentice Hall, 1966).

15. Toni Cade, "On The Issue of Roles" in Cade, ed., *The Black Woman: An Anthology* (New York: American Library, 1970), pp. 101–12.

16. Helen H. King, "The Black Woman and Women's Lib," *Ebony*, March 1971, pp. 68–76; "Letters to the Editor," *Ebony*, May 1971, pp. 20–23; Letha A. Lee See, "Tensions Between Black Women and White Women: A Study," 4 *Affilia*, no. 2 (1989), pp. 31–45.

17. "Letters to the Editor," *Ebony*, May 1971, pp. 20–23.

18. Title VII of the Civil Rights Act of 1964, 42 U.S.C. section 2000e et seq.; Revised Order No. 4, 41, C.F.R. section 60 et seq. part 60–2 revised order No. 4. The Equal Pay Act of 1963, 20 U.S.C. section 201 et seq. (Fair Labor Standards Act), section 206(d)t had been passed earlier.

19. Mary Frances Berry, *Why ERA Failed: Politics, Women's Rights, and the Amending Process of the Constitution* (Bloomington: Indiana University Press, 1986), pp. 63–64.

20. Ibid., *Roe* v. *Wade*, 410 U.S. 113 (1973).

21. 86 Stat. 235; 20 U.S.C. section 1681–86 (1976); 20 U.S.C. section 1866 (1976); 20 U.S.C., 2301 et seq. (1976).

22. *General Electric Co.* v. *Gilbert*, 429 U.S. 125 (1976); 42 U.S.C. section 2000e(k) (supp. 1974–79); U.S. Congress, House of Representatives, Civil Rights Act of 1964, Pregnancy Discrimination, H. Rep. No. 95–948, 95th Congress, 2d sess., p. 3.

23. 29 C.F.R. section 1604–Appendix (1979).

24. U.S. Department of Labor, Office of the Secretary, Women's Bureau, *Time of Change: 1983 Handbook on Women Workers*, Bulletin No. 298, pp. 16–17.

25. Ibid.

26. Jessie Bernard, *The Future of Marriage* (New York: Bantam Press, 1972), p. 72; Jessie Bernard, "The Good Provider Role: Its Rise and Fall," *American Psychologist* 36 (1981), pp. 1–12.

27. Lillian B. Rubin, *Worlds of Pain: Life in the Working Class Family* (New York: Basic Books, 1976), p. 102.

28. 41 C.F.R. Section 60–2.24(h) (1979).

29. Dorothy E. Bradbury, Children's Bureau, *Five Decades of Action for Children* (Washington, D.C.: Government Printing Office, 1962), pp. 96–98.

30. "U.S. Urged to Aid Day Care," *New York Times*, May 2, 1961, p. 31; "President Signs Relief Expansion," *New York Times*, May 9, 1961, p. 19.

31. Marjorie Hunter, "President Seeks Broad Reforms in Aid For Needy," *New York Times*, February 2, 1962, p. 1; "Funds for Day Care Voted by Congress," *New York Times*, May 17, 1963, p. 22.

32. Gilbert Steiner, *The Children's Cause* (Washington, D.C.: Brookings Institution, 1976), pp. 22–24; Margaret O'Brien Steinfels, *Who's Minding the Children? The History and Politics of Day Care in America* (New York: Simon and Schuster, 1973), ch. 2; J. McVicker Hunt, *Intelligence and Experience* (New York: Ronald Press, 1961), p. 362.

33. Benjamin Bloom, *Stability and Change in Human Characteristics* (New York: John Wiley & Sons, 1964), pp. 201–5, 228, 231 discussed in *New York Times*, April 17, 1968, sec. 6, p. 9.

34. Steiner, *The Children's Cause*, pp. 22–35. Joseph A. Califano, Jr., "Head Start: A Retrospective View of the Founders," Edward Zigler and J. Valentine, *Project Head Start: A Legacy of the War on Poverty* (New York: The Free Press, 1979), pp. 43–49.

35. John R. Nelson, Jr., "The Politics of Federal Day Care Regulation," in Edward Zigler and Edmund Gordon, eds., *Day Care: Scientific and Social Policy Issues*; Steiner, *The Children's Cause*, pp. 22–35.

36. Earl Caldwell, "Black Panthers Serving Youngsters a Diet of Food and Politics," *New York Times*, June 15, 1969, pp. 57, 196; Echols, *Daring to Be Bad*, pp. 223–38.

37. Earl Caldwell, "Black Panthers Serving Youngsters," p. 57.

38. Ibid.; John Hope Franklin and Alfred Moss, Jr., *From Slavery to Freedom: A History of Negro Americans* (New York: Knopf, 1988), pp. 459–60.

39. Echols, *Daring to Be Bad*, pp. 223–38.

40. Steinfels, *Who's Minding the Children?*, pp. 80–81, 280; Joel F. Handler and Ellen Hollingsworth, "Work, Welfare and the Nixon Reform Proposals," *Stanford Law Review* 22 (1970), pp. 907–42.

41. Nelson, "The Politics of Federal Day Care Regulation," in Zigler and Gordon, eds., *Day Care*, pp. 280–81; Walter Rugaber, "Nixon Asks Overhaul of Welfare, With Work or Training Required; Urges U.S. Aid States and Cities," *New York Times*, August 9, 1969, p. 1; "Nixon's Message to Congress on Welfare Plan," *New York Times* August 12, 1969, p. 18.

42. Edward Zigler, "A New Child Care Profession: The Child Development Associate," *Young Children*, December, 1971, pp. 71–74.

43. Steiner, *Children's Cause*, p. 62.

44. Henry Aaron, *Why Is Welfare So Hard to Reform* (Washington, D.C.: Brookings Institution, 1973), pp. 20–25; Michael Katz, *In the Shadow of the Poorhouse* (New York: Basic Books, 1986), p. 269; "City's H.R.A. Head Scores Nixon Idea," *New York Times*, August 12, 1969, p. 1.

45. Ibid.

46. Testimony of Elinor Guggenheimer on Child Care and Family Services, *Women's Role in Contemporary Society: The Report of the New York City Commission on Human Rights*, September 21–25, 1970 (New York: Avon Books, 1972), pp. 461–62.

47. Jack Rosenthal, "Plan for Health and Social Services to Children Gains in Congress," *New York Times*, June 14, 1971, p. 22; Marjorie Hunter, "Senate Approves a Broad System of Child Service," *New York Times*, September 10, 1971, p. 1; Nancy Hicks, "Specialists Hail Child Care Bill as a Step in Changing Program," *New York Times*, September 12, 1971, p. 28.

48. Jack Rosenthal, "Advocates of Child Care Bill Press Nixon to Sign It, But a Veto Appears Likely," *New York Times*, December 9, 1971, p. 11; Jack Rosenthal, "President Vetoes Child Care Plan as Irresponsible," *New York Times*, December 10, 1971, pp. 1, 20.

49. Letter to the Editor from Arnold A. Hutschnecker, M.D., *New York Times*, October 15, 1988, p. A30.

50. Memorandum to H.R. Haldeman from Charles Colson, subject "Conservatives," December 8, 1971, including handwritten notes; memorandum from Patrick Buchanan to Haldeman attached to his draft of a veto message, December 9, 1971; draft veto message by John Andrews, December 8, 1971; Haldeman Collection Box 87, National Archives and Records Administration, Washington, D.C.

51. *Public Papers of the President*, Nixon, "Veto of the Economic Opportunity Amendments of 1971," December 10, 1971, no. 387, pp. 1174–1178; *Congressional Record*, September 9, 1971, 31224–31263; Steiner, *Children's Cause*, pp. 90–117.

52. Robert H. Bremner, et al., *Children and Youth in America: A Documentary History*, II, 1866–1932 (Cambridge: Harvard University Press, 1971), p. 365; see also Ehrenreich and English, *For Her Own Good*, p. 131; Steiner, *Children's Cause*, pp. 153–57.

53. Carl Degler, *At Odds: Women and the Family in America from the Revolution to the Present* (New York: Oxford University Press, 1980), pp. 467–69.

54. Steiner, *Children's Cause*, pp. 174–75; Rochelle Beck, "Beyond the Stalemate in Child Care Public Policy," in Zigler and Gordon, eds., *Day Care*, pp. 307–10.

55. Steiner, *Children's Cause*, pp. 174–75; Beck, "Beyond the Stalemate."

56. Nelson, "The Politics of Federal Day Care Regulation," in Zigler and Gordon, eds., *Day Care*, pp. 280–81.

57. The Nixon administration also sponsored a National Center for Voluntary Action to persuade citizens to offer their services in housing, health, education and child care to avoid the need for government programs, Doris B. Gold, "Women and Voluntarism," in Vivian Gornick and Barbara Moran, eds., *Women in Sexist Society* (New York: New American Library, 1971), p. 534.

58. John Herbers, "McGovern Offers Broad Urban Plan," *New York Times*, October 22, 1972, p. 58; James F. Clarity, "Mrs. Nixon Quits Day-Care Unit," *New York Times*, February 9, 1973, p. 41.

59. Eileen Shanahan, "Women's Group Vows Poverty Fight," *New York Times*, February 20, 1973, p. 38; UPI, "Working Mothers Protest in Capital on Day Care Cuts," *New York Times*, April 11, 1973, p. 44; "300 Mothers Protest Cuts in Support for Day Care," Chinatown, *New York Times*, April 11, 1973, p. 51. Chinese women garment workers in Los Angeles organized a Little Friends play group to take care of their children. They too suffered budget cuts; Susie Ling, "The Mountain Movers: Asian American Women's Movement in Los Angeles," *Amerasia* 15, no. 1 (1989), pp. 51–67.

60. Gilbert Steiner, *The Futility of Family Policy* (Washington, D.C.: Brookings Institution, 1981), pp. 92–93.

61. ". . . *To Form a More Perfect Union . . .*" *Justice for American Women*, Report of The National Commission on the Observance of International Women's Year (Washington, D.C.: Government Printing Office, June 1976); President Ford issued the Executive Order creating the Commission and appointed 35 of its members including Assistant to the President Jill Ruckelshaus as Presiding Officer, the Congress appointed four members.

62. Eileen Shanahan, "Ford Vetoes Bill for Day Care Aid," *New York Times*, April 7, 1976, p. 9; Caroline Rand Herron and R. V. Deneberg, "A Block on Just One Block Grant," *New York Times*, April 11, 1976, sec. 4, p. 2; editorial, "The Day Care Vote," *New York Times*, May 4, 1976, p. 36; Nancy Hicks, "House Overrides the Veto of Day Care Bill, 301–101," *New York Times*, May 5, 1976, p. 1; Nancy Hicks, "President's Veto of Day Care Bill Upheld in Senate," *New York Times*, May 6, 1976, p. 1.

63. U.S. Department of Labor, Office of the Secretary, Women's Bureau, *Time of Change: 1983 Handbook on Women Workers*, Bulletin No. 298, pp. 2–22; conversation with Martin O'Connell, November 29, 1989, Bureau of the Census, Population Fertility Branch; Bureau of the Census, Current Population Survey, June 1977 Special Tabulation. There were 4,370,000

children under five of employed mothers in 1977. 33.9 percent were cared for at home, 14.4 percent by the father, 12.6 percent other relatives, 7.0 percent nonrelatives; 40.7 percent were cared for elsewhere, 18.3 percent in a relative's home, 22.5 percent in a nonrelative's home; 13.0 percent were in a day-care center or nursery; .4 percent were latch key; 11.4 percent were cared for by their mothers at work, which meant she either worked at home or took them to work with her; .6 percent were in other arrangements. By telephone, November 29, 1989, unpublished tabulation no. 15, March 1977 Current Population Survey, Bureau of Labor Statistics, p. 378.

64. Steiner, *The Futility of Family Policy*, pp. 32–46; James Wooten, "Carter Scores Ford on Foreign Policy—Assails Policy Toward Women," *New York Times*, October 3, 1976, p. 32. Carter told leaders of 60 national women's organizations he would establish federally subsidized day-care centers across the nation operated by state and local groups. He did not keep the promise.

65. Steiner, *The Futility of Family Policy*, pp. 32–46; personal recollections while Assistant Secretary for Education in HEW, 1977–1980.

66. Steiner, *The Futility of Family Policy*, pp. 94–95. Personal recollections; Suzanne Woolsey, the Associate Director at the Office of Management and Budget, responsible for clearing the testimony had written an article, "Pied Piper Politics and the Child-Care Debate," 106 Proceedings of the American Academy of Arts and Sciences (*Daedalus*, Spring 1977, pp. 127–45), in which she reached the same conclusions as Martinez's testimony. "Neither the evidence on parental preferences in day care nor the evidence on day care as part of the solution for other social ills suggests that a single solution to the day-care problem should be promoted. The data do not, however, support the contention that a heavy federal subsidization of institutional day care is desired by parents or would significantly promote other broad social goals," p. 129.

67. Mary Frances Berry, *Why ERA Failed: Politics, Women's Rights, and the Amending Process of the Constitution* (Bloomington: Indiana University Press, 1986), pp. 82–84.

CHAPTER VII

The Mother-Care Tradition Renewed, 1980–1988

1. Ronald Reagan, *Ronald Reagan's Call to Action* (New York: Warner Books, 1976), p. 137; Janet K. Boles, "Women's Rights and the Gender Gap," in

Tinsley Yarbrough, ed., *The Reagan Administration and Human Rights* (New York: Praeger Publishers, 1985), pp. 55–81.

2. Janet K. Boles, "Women's Rights."

3. U.S. Department of Labor, Bureau of Labor Statistics, *Working Women: A Chartbook*, Bulletin No. 2385, August, 1991, pp. 21–22.

4. Ibid., pp. 15–16; Mary Frances Berry, *Why ERA Failed: Politics, Women's Rights, and the Amending Process of the Constitution* (Bloomington: Indiana University Press, 1986), pp. 82–85.

5. Ibid., p. 75.

6. Ibid., pp. 65–71.

7. Betty Friedan, *The Second Stage* (New York: Summit Books, Simon & Schuster, 1981), pp. 18–19, 24.

8. Berry, *Why ERA Failed*, pp. 83–85.

9. Ibid., pp. 5–10, 81–83.

10. Carol Fesenthal, *The Biography of Phyllis Schlafly: Sweetheart of the Silent Majority* (Chicago: Regnery Gateway, 1982), p. 239.

11. Jane Sherron De Hart Mathews and Donald G. Mathews, *Sex, Gender, and the Politics of ERA* (New York: Oxford University Press, 1990), pp. 160–80.

12. Berry, *Why ERA Failed*, p. 65.

13. Ibid., pp. 108–9.

14. Ibid.

15. Ibid, pp. 107–10

16. *Grove City College* v. *Bell*, 79 L.Ed. 2d 516 (1984). The case interpreted Title IX of the Education Amendments of 1972 in a way that restricted protection against sex discrimination in education.

17. Berry, *Why ERA Failed*, pp. 118–19.

18. Ibid., pp. 115–17.

19. Ibid., pp. 116–18.

20. Ibid., p. 119.

21. Library of Congress issue brief, 1979; "Child Care, the Federal Role," by Margaret Malone, Issue Brief No. IB 77034 (1979), p. 12; Douglas J. Besharov and Paul N. Tramontozzi, "The Costs of Federal Child Assistance," Issue Paper, American Enterprise Institute, April 20, 1988, p. 22; the child-care provision was changed from a deduction to a credit in 1976.

22. David Stockman, *The Triumph of Politics: The Inside Story of the Reagan Revolution* (New York: Harper and Row, 1986, Avon paperback ed., 1987), pp. 1–15; 147–52.

23. Eugenia Hargrave, "Income Tax Treatment of Child and Dependent Care Costs: The 1981 Amendments," *University of Texas Law Review* 60 (1982),

pp. 321–354; Deborah Rankin, "When Uncle Sam Is the Baby Sitter," *New York Times*, September 13, 1981, sec. 3, p. 14; "N.A.A.C.P. Asserts Reagan Budget Profits the Rich at the Expense of the Poor," *New York Times*, April 14, 1981, p. 16; Jane Byrant Quinn, "Federal Help on Day Care Shifted from Poor to Middle Class," *Washington Post*, November 23, 1981, p. H39.

24. "Day Care Center Owner Charged in Child's Death," *New York Times*, December 3, 1981, p. 18; telephone conversation with Michelle Wade of Contra Costa County, California, District Attorney's office, January 1992; Michael Marriott, "Two Children Die at Day Care House in S.E.," *Washington Post*, April 28, 1982, p. C6; Marriott, "Tragedy Points Up Problem of Day Care Licensing," *Washington Post*, April 29, 1982, p. C1.

25. Katharine McDonald, "Boy, 7, Testifies for Second Day," *Washington Post*, January 24, 1985, p. A3; "Child Molestation Testimony Reveals Inherent Problems," *Washington Post*, January 28, 1985, p. A3; Jay Matthews, "Child Molestation Case a Long Way From Trial," *Washington Post*, May 10, 1985, p. E1; Matthews, "Most Charges Dropped in McMartin Case," *Washington Post*, June 13, 1985, p. A5; Robert Reinhold, "Long Child Molestation Trial Viewed as System Run Amok," *New York Times*, July 27, 1989, p. A1. Two years and three months after it began the McMartin case was "teetering on the brink" of a mistrial. The jurors gradually became victims of illness or discharge for sleeping and only one of six alternate jurors was left. By that time the case had cost almost 15 million dollars.

26. "Improving Child Care Services: What Can Be Done?" U.S. House, Hearings Before the Select Committee on Children, Youth, and Families, 98th Congress, 2d sess. (1984); Judy Mann, "Investment," *Washington Post*, March 16, 1984, p. C1.

27. See note 26 above; editorial, "Not Just Women's Issues," *New York Times*, August 17, 1984, p. 24.

28. Ibid.

29. Gallup Poll, 1986, taken between May 17 and 26, 1985; 43 percent in favor, 46 percent against, and 12 percent with no opinion.

30. Louise Saul, "More Companies Offer Child-Care as Job Inducement," *New York Times*, May 3, 1987, sec. 11, p. 1; Keith Schneider, "Broader Family Care Urged at Labor Session," *New York Times*, April 1, 1987, sec. 2, p. 5; Penny Singer, "Women's Issues Move to the Fore in Unions," *New York Times*, June 14, 1987, sec. 22, p. 16.

31. Glenn Collins, "Latch Key Children: A New Profile Emerges," *New York Times*, October 14, 1987, sec. 3, p. 1; Glenn Collins, "Jobs and Child Care Studied," *New York Times*, May 11, 1987, sec. 3, p. 11.

32. U.S. Bureau of the Census Report, May 1987, "Who's Minding the Kids?";

Spencer Rich, "Women Pay $11.1 Billion for Child Care While at Work," *Washington Post*, May 8, 1987, p. A5.

33. Anne L. Radigan, "Concept and Compromise, the Evolution of Family Leave Legislation in the U.S. Congress" (Women's Research and Education Institute, Washington, D.C., 1988), p. 5. Personal observations; conversations with Pat Schroeder, Judith Lichtman of the Women's Legal Defense Fund, Pat Reuss, Executive Director of the Women's Equity Action League; Pat Schroeder, *Champion of the Great American Family: A Personal and Political Book* (New York: Random House, 1989), pp. 44–56.

34. *Cal. Fed. Sav. & Loan Ass'n* v. *Guerra*, 479 U.S. 272 (1987).

35. Anne L. Radigan, "Concept and Compromise," pp. 5–15.

36. Ibid.

37. Ibid.

38. Ibid.

39. Amy K. Berman, "H.R. 4300, The Family and Medical Leave Act of 1986: Congress' Response to the Changing American Family," *Cleveland State Law Review* 35 (1987), pp. 479–82; Schroeder, *Champion of the Great American Family*, pp. 41–53.

40. Radigan, "Concept and Compromise," pp. 19–23; Schroeder, *Champion of the Great American Family*, pp. 54–55.

41. Radigan, "Concept and Compromise," pp. 19–29.

42. Amy K. Berman, "H.R. 4300, The Family and Medical Leave Act of 1986," pp. 479–82.

43. Edward Zigler, "For Many Father's Day Is No Field Day: Parental Leave for Men Too," *New York Times*, June 14, 1986, p. 27; letter to the editor from Isabelle Pinzler, "Equality Means that Men, Too, Are Responsible for Child Care," *New York Times*, June 29, 1986, sec. 4, p. 22.

44. See note 41.

45. *Cal Fed. Sav. & Loan Ass'n* v. *Guerra*, 479 U.S. 272 (1987).

46. See note 41.

47. Ibid.

48. Katherine McFate, "Welfare: Dependency vs. Reform," Judith Gueron, President of the Manpower Demonstration Research Corporation, a New York based, nonprofit research group, which evaluated 11 state WIN programs, reported that effectiveness was uneven. Joint Center for Political Studies, *Focus* 16 (1988), pp. 3–4.

49. Conversations with Andrew Brimmer who was a Commerce Department Assistant Secretary and Roger Wilkins who was Assistant Attorney General for Community Relations.

50. Roosevelt's January 4, 1935, State of the Union address was not about

welfare. He proposed a publicly funded jobs program, calling the unavailability of work for able-bodied people "a narcotic, a destroyer of the human spirit." *Public Papers and Addresses of Franklin Roosevelt, 1935*, pp. 20–21.

51. H.R. 1720, December 16, 1987; Spencer Rich, "Panel Clears Welfare Bill," *Washington Post*, September 28, 1988, p. A4. See, for example, Troy Duster, "Crime, Youth Unemployment and the Black Urban Underclass," *Crime and Delinquency* 33, no. 2 (April 1987), pp. 300–16.

52. AP wire, *Washington Post*, May 6, 1987, p. A16.

53. H.R. 1720, 133 *Congressional Record* (1987); House Reports No. 100–159, Pt. 1 (Committee on Ways and Means), Pt. 2 (Committee on Education and Labor), and Pt. 3 (Committee on Energy and Commerce) and No. 100–998 (Committee of Conference); S. 1511, 134 *Congressional Record* (1988).

54. "Family Support Act of 1988," Public Law 100–485, 100th Congress; Volume 102 of the Statutes at Large of the U.S., p. 2343 (October 21, 1988), Title II; sections 301–302 are the child-care provisions.

55. Ibid.

56. In fact, access to child care became a major problem in implementing the program, Julie Johnson, "Child Care Lack Dims Welfare Program's Future," *New York Times*, December 12, 1989, p. A20.

57. William Stevens, "Welfare Bill's Radical Goals Would Take Years," *New York Times*, October 2, 1988, p. 20; Spencer Rich, "New Welfare Approach to Be Nationwide," *Washington Post*, October 14, 1988, p. A3.

58. The Department of Health and Human Services wanted to count people as participants in the program even if they were not being given the services required in addition to job training. The services such as education, child care, and support were very expensive and the administration was essentially trying to cut the program back to workfare with some job training as Hawkins had predicted. Martin Tolchin, "Welfare Changes Endangered, Governors Say," *New York Times*, May 21, 1989, p. 27; telephone conversation January 1992 with staff, Administration of Children and Families, and Social Services Block Grant Program, Department of Health and Human Services.

CHAPTER VIII

Toward a National Child-Care Policy, 1988–1990

1. Labor Force Statistics, Bureau of Labor Statistics.

2. U.S. Census Bureau Report, "Who's Minding the Kids?," May 1987. Em-

ployed mothers paid an estimated $11.1 million for child care while they worked; Spencer Rich, "Women Pay $11.1 Billion for Child Care While at Work," *Washington Post*, May 8, 1987, p. A5. The National Governors Conference announced a major effort on the part of states to help with child care. By the next April, "Who Cares for the Children" was a public television documentary supplemented with conferences, workshops, and a publication on child care; memorandum from Irene Natividad, a board member of the Child Care Action Campaign, January 22, 1990.

3. Sara Rimer, "Women, Jobs and Children: A New Generation Worries," *New York Times*, November 27, 1988, p. A1.

4. Conversations with Molly Yard, President of NOW; Karen DeCrow, past NOW president, reiterated the long history of NOW's advocacy of child care since 1967 in the April 1989 issue of *NOW National Times*, p. 4. In 1970 she pointed out NOW had asked for free universal 24-hour care to fit whatever needs parents had within that 24-hour spectrum.

5. Gilbert Steiner, *The Children's Cause* (Washington, D.C.: Brookings Institution Press, 1976), pp. 171–75; Pat Schroeder, *Champion of the Great American Family* (New York: Random House, 1989), pp. 57–86.

6. Steiner, *The Children's Cause*, pp. 171–75; Calvin Tompkins, "Profiles: A Sense of Urgency," *The New Yorker*, March 27, 1989, pp. 48–74, sketch of life and career of Edelman.

7. Tompkins, "Profiles: A Sense of Urgency," *The New Yorker*, March 27, 1989, pp. 48–74; conversations with Edelman over the years, and more specifically during the summer of 1988 while child care was being negotiated.

8. Tompkins, "Profiles: A Sense of Urgency."

9. Ibid.

10. Ibid.

11. Karen Offen, "Defining Feminism: A Comparative Historical Approach," *Signs* 14 (1988), pp. 119–57.

12. Conversation with Molly Yard, August 1988.

13. Conversation with Phyllis Schlafly, May 3, 1988.

14. Act for Better Child Care, H.R. 3660, 100th Congress, 2d sess.; S. 1885, 100th Congress, 2d sess.

15. Ibid.

16. Ibid.

17. Ibid.

18. Ibid.

19. Child Care Services Improvement Act, H.R. 4002 (S. 1678/S. 1679); 100th Congress, 2d sess.

20. 100th Congress, 2d sess., House Education and Labor Committee, Human Resources Subcommittee, February 25, 1988.
21. Ibid.
22. Ibid.
23. Ibid.
24. 100th Congress, 2d sess., Senate Labor and Human Resources Committee, Children, Families, and Drugs and Alcoholism Subcommittee, March 15, 1988.
25. Ibid.
26. 100th Congress, 2d sess., House Education and Labor Committee, Human Resources Subcommittee, April 21, 1988.
27. Schroeder, *Champion of the Great American Family*, p. 60.
28. Linda Greenhouse, "Church State Debate Blocks Day Care Bill," Washington Talk, *New York Times*, September 8, 1988, p. B9. The issue that concerned the bishops was whether federal funds could be used if a church which runs a center as part of its religious mission wants to hire and admit children on the basis of religious faith or on the basis of sex for religious reasons.
29. Ibid.
30. Conversations with Congressman Hawkins and Edelman, summer 1988.
31. Ibid.
32. Bill Peterson, "Bush Proposes Child-Care Tax Credits," *Washington Post*, July 25, 1988, p. A5; Gerald Boyd, "Tax Refund Proposed by Bush in Child Care Plan," *New York Times*, July 25, 1988, p. A1; George Gallup, Jr., *The Gallup Poll*, Public Opinion 1988 (Wilmington, Delaware, 1989), pp. 219, 229.
33. E. J. Dionne, Jr., "New Poll Shows Attacks by Bush Building Lead," *New York Times*, November 9, 1988, p. 1.
34. Letter from Judy Lichtman to WLDF President's Council November 14, 1988; the Leave Bill in the incarnation under discussion would guarantee 10 weeks of unpaid parental leave every two years for the birth, illness, or adoption of a child and 15 weeks of unpaid leave every year for the worker's own serious illness. When the employee returned the employer would be required to provide the same or a comparable job. Existing health insurance coverage would continue during the leave, but other employee benefits such as pensions and life insurance would be frozen. Companies with fewer than fifty employees in the House version and twenty employees in the Senate version would be exempt. The Senate version did not include elder care but the House version did.
35. Ibid.

36. Tom Kenworthy, "Women's Groups Press Congress on Parental Leave," *Washington Post*, September 8, 1988, p. A4; Sandra Sugawara, "Benefit or Burden? Business Lobby Against Parental Leave Bill," *Washington Post*, October 5, 1988, p. F1; Report by National Association of Working Women, *Washington Post*, September 5, 1988, p. 10; ". . . empirically . . . parental leave does not hurt small business." Telephone conversation with Pat Reuss, executive director, Women's Equity Action League, in October and on November 2, 1988.

37. Conversations with Molly Yard and other participants in the child-care and women's rights groups.

38. Helen Dewar and Don Phillips, "Politics Mires Family Issues," *Washington Post*, September 30, 1988, p. A4; Irvin Molotsky, "Day Care and Parental Leave Bill," *New York Times*, October 8, 1988, p. 7.

39. Helen Dewar, "Child Care-Parental Leave Bill Dies," *Washington Post*, November 14, 1988, p. 1; letter from Lichtman to WLDF President's Council November 14, 1988.

40. See note 39 above.

41. "The Candidates and Poor Children," editorial, *New York Times*, September 25, 1988, p. E24.

42. Julie Johnson, "Child Care No Shortage of Proposals," "A Push by Conservatives as Well as Liberals," *New York Times*, March 26, 1989, p. E5.

43. Ibid.

44. Ibid.

45. Ibid.; Tompkins, "Profiles: A Sense of Urgency," p. 71; the bill came to the Senate floor on Wednesday, June 14, 1989. U.S. Congress, Senate, Committee on Labor and Human Resources, Act for Better Child Care Services of 1989, 101st Congress, 1st sess., S. Rept. 101–17; Senators Kassebaum, Coats, Thurmond, Durenberger, and Cochran voted nay.

46. Shapiro, Robert Greenstein, "Making Work Pay: A New Agenda for Poverty Policies," Issue Paper, March 21, 1989, pp. 10–16; Center on Budget and Policy Priorities. *Internal Revenue Code of 1986*, Section 129, Dependent Care Assistant Programs; Section 32, Earned Income; Peter Passell, "Economic Scene a Breakthrough on Poverty?," *New York Times*, March 1, 1989, p. D2; "Early Childhood and Development Act of 1989," Report on H.R. 3, Report 101–190, Part 1, 101st Congress, 1st sess., July 27, 1989.

47. Frank Swoboda, "Democrats Push Early Test of Minimum Wage, Parental Leave Issues," *Washington Post*, February 14, 1989, p. E1, 52.

48. Pat Schroeder, "We Need a Law to Ensure Family Leave," Ronald C. Pilenzo, "Don't Pass a Law: Keep Benefits Flexible," Face-Off (Granting Employees Parental Leave), *USA Today*, February 13, 1989, p. 6A. By May

24, Schroeder knew that the bill would not get to the House floor. Conversation with Pat Schroeder, May 24, 1989; Frank Swoboda, " 'Family Issues' Fight Coming to a Head," *Washington Post*, April 20, 1989, p. A17.

49. Marian Wright Edelman, "Pass That Child Care Bill," *Washington Post*, June 20, 1989, p. A23.

50. U.S. Congress, Senate, Committee on Labor and Human Resources, Act for Better Child Care Services of 1989, 101st Congress, 1st sess., S. Rept. 101–17; *Congressional Record*, June 20, 1989, pp. S6973–S6975.

51. *Congressional Record*, June 20, 1989, pp. S6972–S6975, S6952–S6963.

52. Julie Kosterlitz, "Tough to Typecast," *National Journal* 21 (1989), pp. 2088–92; conversations with CDF staffer Helen Blank and Marian Edelman.

53. *Congressional Record*, June 20, 1989, pp. S6953–S6954; Kassebaum voted for the compromise bill on final passage and was a member of the conference committee between the House and Senate. She voted for it essentially because nothing better was available. Conversation with Nancy Kassebaum, May 20, 1990.

54. *Congressional Record*, June 23, 1989, pp. S7394–S7396, S7401–S7418, S7438–S7499.

55. Ibid.; the maximum amount anyone could make and qualify for benefits under any of the credits was $28,000; also benefits would be phased out as income increased. None of the credits was large enough to permit the actual buying of care or health insurance.

56. Helen Dewar, "Child-Care Legislation Advances, Senate Democrats' Bill Offers Grants, Credits as Veto Is Threatened," *Washington Post*, June 24, 1989, p. A1.

57. William Safire, "Candidate for Veto," *New York Times*, June 29, 1989, p. A23.

58. Thomas B. Edsall, "Disputes over Social Issues Mark Partisan Upheaval in Congress," *Washington Post*, July 6, 1989, p. A14. "The Child Care Bill," an editorial in the *Washington Post*, June 22, 1989, p. A26 complained that sponsors ". . . have abandoned principles they would otherwise uphold and agreed to give funds to sectarian programs. . . . Badly as the sponsors want child care, they cannot want it this badly; the provision needs to be fixed."

59. Augustus Hawkins, "Child Care: Building on What Works," *Focus*, Joint Center For Political Studies, January/February 1989, pp. 7–8. Liberals and conservatives liked the earned income credit; liberals because it provided more money to the poor and conservatives because it did not require a government bureaucracy and went to poor people who were working and not

on welfare. Susan B. Garland and Howard Gleckman, "Washington Outlook," "The Rich Aren't the Only Ones Who May Get a Tax Break," *Business Week*, August 21, 1989, p. 37.

60. Jodie Allen, "Senate Child Care Measure's Missing Component: Old Fashioned Analysis," *Washington Post*, July 12, 1989, p. F3. Twenty-two percent of senior level appointments were women by early 1990. The first thing Adis Avila, one of the appointees as Assistant Secretary for Administration in the Agriculture Department, did was to establish an on-site child-care center. Memorandum from Irene Natividad to Mary Frances Berry, January 22, 1990; Susan F. Rasky, "House Panel Approves $16 Billion Child Care Bill," *New York Times*, July 20, 1989, p. A18.

61. Letter from Edelman to Downey and Miller, November 14, 1989; Dorothy Gilliam, "Child Care Bill Is Sacrificed," *Washington Post*, November 16, 1989, p. D3; David Johnstone, "Congress Plans to Put Off Action on Child Care Because of Impasse," *New York Times*, November 17, 1989, p. A18; Frank Swoboda, "Hill Democrats Postpone Action on Child-Care Proposals," *Washington Post*, November 16, 1989, p. A11.

62. "A Welcome Shift on Child Care," *New York Times* editorial, October 11, 1989, p. A30, "Millions of working parents depend on church-sponsored day care, but resistance to any form of public funding of sectarian child care program is widespread." Frank Swoboda, "Court Test Likely on Child Care," *Washington Post*, October 12, 1989, p. A8; Leah Latimer, "Suffer the Children: The Church-State Day Care Controversy," *Washington Post*, September 3, 1989, p. C5, "In the end parents will have to decide: Does it matter if toddlers sing 'Jesus Loves Me'? And how much evangelizing can you do with two-year-olds anyway?"

63. Letter from Edelman to Downey and Miller, November 14, 1989; letter from Members of Congress Harold Ford, Robert Matsui, William J. Coyne, Michael Andrews, Dan Rostenkowski, Barbara Kennelly, Don J. Pease, Nancy J. Johnson, Hank Brown, E. Clay Shaw, Don Lindquist to Marian Wright Edelman, November 17, 1989; David Johnstone, "Congress Plans to Put Off Action on Child Care Because of Impasse," *New York Times*, November 17, 1989, p. A18.

64. Congressman George Miller, letter to the *Washington Post*, November 25, 1989, p. A21, "I have no doubt a . . . child care bill will be law by the time the next funding cycle comes around and that it will contain an entitlement that means real child care services for working families, not empty promises." He thought there was so much disagreement that the bill would not have passed anyway this time. He promised also to work to "ensure that it contains the crucial improvements in training, wages and quality . . ."

which were in the Education and Labor bill but which the conferees agreed to delete.

65. Memorandum to Mary Frances Berry from Irene Natividad, past chair of NWPC and a member of the Board of Directors of Child Care Action Campaign, January 22, 1990.

66. State of the Union Message, January 31, 1990, *New York Times*, February 1, 1990, p. D22.

67. Frank Swoboda, "30 Billion Child-Care Bill Passes House; Veto Threatened," *Washington Post*, March 30, 1990, p. 1; Steven A. Holmes, "House, 265–145, Votes to Widen Day Care Programs in the Nation," *New York Times*, March 30, 1990, p. A14.

68. Steven A. Holmes, "House Passes Measure on Family Leave," *New York Times*, May 11, 1990, p. B6; Tom Kenworthy, "House Approves Bill Granting Unpaid Job Leave to Workers," *Washington Post*, May 11, 1990, p. 1; conversation with Senator Nancy Kassebaum; Steven A. Holmes, "House Backs Bush Veto of Family Leave Bill," *New York Times*, July 26, 1990, p. A16.

69. The Child Care Bill, Public Law 101–508, November 5, 1990, was included in the Omnibus Budget Reconciliation Act of 1990. Karen DeWitt, "U.S. Plan on Child Care Is Reported to Be Stalled," *New York Times*, January 27, 1991, p. A13.

70. Telephone conversation with staff of the Child Care Task Force, and the Title XX social services Block Grant program, Department of Health and Human Services, January 13, 1992.

71. Ibid.

CHAPTER IX

The Next Agenda

1. Saundra Torry, "Female Lawyers Face Persistent Bias, ABA Told," *Washington Post*, August 9, 1988, p. 1; according to the ABA Commission on women these were the latest data available as of January, 1992.

2. Jennifer A. Kingson, "Women in the Law Say Path Is Limited by 'Mommy Track,' " *New York Times*, August 8, 1988, p. 1; the president of the Washington, D.C., Bar Association, Phillip A. Lacovara, addressed these concerns typically. He wanted to make sure that the membership understood that this was not solely a women's issue. Over time he hoped attitudes would change about billable hours and what is required to get ahead. In the short run all employers should provide a menu of "flex-time, part-time positions

for working mothers, extended maternity leave with off-site professional work, and on site or group day care, or at least emergency day care and comparable programs for fathers who share child rearing with working spouses." But, "This is not the place to debate the sexually stereotyped bromide that 'a woman's place is in the home' or to debate the principle that both parents should have equal responsibility for rearing children and should equally adjust their careers to accommodate these nurturing roles." *The Washington Lawyer* 3 (1988), p. 6.

3. Sara Rimer, "Women, Jobs and Children: A New Generation Worries," *New York Times*, November 27, 1988, p. A1.

4. Felice N. Schwartz, "Management Women and the New Facts of Life," *Harvard Business Review* 89 (1989), pp. 65–76; her views fell within a tradition of social science support for the idea. Alice Rossi, "A Biosocial Perspective on Parenting," *Daedalus* 106 (1977), pp. 1–32, discusses the need to change work patterns for some women to fit their responsibilities for children; Kenneth Keniston and the Carnegie Council on Children, *All Our Children: The American Family Under Pressure* (New York: Harcourt Brace Jovanovich, 1977), suggested such an approach to meet child development needs.

5. Schwartz, "Management Women and the New Facts of Life," pp. 65–76.

6. Ibid.

7. Pat Schroeder, letter to the editor, *New York Times*, April 2, 1989, p. E30.

8. Ibid.

9. Conversation with Eleanor Smeal, March 16, 1989; Lewin, " 'Mommy Career Track' Sets Off Furor," *New York Times*, March 8, 1989, p. A18; Irene Natividad, "Do Women in Business Need a Mommy Track?" *Women's Political Times* 14 (1989), p. 3.

10. Lewin, " 'Mommy Career Track' Sets Off Furor," p. A18.

11. Sylvia Hewlett, letter to the editor of the *Harvard Business Review* 89 (1989), pp. 208–9.

12. Meredith Chen, "Women at Work: A New Debate Is Born," *Los Angeles Times*, March 19, 1989, sec. 4, p. 3; in the article a number of people were asked whether Schwartz's "mommy track" would help women to meet their career and personal goals or pigeonhole women and institutionalize unequal treatment.

13. Cindy Skrzycki, "Mommy Track Author Answers Her Many Critics," *Washington Post*, March 19, 1989, p. 1.

14. *Harvard Business Review* 89 (1989), pp. 184–210, published over 60 letters responding to Schwartz's article. Betty Friedan wrote that a positive aspect was that "At a time when the rights women have fought for are in jeopardy,

such outrage and discussion can keep those rights from being abolished,"
p. 200. Schwartz insisted she was dealing with the "flexibility women need
right now while they continue to bear the primary responsibility for child-
rearing," pp. 184–85; Kathy Bonk of the Communications Consortium was
given the task of organizing the women's organizations' response to Schwartz.
Memorandum to Mary Frances Berry from Irene Natividad, former Chair
NWPC, January 22, 1990.

15. Alison Leigh Cowan, "New Harvard Business Review Chief," *New York
Times*, December 4, 1989, p. D1; in 1992 Kanter stepped down as editor
of the *Review*; Felice Schwartz, *Breaking With Tradition: Women and Work,
the New Facts of Life* (New York: Warner Books, 1992).

16. Ed Bruske, "300,000 March Here for Abortion Rights," *Washington Post*,
April 10, 1989, p. 1; Robin Toner, "Right to Abortion Draws Thousands
to Capital Rally," *New York Times*, April 10, 1989, p. A1; Christine Spolar,
"Abortion-Rights Rally Draws Half a Million Marchers," *Washington Post*,
April 6, 1992, p. A1; Karen De Witt, "Huge Crowd Backs Right to Abortion
in Capital March," *New York Times*, April 6, 1992, p. A1; Christine Spolar,
"Departments Accuse Each Other of Doing a Number on Crowds," *Washington Post*, June 8, 1992, p. B1. The U.S. Park Police insisted no more
than 250,000 people participated in the march and were accused of down-
sizing the figures because the Bush administration opposes abortion rights.
The local police reported that at least 500,000 people marched.

17. Marjorie Williams, "Mothers and Daughters on the March," *Washington
Post*, April 10, 1989, p. B1; Martha Sherill, "Hollywood's Activists, Taking
Up the Banner," *Washington Post*, April 10, 1989, p. B1; E. J. Dionne,
Jr., "Tepid Black Support Worries Advocates of Abortion Rights," *New York
Times*, April 16, 1989, p. A1; personal observations.

18. Bruske, "300,000 March Here for Abortion Rights," p. 1; Toner, "Right to
Abortion Draws Thousands to Capital Rally," p. 1; Williams, "Mothers and
Daughters on the March," p. B1; Sherill, "Hollywood's Activists, Taking
Up the Banner," p. B1.

19. *Wards Cove Packing Co. v. Atonio*, 109 S.Ct. 2115 (1989); the case involved
cannery workers at a salmon processing facility. Minorities held most unskilled positions while whites predominated in higher paid, skilled positions.
The employer had separate hiring channels for unskilled and skilled jobs
so that a person once on the unskilled track could never apply for a skilled
job or get promoted to one. In addition, the employer never promoted from
within and only hired people at the entry level and maintained segregated
living and eating facilities for the employees. The Court rejected the minority
employee's complaint that this pattern and practice constituted illegal dis-

crimination under Title VII. The ruling applied as well to pay equity cases and other sex discrimination in employment complaints.

20. *Martin* v. *Wilks*, 109 S.Ct. 2180 (1989); the consent decree called for the hiring and promotion of blacks and whites in equal numbers until the fire department reflected the local labor market.

21. *Lorance* v. *AT&T Technologies Inc.*, 109 S.Ct. 2261 (1989). Until 1979 the firm had plant-wide seniority for promotions. In 1979 the rules were changed to job seniority, so that even if a person had plant-wide seniority he or she could not use it when the time came to move into higher-paying jobs. The company did not enforce the rule and continued to operate on the basis of plant-wide seniority. But in 1982 the three women plantiffs were demoted from their jobs when the company applied the new rules.

22. *Price Waterhouse* v. *Hopkins*, 109 S.Ct. 1775 (1989); Albert B. Crenshaw, "Judge Orders Partnership for Woman," *Washington Post*, May 15, 1990, p. A1 and A9. On remand, U.S. District Judge Gerhard Gesell ordered Price Waterhouse to give Linda Hopkins a partnership, and to pay her about $350,000 to make up for earnings lost as a result of illegal sexual stereotyping.

23. *Patterson* v. *McLean Credit Union*, 109 S.Ct. 2363 (1989).

24. Thurgood Marshall, "Remarks of Thurgood Marshall, Associate Justice, Supreme Court of the United States, at the Second Circuit Judicial Conference," September 1989, pp. 2, 5, copy in my possession.

25. Personal observations.

26. *Webster* v. *Reproductive Health Services*, 109 S.Ct. 3040 (1989); *United States Law Week* 57 (July 3, 1989), p. 5023.

27. Ibid., pp. 5031–35.

28. Ibid.

29. Ibid.

30. Four articles from *New York Times*, July 4, 1989, Linda Greenhouse, "Supreme Court, 5–4, Narrowing *Roe* v. *Wade*, Upholds Sharp State Limits on Abortion," p. 1; E. J. Dionne, Jr., "On Both Sides, Advocates Predict a 50-State Battle," p. A10; David Johnstone, "Confusion Followed by Confrontation as Ruling Stirs the Waiting Crowd," p. A10; Gina Kolata, "Doctors' Tools Limited in Testing Fetal Viability," p. A10.

31. See note 30 above.

32. Andrew Kohut and Larry Hugick, "55% Oppose High Court on Abortion, Poll Finds," *Washington Post*, July 12, 1989, p. A7.

33. T. R. Reid and Paula Yost, "Florida Plans Speedy Abortion Review," *Washington Post*, July 6, 1989, p. A10; R. W. Apple, Jr., "An Altered Political Climate Suddenly Surrounds Abortion," *New York Times*, October 13, 1989,

p. A1; editorial, "Abortion, the Voters and the Court," *New York Times*, November 13, 1989, p. A20; Andrew Rosenthal, "G.O.P. Leaders Urge Softer Line About Abortion," *New York Times*, November 10, 1989, p. A2.

34. Apple, "An Altered Political Climate," p. A1; editorial, "Abortion, the Voters and the Court," p. A20; Rosenthal, "G.O.P. Leaders Urge Softer Line About Abortion," p. A2.

35. S. 1912/H.R. 3700, 101st Congress, 1st sess.; Robin Toner, "Rallies for Abortion Rights Span Nation," *New York Times*, November 13, 1989, p. A14.

36. Claudia Wallis, "Onward, Women!," *Time*, December 4, 1989, pp. 80–82, 85–86, 89.

37. Lisa Belkin, "Bars to Equality of Sexes Seen as Eroding, Slowly," *New York Times*, August 20, 1989, pp. A1, 25.

38. "The 1990 Election," *New York Times*, November 8, 1990, p. B4; Maralee Schwartz and E. J. Dionne, Jr., "Abortion Showdown a Tossup," *Washington Post*, November 10, 1990, pp. A8–9.

39. Steven A. Holmes, "Bush Vetoes a Bill to Give Workers Family Leave," *New York Times*, June 30, 1990, p. A1; editorial, "Parental Leave: Leave It at That," *New York Times*, May 10, 1990, p. A32; letters to editor from American Association of Retired Persons President Louis Crooks and Judith Lichtman, president of WLDF, *New York Times*, May 20, 1990, p. E20.

40. Transcript, "The MacNeil/Lehrer NewsHour," Public Broadcasting Service, May 17, 1990.

41. Clifford Krauss, "House Backs Bill for Family Leave Up to 90 Days," *New York Times*, November 14, 1991, p. A1; Jason De Parle, "U.S. Loses Lead to States on Family Leave Policies," *New York Times*, September 21, 1991, p. A1.

42. Helen Dewar and Ann Devroy, "White House Sees Victory in Vote on Thomas Today," *Washington Post*, October 15, 1991, p. A1; Andrew Rosenthal, "President Tries to Quell Furor on Interpreting Scope of New Law," *New York Times*, November 22, 1991, p. A1. The vote was 93–5 in the Senate and 381–38 in the House.

43. Christine Spolar, "Abortion-Rights Rally Draws Half a Million Marchers," *Washington Post*, April 6, 1992, p. A1; Karen De Witt, "Huge Crowd Backs Right to Abortion in Capital March," *New York Times*, April 6, 1992, p. A1.

44. Linda Greenhouse, "High Court Takes Pennsylvania Case on Abortion Right," *New York Times*, January 22, 1992, p. 1.

45. See note 43.

46. *Planned Parenthood of Southeastern Pennsylvania et al. v. Robert Casey et*

al., *United States Law Week* 60, pp. 4795, 4798; Linda Greenhouse, "Slim Margin, Moderates on the Court Defy Predictions," *New York Times*, July 5, 1992, p. E1.

47. *Planned Parenthood* v. *Casey*, p. 4806.

48. Ibid., p. 4826.

49. Ruth Marcus, "5–4 Court Declines to Overrule Roe," *Washington Post*, June 30, 1992, p. 1; Linda Greenhouse, "High Court, 5–4, Affirms Right to Abortion but Allows Most of Pennsylvania's Limits," *New York Times*, June 30, 1992, p. A1; Robin Toner, "Ruling Eases Bush's Peril for Now but Leaves Him with a Problem," *New York Times*, June 30, 1992, p. A1.

50. Tamar Lewin, "Long Battles Over Abortion Are Seen," *New York Times*, June 30, 1992, p. A18.

51. WLDF President Judith Lichtman, to Mary Frances Berry, July 2, 1992.

52. *Planned Parenthood* v. *Casey*, p. 4801.

53. 1992 Democratic Platform—"A New Covenant with the American People"; the Republican Platform—"A New Call for Unity."

54. Ibid.

55. Labor Force Statistics Staff, Bureau of Labor Force Statistics; Robin Toner, "Right to Abortion Draws Thousands to Capital Rally," *New York Times*, April 10, 1989, p. A1.

56. Susan Antilla, "Analyst Looks to Family Trends to Guide Wall Street," *USA Today*, April 22, 1991, p. 9B; Tamar Lewin, "For Some Two-Paycheck Families, the Economics Don't Add Up," *New York Times*, April 21, 1991, p. E18.

57. Michelle Osborn, "Women Change Career Paths: More Stay Home with Children," *USA Today*, May 10, 1991; Paul Taylor, "Struggling to Be a Woman for All Seasons," *Washington Post*, May 12, 1991, p. A1; Paul Taylor, "Work Losing Romanticized Aura of the '80s," *Washington Post*, May 12, 1991, p. A18.

58. The analysis of the financial consequences of the child-care bill is based on Nancy Duff Campbell and Letitia Lee, "Changes in the Earned Income Tax Credit Under the Revenue Reconciliation Act of 1990," National Women's Law Center; conversation with Nancy Duff Campbell, May 15, 1991. The child-care legislation was officially part of the Omnibus Budget Reconciliation Act of 1990 signed into law by President Bush on November 5, 1990.

Bibliography

Primary Collections

Haldeman Collection, Box 87, National Archives and Records Administration, Washington, D.C.

Cases Cited

Cal Fed. Sav. & Loan Ass'n v. *Guerra*, 479 *U.S.* 272 (1987).
EEOC v. *Sears, Roebuck & Co.*, 39 *FEP Cases* 1672 (N.D. Ill. 1986).
General Electric Co. v. *Gilbert*, 429 *U.S.* 125 (1976).
Grove City College v. *Bell*, 79 *L.Ed.* 516 (1984).
Lorance v. *AT&T Technologies Inc.*, 109 *S.Ct.* 2261 (1989).
Martin v. *Wilks*, 109 *S.Ct.* 2180 (1989).
Mercein v. *People ex. rel. Barry*, 25 *Wend.* 641 (New York 1840).
Muller v. *Oregon*, 208 *U.S.* 412 (1908) 421–22.
Patterson v. *McLean Credit Union*, 109 *S.Ct.* 2363 (1989).
Planned Parenthood of Southeastern Pennsylvania v. *Casey*, 60 *United States Law Week* 4795 (1992).
Price Waterhouse v. *Hopkins*, 109 *S.Ct.* 1775 (1989).

Roe v. *Wade*, 410 *U.S.* 113 (1973).

Smith v. *Commissioner of Internal Revenue*, 40 *U.S. Tax Appeals Reports* 1038 (1939).

United Auto Workers v. *Johnson Controls, Inc.*, 59 *United States Law Week* 4209–4219 (1991).

Wards Cove Packing Co. v. *Atonio* 109 *S.Ct.* 2115 (1989).

Webster v. *Reproductive Health Services*, 109 *S.Ct.* 3040 (1989).

Books

Aaron, Henry. *Why Is Welfare So Hard to Reform*. Washington, D.C.: Brookings Institution, 1973.

Addams, Jane. *Twenty Years at Hull House*. New York: Macmillan, 1910.

Ambrose, Stephen. *Eisenhower*. 2 vols. New York: Simon and Schuster, 1984.

Armes, Ethel, ed. *Nancy Shippen: Her Journal Book*. Philadelphia: J.B. Lippincott Co., 1935.

Babcock, Barbara Allen, Ann E. Freedman, Eleanor Holmes Norton, and Susan C. Ross. *Sex Discrimination and the Law, Causes and Remedies*. Boston: Little, Brown & Co., 1975.

Becker, Susan. *The Origins of the Equal Rights Amendment: American Feminism Between the Wars*. Westport, Conn.: Greenwood Press, 1981.

Beecher, Catherine E. *Treatise on Domestic Economy*. Rev. 3rd ed. New York: Harper and Row, 1847.

Berger, Brigitte, and Peter Berger. *The War Over the Family: Capturing the Middle Ground*. New York: Anchor Press/Doubleday, 1983.

Bernard, Jessie. *The Future of Marriage*. New York: Bantam Press, 1972.

Berry, Mary Frances. *Why ERA Failed: Politics, Women's Rights, and the Amending Process of the Constitution*. Bloomington: Indiana University Press, 1986.

Berry, Mary Frances, and John Blassingame. *Long Memory: The Black Experience in America*. New York: Oxford University Press, 1982.

Billingsley, Andrew. *Black Families in White America*. Englewood Cliffs, N.J.: Prentice Hall, 1966.

Blake, Nelson Manfred. *The Road to Reno: A History of Divorce in the United States*. New York: Macmillan, 1962.

Blassingame, John W. *Slave Testimony: Two Centuries of Letters, Speeches, Interviews and Autobiographies*. Baton Rouge: Louisiana State University Press, 1977.

———. *The Slave Community*. New York: Oxford University Press, 1979.

Bleier, Ruth. *Science and Gender: A Critique of Biology and Its Theories on Women.* New York: Pergamon Press, 1984.

Bloom, Benjamin. *Stability and Change in Human Characteristics.* New York: John Wiley & Sons, 1964.

Boswell, John. *The Kindness of Strangers: The Abandonment of Children in Western Europe From Late Antiquity to the Renaissance.* New York: Pantheon Books, 1988.

Brace, Charles Loring. *The Dangerous Classes of New York and Twenty Years of Work Among Them.* New York: Wynkoop and Hallenbeck, 1872.

Brant, Irving. *James Madison: The Virginia Revolutionist, 1751–1789.* Indianapolis: Bobbs-Merrill Co., 1941.

Brazelton, T. Berry. *Working and Caring.* Reading, Mass.: Addison-Wesley Publishing Co., 1985.

Bremner, Robert H., John Barnard, Tamara K. Hareven, Robert M. Mennell. *Children and Youth in America: A Documentary History.* 3 vols. Cambridge: Harvard University Press, 1970.

Brenzel, Barbara M. *Daughters of the State: A Social Portrait of the First Reform School for Girls in North America, 1856–1905.* Cambridge, Mass.: MIT Press, 1983.

Brown, Dorothy. *American Women in the 1920s Setting a Course.* Boston: Twayne Publishers, 1987.

Byerly, Virginia. *Hard Times Cotton Mill Girls: Personal Histories of Womanhood and Poverty in the South.* Ithaca, N.Y.: ILR Press, 1986.

Calhoun, Arthur W. *A Social History of the American Family from Colonial Times to the Present.* New York: Arno Press, 1973.

Chafe, William. *The American Woman: Her Changing Social, Economic, and Political Roles, 1920–1970.* New York: Oxford University Press, 1972.

Chodorow, Nancy. *The Reproduction of Mothering: Psychoanalysis and the Sociology of Gender.* Berkeley and Los Angeles: University of California Press, 1978.

Clinton, Catherine. *The Plantation Mistress: Woman's World in the Old South.* New York: Pantheon Books, 1982.

Cornish, Dudley. *The Sable Arm: Negro Troops in the Union Army, 1864–1865.* New York: Longman Green, 1956.

Cott, Nancy. *The Bonds of Womanhood: Woman's Sphere in New England, 1780–1835.* New Haven: Yale University Press, 1977.

———. *The Grounding of Modern Feminism.* New Haven: Yale University Press, 1987.

Cott, Nancy, ed. *Root of Bitterness: Documents of the Social History of American Women.* Boston: Northeastern University Press, 1986.

Cott, Nancy F., and Elizabeth H. Pleck, eds. *A Heritage of Her Own.* New York: Simon & Schuster, 1979.

Culley, Margo, ed. *A Day at a Time: The Diary Literature of American Women from 1764 to the Present.* Old Westbury, New York: Feminist Press, 1985.

Daniel, Pete. *The Shadow of Slavery, 1901–1969.* Urbana: University of Illinois, 1972.

Degler, Carl. *At Odds: Women and the Family in America from the Revolution to the Present.* New York: Oxford University Press, 1980.

Demos, John. *Entertaining Satan: Witchcraft and the Culture of Early New England.* New York: Oxford University Press, 1982.

———. *A Little Commonwealth: Family Life in Plymouth Colony.* New York: Oxford University Press, 1970.

———. *Past, Present and Personal: The Life Course in American History.* New York: Oxford University Press, 1986.

Diner, Hasia. *Erin's Daughters in America: Irish Immigrant Women in the Nineteenth Century.* Baltimore: Johns Hopkins University Press, 1983.

Dublin, Thomas. *Women at Work: The Transformation of Work and Community in Lowell, Massachusetts, 1826–1860.* New York: Columbia University Press, 1979.

DuBois, Ellen Carol. *Feminism and Suffrage: The Emergence of an Independent Women's Movement in America.* Ithaca, N.Y.: Cornell University Press, 1978.

DuBois, Ellen Carol, ed. *Elizabeth Cady Stanton/ Susan B. Anthony: Correspondence, Writing, Speeches.* New York: Schocken Books, 1981.

Du Bois, W. E. B., ed. *Efforts for Social Betterment Among Negro Americans.* No. 14. Atlanta: Atlanta University Publications, 1909.

———. *Some Efforts of Negroes for Social Betterment.* No. 3. Atlanta: Atlanta University Publications, 1898.

Dudden, Faye. *Serving Women: Household Service in Nineteenth Century America.* Middletown, Conn.: Wesleyan University Press, 1983.

Duster, Alfreda, ed. *Crusade For Justice: The Autobiography of Ida B. Wells.* Chicago: University of Chicago Press, 1971.

Echols, Alice. *Daring to Be Bad: Radical Feminism in America 1967–1975.* Minneapolis: University of Minnesota Press, 1989.

Ehrenreich, Barbara, and Deirdre English. *For Her Own Good: 150 Years of the Experts' Advice to Women.* New York: Doubleday, 1978.

Ellet, Elizabeth. *Pioneer Women of the West.* New York: Charles Scribner's Sons, 1856.

Evans, Sara. *Born for Liberty: A History of Women in America.* New York: The Free Press, 1986.

————. *Personal Politics: The Roots of Women's Liberation in the Civil Rights Movement and the New Left.* New York: Knopf, 1979.

Fallows, Deborah. *A Mother's Work.* Boston: Houghton Mifflin, 1985.

Faludi, Susan. *Backlash: The Undeclared War Against American Women.* New York: Crown Publishers, 1991.

Falwell, Jerry. *Listen America.* New York: Doubleday, 1980.

Faragher, John Mack. *Women and Men on the Overland Trail.* New Haven: Yale University Press, 1979.

Flexner, Eleanor. *Century of Struggle: The Woman's Rights Movement in the United States.* 2nd ed. Cambridge, Mass.: Harvard University Press, 1959, 1972.

Fliegelman, Jay. *Prodigals and Pilgrims: The American Revolution Against Patriarchal Authority, 1750–1800.* Cambridge, England: Cambridge University Press, 1982.

Foner, Eric. *Reconstruction: America's Unfinished Revolution, 1863–1877.* New York: Harper & Row, 1988.

Foner, Philip, ed. *Women and the American Labor Movement.* New York: Macmillan Co., 1979.

Franklin, John Hope, and Alfred Moss, Jr. *From Slavery to Freedom: A History of Negro Americans.* 6th ed. New York: Knopf, 1988.

Friedan, Betty. *The Second Stage.* New York: Simon & Schuster, 1981.

————. *The Feminine Mystique.* New York: W. W. Norton, 1963.

Friedman, Lawrence. *The History of American Law.* New York: Simon & Schuster, 1985.

Gallup, George. *The Gallup Poll Public Opinion, 1935–1971.* New York: Random House, 1972.

Gatlin, Rochelle. *American Women Since 1945.* Jackson: University Press of Mississippi, 1987.

Geary, James W. *We Need Men: The Union Draft in the Civil War.* DeKalb: Northern Illinois University Press, 1991.

Geertz, Clifford. *The Interpretation of Cultures.* New York: Basic Books, 1973.

Gerson, Noel B. *Light Horse Harry: A Biography of Washington's Great Cavalryman General Henry Lee.* Garden City, N.Y.: Doubleday & Co. Inc., 1966.

Giddings, Paula. *When and Where I Enter: The Impact of Black Women on Race and Sex in America.* New York: William Morrow & Co., 1984.

Gilder, George. *Wealth and Poverty.* New York: Basic Books, 1981.

Gilligan, Carol. *In a Different Voice: Psychological Theory and Women's Development.* Cambridge: Harvard University Press, 1982.

Gilligan, Carol, Janie Victoria Ward, and Jill McLean Taylor, with Betty Bardige, ed. *Mapping the Moral Domain: A Contribution of Women's Thinking to Psychological Theory and Education.* Cambridge: Harvard University Press, 1989.

Glenn, Evelyn Nakano. *Issei, Nisei, War Bride: Three Generations of Japanese-American Women in Domestic Service.* Philadelphia: Temple University Press, 1986.

Gordon, Linda. *Woman's Body, Woman's Right: Birth Control in America.* New York: Penguin Books, 1977, 1983.

Graves, Mrs. A. J. *Woman in America: Being an Examination into the Moral and Intellectual Condition of American Female Society.* New York: Harper and Bros., 1841.

Greenwald, Maurine. *Women, War, and Work.* Ithaca: Cornell University Press, 1990.

Grimké, Angelina. *An Appeal to the Women of the Nominally Free States.* 2d ed. Boston: Isaac Knapp, 1838.

Grossberg, Michael. *Governing the Hearth: Law and Family in Nineteenth-Century America.* Chapel Hill: University of North Carolina Press, 1985.

Gutman, Herbert. *The Black Family in Slavery and Freedom, 1750–1925.* New York: Vintage Books, 1977.

Harrison Cynthia. *On Account of Sex: The Politics of Women's Issues.* Berkeley: University of California Press, 1988.

Hayden, Delores. *Redesigning the American Dream: The Future of Housing, Work and Family.* New York: W. W. Norton, 1984.

Hendrick, Burton. *The Life of Andrew Carnegie.* 2 vols. Garden City, N.Y.: Doubleday Doran and Co., 1932.

Hewlett, Sylvia. *A Lesser Life: The Myth of Women's Liberation in America.* New York: William Morrow and Co., 1986.

Hiner, N. Ray, and Joseph M. Hawes, eds. *Growing Up in America: Children in Historical Perspective.* Urbana: University of Illinois Press, 1985.

Hochschild, Arlie. *The Second Shift: Working Parents and the Revolution at Home.* New York: Viking, 1989.

Hoff, Joan. *Law, Gender and Injustice.* New York: New York University Press, 1991.

Hole, Judith, and Ellen Levine. *Rebirth of Feminism.* New York: Quadrangle Books, 1971.

Honey, Maureen. *Creating Rosie the Riveter: Class, Gender, and Propaganda.* Amherst: University of Massachusetts Press, 1984.

Hunt, J. McVicker. *Intelligence and Experience.* New York: Ronald Press, 1961.

Jaggar, Alison M., and Paula S. Rothenberg. *Feminist Frameworks: Alternative Theoretical Accounts of the Relations Between Women and Men.* 2d ed. New York: McGraw-Hill, 1979, 1984.

James, Edward T., Janet Wilson James, and Paul Boyer. *Notable American Women: A Biographical Dictionary.* Cambridge, Mass.: Harvard University Press, Belknap Press, 1971.

Jeffrey, Julie Roy. *Frontier Women: The Trans-Mississippi West, 1840–1880.* New York: Hill and Wang, 1979.

Johnson, Michael P., and James L. Roark. *Black Masters: A Free Family of Color in the Old South.* New York: W. W. Norton, 1984.

Jones, Jacqueline. *Labor of Love, Labor of Sorrow: Black Women's Work and the Family from Slavery to the Present.* New York: Basic Books, 1985.

Kaestle, Carl. *The Evolution of an Urban School System, New York City, 1750–1850.* Cambridge: Harvard University Press, 1973.

Kaledin, Eugenia. *Mothers and More: American Women in the 1950s.* Boston: Twayne Publishers, 1984.

Kamerman, Sheila, and Alfred Kahn. *Maternity Policy and Working Women.* New York: Columbia University Press, 1983.

Karlsen, Carol. *The Devil in the Shape of a Woman: Witchcraft in Colonial New England.* New York: W. W. Norton, 1987.

Katz, Michael. *In the Shadow of the Poorhouse.* New York: Basic Books, 1986.

Keniston, Kenneth, and the Carnegie Council on Children. *All Our Children: The American Family Under Pressure.* New York: Harcourt Brace Jovanovich, 1977.

Kerber, Linda. *Women of the Republic: Intellect and Ideology in Revolutionary America.* Chapel Hill: University of North Carolina Press, 1980.

Kessler-Harris, Alice. *Out to Work: A History of Wage-Earning Women in the United States.* New York: Oxford University Press, 1982.

Koehler, Lyle. *A Search for Power: The Weaker Sex in Seventeenth Century New England.* Urbana: University of Illinois Press, 1980.

Koger, Larry. *Black Slaveowners: Free Black Slave Masters in South Carolina, 1790–1860.* Jefferson, N.C.: McFarland & Co., 1985.

Kuhn, Anne L. *The Mother's Role in Childhood Education: New England Concepts, 1830–1860.* New Haven: Yale University Press, 1947.

Lebsock, Suzanne. *The Free Women of Petersburg.* New York: W. W. Norton, 1984.

Lemons, J. Stanley. *Woman Citizen: Social Feminism in the 1920's.* Urbana: University of Illinois Press, 1973.

Lerner, Gerda. *The Creation of Patriarchy.* New York: Oxford University Press, 1986.

Levin, David. *Cotton Mather: The Young Life of the Lord's Remembrancer, 1633–1703.* Cambridge: Harvard University Press, 1978.

Litwack, Leon. *Been in the Storm So Long: The Aftermath of Slavery*. New York: Knopf, 1979.

Malone, Dumas. *Jefferson and His Time, Jefferson the Virginian*. Vol. I. Boston: Little, Brown and Co., 1948.

Matthews, Glenna. *Just a Housewife: The Rise and Fall of Domesticity in America*. New York: Oxford University Press, 1987.

May, Elaine Tyler. *Homeward Bound: American Families in the Cold War Era*. New York: Basic Books, 1988.

McCaughey, Elizabeth P. *From Loyalist to Founding Father: The Political Odyssey of William Samuel Johnson*. New York: Columbia University Press, 1980.

McFarlane, Alan, ed. *The Diary of Ralph Josselin, 1616–1683*. London: Oxford University Press, 1976.

McPherson, James. *Battle Cry of Freedom: The Civil War Era*. New York: Oxford University Press, 1988.

Mead, Margaret, and Frances Bagley Kaplan, eds. *American Women: The Report of the President's Commission on the Status of Women and Other Publications of the Commission*. New York: Charles Scribner's Sons, 1965.

Milkman, Ruth. *Gender at Work: The Dynamics of Job Segregation by Sex During World War II*. Urbana: University of Illinois Press, 1987.

Mintz, Steven, and Susan Kellogg. *Domestic Revolutions: A Social History of American Family Life*. New York: The Free Press, 1988.

Moore, Virginia. *The Madisons*. New York: McGraw-Hill, 1979.

Morgan, Edmund. *The Puritan Family: Essays on Religion and Domestic Relations in Seventeenth-Century New England*. Reprint ed. New York: Harper & Row, 1966.

Morgan, Hal, and Kerry Tucker. *Companies That Care: The Most Family Friendly Companies in America—What They Offer and How They Got That Way*. New York: Simon and Schuster/Fireside, 1991.

Morris, Richard B., and William Greenleaf. *U.S.A. The History of a Nation*. Chicago: Rand McNally, 1969.

Moynihan, Daniel P. *The Negro Family: The Case for National Action*. Washington, D.C.: Government Printing Office, 1965.

Murray, Pauli. *Song in a Weary Throat: An American Pilgrimage*. New York: Harper and Row, 1987.

Musto, David. *The American Disease: Origins of Narcotic Control*. Expanded ed. New Haven: Yale University Press, 1973; New York: Oxford University Press, 1987.

Norton, Mary Beth, David Katzman, Paul Escott, Howard Chudacoff, Thomas Paterson, and William Tuttle. *A People and a Nation: A History of the United States*. Boston: Houghton Mifflin, 1990.

O'Neill, William L. *Divorce in the Progressive Era*. New Haven: Yale University Press, 1967.

Oppenheimer, Valerie. *The Female Labor Force in the United States: Its Growth and Changing Composition*. Berkeley: University of California Press, 1967.

Otis, D. S. *The Dawes Act and the Allotment of Indian Lands*. Ed. by Francis Prucha. Norman: University of Oklahoma Press, 1973.

Palmer, Phyllis. *Domesticity and Dirt: Housewives and Domestic Servants in the United States, 1920–1945*. Philadelphia: Temple University Press, 1989.

Proceedings: Constitutional Convention of South Carolina. Charleston, S.C.: Denny & Perry, 1868; reprint: New York: Arno Press and *The New York Times*, 1968.

Radigan, Anne L. *Concept and Compromise, the Evolution of Family Leave Legislation in the U.S. Congress*. Washington, D.C.: Women's Research and Education Institute, 1988.

Reagan, Ronald. *Ronald Reagan's Call to Action*. New York: Warner Books, 1976.

Riley, Glenda. *The Female Frontier: A Comparative View of Women on the Prairie and the Plains*. Lawrence: University Press of Kansas, 1988.

Rosengartner, Theodore. *Tombee: Portrait of a Cotton Plantation*. New York: McGraw-Hill, 1987.

Ross, Dorothy. *G. Stanley Hall: The Psychologist as Prophet*. Chicago: University of Chicago Press, 1972.

Rossi, Alice, ed. *The Feminist Papers from Adams to De Beauvoir*. New York: Columbia University Press, 1973.

Rouse, Jacqueline. *Lugenia Burns Hope: A Black Southern Reformer*. Athens: University of Georgia Press, 1989.

Rubin, Lillian B. *Worlds of Pain: Life in the Working Class Family*. New York: Basic Books, 1976.

Ruggie, Mary. *The State and Working Women: A Comparative Study of Britain and Sweden*. Princeton: Princeton University Press, 1984.

Ruiz, Vicki. *Cannery Women Cannery Lives: Mexican Women, Unionization, and the California Food Processing Industry, 1930–1950*. Albuquerque: University of New Mexico Press, 1987.

Rupp, Leila J., and Verta Taylor. *Survival in the Doldrums: The American Women's Rights Movement, 1945 to the 1960s*. New York: Oxford University Press, 1987.

Ryan, Mary P. *Cradle of the Middle Class: The Family in Oneida County, New York, 1790–1865*. Cambridge: Harvard University Press, 1981.

Salmon, Marylynn. *Women and the Law of Property in Early America*. Chapel Hill: University of North Carolina Press, 1986.

Scarr, Sandra. *Mother Care/Other Care*. New York: Basic Books, 1984.

Scharf, Lois. *To Work and to Wed: Female Employment, Feminism, and the Great Depression*. Westport, Ct.: Greenwood Press, 1980.

Schlafly, Phyllis. *The Power of the Positive Woman*. New Rochelle, N.Y.: Arlington House, Publishers, 1977.

Scholten, Catherine M. *Childbearing in American Society, 1650–1850*. New York: New York University Press, 1985.

Schroeder, Pat. *Champion of the Great American Family: A Personal and Political Book*. New York: Random House, 1989.

Schwartz, Felice. *Breaking With Tradition: Women and Work, the New Facts of Life*. New York: Warner Books, 1992.

Scott, Joan Wallach. *Gender and the Politics of History*. New York: Columbia University Press, 1988.

Shapiro, Michael Steven. *Child's Garden: The Kindergarten Movement from Froebel to Dewey*. University Park and London: Pennsylvania State University Press, 1983.

Sidel, Ruth. *Women and Children Last: The Plight of Poor Women in Affluent America*. New York: Viking, 1981.

Sklar, Kathryn Kish. *Catharine Beecher: A Study in American Domesticity*. New York: W. W. Norton, 1976.

Smith, Daniel Blake. *Inside the Great Houses: Planter Family Life in Eighteenth-Century Chesapeake Society*. Ithaca: Cornell University Press, 1980.

Smith, Page. *John Adams*. Vol. I, 1735–1784. Garden City, N.Y.: Doubleday and Co. Inc., 1962.

Stansell, Christine. *City of Women: Sex and Class in New York, 1789–1860*. Urbana: University of Illinois Press, 1986.

Steiner, Gilbert. *The Futility of Family Policy*. Washington, D.C.: Brookings Institution, 1981.

Steiner, Gilbert, with Pauline H. Milius. *The Children's Cause*. Washington, D.C.: Brookings Institution, 1976.

Steinfels, Margaret O'Brien. *Who's Minding the Children? The History and Politics of Day Care in America*. New York: Simon & Schuster, 1973.

Sterling, Dorothy, ed. *We Are Your Sisters*. New York: W. W. Norton, 1984.

Stockman, David. *The Triumph of Politics: The Inside Story of the Reagan Revolution*. New York: Harper and Row, 1986.

Strasser, Susan. *Never Done: A History of American Housework*. New York: Pantheon Books, 1982.

Tanner, Nancy Makepeace. *On Becoming Human*. Cambridge, England: Cambridge University Press, 1981.

Tentler, Leslie Woodcock. *Wage-Earning Women: Industrial Work and Family*

Life in the United States, 1900–1930. New York: Oxford University Press, 1979.

Tiger, Lionel, and Robin Fox. *The Imperial Animal*. New York: Holt, Rinehart and Winston, 1971.

Ulrich, Laurel Thatcher. *Good Wives: Images and Reality in the Lives of Women in Northern New England*. New York: Random House, 1982.

Van Doren, Mark, ed. *The Correspondence of Aaron Burr and His Daughter Theodosia*. New York: Covici, Friede, 1929.

Ware, Susan. *Holding Their Own: American Women in the 1930's*. Boston: Twayne Publishers, 1982.

Wattenberg, Ben J. *The Birth Dearth*. New York: Pharos Books, 1987.

Weiner, Lynn Y. *From Working Girl to Working Mother: The Female Labor Force in the United States, 1820–1980*. Chapel Hill: University of North Carolina Press, 1985.

White, Burton. *A Parent's Guide to the First Three Years*. Englewood Cliffs, N.J.: Prentice Hall, 1981.

White, Deborah Gray. *Ain't I a Woman: Female Slaves in the Plantation South*. New York: W. W. Norton, 1985.

Zahnhiser, Marvin. *Charles Cotesworth Pinckney*. Chapel Hill: University of North Carolina Press, 1967.

Zainaldin, Jamil. *Law in Antebellum Society*. New York: Alfred A. Knopf, 1983.

Zelizer, Viviana A. *Pricing the Priceless Child: The Changing Social Value of Children*. New York: Basic Books, 1985.

Zigler, Edward, and Edmund Gordon, eds. *Day Care: Scientific and Social Policy Issues*. Boston: Auburn House Publishing Co., 1982.

Articles

Berman, Amy K. "H.R. 4300, The Family and Medical Leave Act of 1986: Congress' Response to the Changing American Family." *Cleveland State Law Review* 35 (1987): 479–82.

Bernard, Jessie. "The Good Provider Role: Its Rise and Fall." *American Psychologist* 36 (1981) 1:1–12.

Besharov, Douglas J., and Paul N. Tramontozzi. *The Costs of Federal Child Assistance*. Issue paper. Washington, D.C.: American Enterprise Institute, 1988.

Boles, Janet K. "Women's Rights and the Gender Gap." In *The Reagan Administration and Human Rights*, Tinsley Yarbrough, ed. New York: Praeger Publishers, 1985.

Brobeck, Stephen. "Images of the Family: Portrait Paintings as Indices of American Family Culture, Structure and Behavior, 1730–1860." In *Journal of Psychohistory* 5 (Summer 1977): 81–106.

Cade, Toni. "On the Issue of Roles." In *The Black Woman: An Anthology*, Toni Cade, ed. New York: American Library, 1970.

Califano, Joseph A., Jr. "Head Start: A Retrospective View of the Founders." In *Project Head Start: A Legacy of the War on Poverty*, Edward Zigler and J. Valentine, eds. New York: The Free Press, 1979.

Campbell, Nancy Duff, and Letitia Lee. "Changes in the Earned Income Tax Credit Under the Revenue Reconciliation Act of 1990." Washington, D.C.: National Women's Law Center.

Cancian, Francesca M. "The Feminization of Love." *Signs* 11 (1986): 692–709.

Cleaver, Nancy. "Are You a Dud as Dad?" *American Home*, August 1950, 21.

Cobb, Nathan. "The Baby Gurus." *Boston Globe Magazine*, June 17, 1990, 14.

Cohen, Susan, and Mary Fainsod Katzenstein. "The War Over the Family Is Not Over the Family." In *Feminism, Children and the New Families*, Sanford Dornbusch and Myra H. Strober, eds. New York: The Guilford Press, 1988.

Cott, Nancy F. "Feminist Politics in the 1920s: The National Woman's Party." *Journal of American History* 71 (1984): 43–68.

Crozier, Blanche. "Marital Support." *Boston University Law Review* (1935): 28–58.

DeCrow, Karen. *NOW National Times*, April 1989, 4.

Dill, Bonnie Thornton. "Our Mothers' Grief: Racial Ethnic Women and the Maintenance of Families." Memphis: Center for Research on Women, Memphis State University, Research Paper No. 4, 1986.

Duster, Troy. "Crime, Youth Unemployment, and the Black Urban Underclass." *Crime and Delinquency* 33 (April 1987): 300–16.

"Elizabeth Geer Diary and Letter [1847]." *Transactions* 35 (1907).

Fineman, Howard. "What's a Pair of Paradigms? The Newest Odd Couples." *Newsweek*, May 13, 1991, 35.

Foster, John N. "Ten Years of Child Saving Work in Michigan." *Proceedings of the National Conference of Charities and Corrections* (1884): 132–42.

Freeman, Jo. "The Women's Liberation Movement: Its Origins, Organizations, Activities and Ideas." In *Women: a Feminist Perspective*, Jo Freeman, ed., Palo Alto, Calif.: Mayfield Publishing Co., 1975, 1979.

Frug, Mary Joe. "Securing Job Equality for Women: Labor Market Hostility to Working Mothers." *Boston University Law Review* 59 (1979): 55–103.

Garland, Susan B., and Howard Gleckman. "The Rich Aren't the Only Ones Who May Get a Tax Break." *Business Week*, August 21, 1989, 37.

Gold, Doris B. "Women and Voluntarism." In *Women in Sexist Society*, Vivian Gornick and Barbara Moran, eds. New York: New American Library, 1971.

Goldin, Claudia. "Female Labor Participation: The Origin of Black-White Differences." *Journal of Economic History* 37 (March 1977): 87–108.

Gordon, Linda. "Social Insurance and Public Assistance: The Influence of Gender in Welfare Thought in the United States, 1890–1935." *American Historical Review* 97 (1992): 19–54.

Greenstein, Robert. "Making Work Pay: A New Agenda for Poverty Policies." Washington, D.C.: Center on Budget and Policy Priorities, 1989.

Guggenheimer, Elinor. [Testimony on Child Care and Family Services]. In *Women's Role in Contemporary Society: The Report of the New York City Commission on Human Rights*. New York: Avon Books, 1972.

Hallowell, Anna. "The Care and Saving of Neglected Children." *Journal of Social Science*, September 1880, 122.

Handler, Joel F., and Ellen Hollingsworth. "Work, Welfare and the Nixon Reform Proposals." *Stanford Law Review* 22 (1970): 907–42.

Hargrave, Eugenia. "Income Tax Treatment of Child and Dependent Care Costs: The 1981 Amendments." *University of Texas Law Review* 60 (1982): 321–54.

Harley, Sharon. "Northern Black Female Workers: Jacksonian Era." In *The Afro-American Woman: Struggles and Images*, Sharon Harley and Rosalyn Terborg-Penn, eds. Port Washington, N.Y.: Kennikat Press, 1978.

Hawkins, Augustus. "Child Care: Building on What Works." *Focus*, January-February 1989, 7–8.

Hewlett, Sylvia. "Letter to the Editor." *Harvard Business Review* 89 (May-June 1989): 208–9.

Karen, Robert. "Becoming Attached." *Atlantic Monthly* 265 (February 1990): 35–50.

King, Helen H. "The Black Woman and Women's Lib." *Ebony*, March 1971, 68.

Kosterlitz, Julie. "Tough to Typecast." *National Journal* 21 (August 19, 1989): 2088–92.

Lacovara, Philip A. "President's Page," *Washington Lawyer* 3 (November-December 1988): 6.

LaFromboise, Theresa, and Anneliese M. Heyle. "Changing and Diverse Roles of Women in American Indian Culture." *Sex Roles* 2 (1990): 455–76.

Lambert, Helen H. "Biology and Equality: A Perspective on Sex Differences." *Signs* 4 (1978): 97–117.

"Letters to the Editor." *Ebony*, May 1971, 20–23.

Ling, Susie. "The Mountain Movers: Asian American Women's Movement in Los Angeles." *Amerasia* 15, no. 1 (1989): 51–67.

Luker, Ralph E. "Missions, Institutional Churches, and Settlement Houses:

The Black Experience, 1885–1910." *Journal of Negro History* 69 (1984): 101–13.

Mathes, Valerie Sher. "Nineteenth-Century Women and Reform: The Women's National Indian Association." *American Indian Quarterly* 14 (1990): 1–18.

May, Martha. "Bread Before Roses: The American Workingmen, Labor Unions and the Family Wage." In *Women, Work and Protest: A Century of U.S. Labor History*, Ruth Milkman, ed. Boston: Routledge, Kegan and Paul, 1985.

McFate, Katherine. "Welfare: Dependency v. Reform." *Focus* 7 (1988): 3–5.

Michel, Sonya. "American Women and the Discourse of the Democratic Family in World War II." In *Behind the Lines: Gender and the Two World Wars*, Margaret Randolph Higonnet et al., eds. New Haven: Yale University Press, 1987.

"The New American Domesticated Male." *Life* 36 (1954): 42–45.

Nixon, Richard M. "Veto of the Economic Opportunity Amendments of 1971, December 10, 1971." In *Public Papers of the President* 387: 1174–78.

Offen, Karen. "Defining Feminism: A Comparative Historical Approach." *Signs* (1988): 119–57.

Perdue, Theda. "Cherokee Women and the Trail of Tears." *Journal of Women's History* 1 (Spring 1989): 14–30.

Polikoff, Nancy. "Why Mothers Are Losing: A Brief Analysis of Criteria Used in Child Custody Determinations." *Women's Rights Law Reporter* 7 (1982): 235.

Riger, Stephanie. "Comment on 'Women's History Goes to Trial.'" *Signs* 13 (1988): 897–903.

Rossi, Alice. "A Biosocial Perspective on Parenting." *Daedalus* 106 (1977): 1–32.

Scharf, Lois. "ER and Feminism." In *Without Precedent: The Life and Career of Eleanor Roosevelt*, Joan Hoff-Wilson and Marjorie Lightman, eds. Bloomington: Indiana University Press, 1984.

Schwartz, Felice N. "Management Women and the New Facts of Life." *Harvard Business Review* 89 (January-February 1989): 65–76.

See, Letha A. Lee. "Tensions Between Black Women and White Women: A Study." *Affilia* 4, no. 2 (1989): 31–45.

Shoemaker, Nancy. "The Rise or Fall of Iroquois Women." *Journal of Women's History* 2 (Winter 1991): 39–57.

Smith-Rosenberg, Carroll. "Female World of Love and Ritual." *Signs* 1 (1975): 1–26.

Tompkins, Calvin. "Profiles: A Sense of Urgency." *The New Yorker*, March 27, 1989, 48–74.

Ulrich, Laurel. "Housewife and Gadder: Themes of Self-Sufficiency and Community in Eighteenth-Century New England." In *To Toil the Livelong Day*, Carol Groneman and Mary Beth Norton, eds. Ithaca: Cornell University Press, 1987.

Wallis, Claudia. "Onward, Women!" *Time*, December 4, 1989, 80–89.

Welter, Barbara. "The Cult of True Womanhood, 1820–1860." *American Quarterly* 18 (1966): 131–75.

Williams, Fannie Barrier. "The Need of Social Settlement Work for the City Negro." *Southern Workman*, September 1904, 501–6.

Williams, Joan C. "Domesticity as the Dangerous Supplement of Liberalism." *Journal of Women's History* 2 (Winter 1991): 128–50.

———. "Deconstructing Gender." *Michigan Law Review* 87 (1989): 797–845.

"Women's History Goes to Trial: EEOC v. Sears Roebuck and Company." *Signs* 11 (1986): 751–79.

Woodman, Harold. "Sequel to Slavery: The New History Views the Old South." *Journal of Southern History* 43 (November 1977): 523–54.

Woolsey, Suzanne. "Pied Piper Politics and the Child-Care Debate." *Daedalus* 106 (Spring 1977): 127–45.

Zigler, Edward. "A New Child Care Profession: The Child Development Associate." *Young Children*, December 1971, 71–74.

Zuckerman, Michael. "Dr. Spock, The Confidence Man." In *The Family in History*, Charles Rosenberg, ed. Philadelphia: University of Pennsylvania Press, 1975.

Government Publications

Bradbury, Dorothy E., *U.S. Children's Bureau: Five Decades of Action for Children*. Washington, D.C.: Government Printing Office, 1962.

De Reid, Ira. "The Negro in the United States." In *Report of the Committee on Socially Handicapped-Dependency and Neglect*. White House Conference on Child Health and Protection, 1930.

Malone, Margaret. "Child Care the Federal Role," Library of Congress. Issue Brief No. IB 77034, 1979.

National Commission on the Observance of International Women's Year," ". . . To Form a More Perfect Union . . ." *Justice for American Women*. Report of The National Commission on the Observance of International Women's Year. Washington, D.C.: Government Printing Office, June 1976.

Pidgeon, Mary Elizabeth. *Employed Mothers and Child Care*. Women's Bureau Bulletin No. 246. Washington, D.C.: Government Printing Office, 1953.

U.S. Bureau of the Census Report. *Who's Minding the Kids?* May 1987.

U.S. Bureau of Education. *Legal Rights of Children.* Circular of Information No. 3. Washington, D.C.: Government Printing Office, 1880.

U.S. Congress. House. Select Committee on Children, Youth and Families. Hearings on Improving Child Care Services: What Can Be Done? 98th Congress, 2d sess., 1984.

U.S. Congress. Senate. Committee on Labor and Human Resources. Act for Better Child Care Services of 1989. 101st Congress, 1st sess., 1989. S. Report 101–17.

U.S. Department of Labor. *Employed Mothers and Child Care.* Women's Bureau Bulletin No. 246. Washington, D.C.: Government Printing Office, 1953.

U.S. Department of Labor. *Time of Change: 1983 Handbook on Women Workers.* Women's Bureau Bulletin No. 298. Washington, D.C.: Government Printing Office, 1983.

U.S. Department of Labor. *Working Women: A Chartbook.* Women's Bureau Bulletin No. 2385. Washington, D.C.: Government Printing Office, 1991.

Wright, Helen Russell. *Children of Wage-Earning Mothers: A Study of a Selected Group in Chicago.* Children's Bureau Publication No. 102. Washington, D.C.: Government Printing Office, 1922.

Unpublished Works

Aron, Cindy. "To Barter Their Souls for Gold: Female Federal Clerical Workers in Nineteenth-Century America." Ph.D. diss., University of Maryland, 1981.

George, Elsie. "The Women Appointees of the Roosevelt and Truman Administrations: A Study of Their Impact and Effectiveness." Ph.D. diss., American University, 1972.

Marshall, Thurgood. "Remarks of Thurgood Marshall, Associate Justice, Supreme Court of the United States, at the Second Circuit Judicial Conference," September 1989.

Memorandum, Irene Natividad to Mary Frances Berry, January 22, 1990.

Television

"The MacNeil/Lehrer NewsHour," Public Broadcasting Service, May 17, 1990.

"Modern Maturity," Public Broadcasting Service, March 3, 1988.

Newspapers

The New York Times, 1939–1992.
USA Today, 1987–1992.
The Wall Street Journal, 1981–1992.
The Washington Post, 1981–1992.

Index